THE
NANTEOS
GRAIL

THE NANTEOS GRAIL

THE EVOLUTION OF A HOLY RELIC

JOHN MATTHEWS, IAN PEGLER
AND FRED STEDMAN-JONES

AMBERLEY

To *the memory of our friend Fred Stedman-Jones (1932–2016),*
who devoted so much of his life to this project.
We hope he likes the final version.

JM *& IP, 2020*

To *the memory of my mother, Anne Pegler, who translated some*
of the Welsh sources found in this book. Also, to the memory of
my father, Roger Pegler, who first took me to Glastonbury and
later told me the story of the Nanteos Cup.

IP, 2020

First published 2022

Amberley Publishing
The Hill, Stroud
Gloucestershire, GL5 4EP

www.amberley-books.com

Copyright © John Matthews, Ian Pegler and Fred Stedman-Jones, 2022

The right of John Matthews, Ian Pegler and Fred Stedman-Jones to be identified as the
Author of this work has been asserted in accordance with the Copyright, Designs and
Patents Act 1988.

British Library Cataloguing in Publication Data.
A catalogue record for this book is available from the British Library.

ISBN 978 1 3981 0622 2 (paperback)
ISBN 978 1 3981 0623 9 (ebook)

1 2 3 4 5 6 7 8 9 10

Typesetting by SJmagic DESIGN SERVICES, India.
Printed in the UK.

Contents

Acknowledgements

We would like to express our thanks to a number of individuals and organizations without whose cooperation we could not have completed this book.

First and foremost, to the estate of the late Fred Stedman-Jones for allowing us access to his extensive archive and for permission to quote extensively from it.

Grateful thanks to the estate of the late W. G. Gray for allowing us to quote from his unpublished autobiography on pp. 146-7.

The letter on p. 170 is printed with permission of the estate of the late Helmut Nickel.

In addition, we would like to thank Caitlín Matthews for her support and assistance throughout the writing of the book, and to David Elkington for proofreading the manuscript several times and pointing out various errors.

To the staff and editors at Amberley for their professionalism and enthusiastic support for the book, especially Shaun Barrington. We would also like to thank the staff at the National Library of Wales, the staff at Ceredigion archive, the staff at the Royal Commission for Ancient and Historical Monuments Wales and Janet Joel.

JM, Oxford
IP, Borth

Loss and Recovery

'Holy Grail Stolen!' read the headlines on 16 July 2014, when the BBC and national newspapers announced that the Nanteos Cup, believed by many to be the Holy Grail, had been stolen from a house in Weston under Penyard, near Ross-on-Wye in Herefordshire. The cup was stolen from the house of its guardian, who had been taken into hospital. Burglars had broken in and stolen the cup, kept wrapped in a small green velvet bag (mistakenly reported in some reports as blue). The fact that nothing else was taken suggests that this was a targeted theft.

For months the search spread out across the country. A reward of £2,000 was offered for its return. Finally, almost exactly a year after the theft was reported, the police announced that they had retrieved the missing vessel and that it would shortly be reunited with its owner. Photographs of the detective in charge of the case, proudly holding the cup, must rank high among the strange images and stories of this remarkable relic.

The Nanteos Cup is a small, dark, wooden vessel, originally 5 inches in diameter and 3 inches in depth, with a shallow base of roughly 1.5 inches diameter. Less than half of the cup now remains, since sufferers who used to borrow it apparently nibbled away pieces of the wood, hoping to ensure that a cure of their particular ailment was successful. The remnant of the cup is kept in a glass bowl within a wooden box that also contains handwritten receipts dating from 1857 to 1901, recording its many 'cures'. It used to be borrowed by local families who left a coin or a valuable item such as a watch as a token of faith. The average loan was three and a half weeks and it was invariably borrowed on behalf of women.

Most contemporary writers state that the cup is made of olive wood or wych elm, but these claims have never been proved, and the examination by 'experts' carried out in 1977 falls far short of any final opinion. Nor has the cup ever been carbon-dated. It could probably be identified scientifically by timber experts and dated from a shaving of the wood, but the guardians of the cup have so far not allowed this. The pragmatic view of Betty Mirylees, its penultimate guardian, was that it 'heals, and nothing would be gained by finding out that it was made in Birmingham'.

There are a number of traditions concerning the cup, the best known being that it is the Holy Grail, the vessel used by Jesus to celebrate the first Eucharist during the Last Supper, and that seven monks took it to the Cistercian abbey of Strata Florida in Mid Wales from Glastonbury, where it had been kept, at the time of the dissolution of their abbey in 1539. The (presumably) same seven monks later carried it to Nanteos, a grand house some miles from Strata Florida. Hearing of the approach of Thomas Cromwell's commissioners (or by the king with his soldiers, according to more imaginative versions) who would most certainly have either destroyed it or taken it away, the monks sought sanctuary with the Powell family at Nanteos. On his deathbed the last monk – who is sometimes identified as the prior, even as the abbot in one account – is said to have revealed the secret of the cup to the family and entrusted them with its care 'until the Church shall claim her own'.

Much of this can be contested, as we shall show in this book, but whatever the truth of these accounts, the cup was definitively reported to be at Nanteos from the 1830s. During the Victorian period, the Powell family themselves said that they had no knowledge of its earlier history, and its reputation as a healing vessel was largely confined to Wales during the nineteenth century. However, during the twentieth century its fame spread astronomically, and its story has been told with great authority in many newspaper and magazine articles and currently on dozens of websites. All too often these accounts contain astonishing accretions that display the ignorance of their authors, many of whom claim copyright of their confused accounts but in fact borrow from older versions to which they have added their own ideas.

One transatlantic version of the story from a website offering reports on this and a number of other 'unexplained mysteries' reads as follows:

> The Abbot accompanied the monks and barely escaped the ravages of Glastonbury; at Strata Florida the monks hid their treasure under a loose floorboard in the Abbey's main chapel; they made contact with the Powell family – partners to the neighbouring Stedman family – in an extensive smuggling operation via a tunnel running nearly a mile from the coast to the Powell's Manor – the monks hid in this coastal tunnel when prying eyes came to the estate.[1]

The fact that none of this can be proven and that no such tunnel has ever been found or even described by local people is indicative of the kind of fictions circulating about the cup.

In this book we explore the long and curious history of the Nanteos vessel, beginning with its possible connection to the story of the Grail, disseminated throughout the Christian world via the legends of King Arthur and his knights. From there we will trace the various stories of the cup's supposed journey from the Holy Land to Strata Florida, how it subsequently came to be in the keeping of the Stedman and later the Powell families, and from there to the revival of interest in the cup throughout the twentieth and into the twenty-first century.

We seek to chronicle the complex and fascinating tale of the cup's journey though time and space, taking in the accounts of the many people who have sought (and some who claimed to have found) the truth about this remarkable relic. We will show how the story has grown through the ages, and how we have reached our current understanding of what it is.

The Nanteos Cup remains a mystery. What we offer here is the unvarnished truth, based upon many years of research, of its long and remarkable history. But in order to understand how it came to be and how it has been interpreted, we need to look at the object with which it has been most consistently connected and compared – the Holy Grail.

John Matthews
Ian Pegler
F. Stedman-Jones

1

The Great Quest

The history of the Grail is one of the most complex stories in the world. It is known about by many, but understood by very few, and its story has spread outwards around the world for thousands of years. There are, indeed, almost as many theories as to its origin as there are days in the year, with new discoveries and identifications appearing in print and across the Internet every year.

There are periods of time when the Grail hid itself so deeply that few even knew of its existence; yet it was never completely forgotten, and no matter how far in time or space we have to travel between one point and another, the Grail always reappears, sometimes taking on a new form, sometimes echoing an older manifestation, but always retaining certain key principles: the ability to transform, to enlighten, to inspire – to lead its seekers into evermore fascinating places. The Nanteos Cup is just one of the shapes taken by the Grail, but its remarkable history continues to haunt the imagination to this day.

Some of the forms taken by the Grail, especially the earliest, may be unfamiliar to followers of the myth, and some readers will doubtless disagree with our interpretation. For many the Grail can *only* be the Cup of Christ, while others see bloodlines and stones and imagery that in the end confuse rather than clarify the story. However, within each of these images and strands of belief and tradition, some recognisable shadow of the Grail can still be seen.

The Essential Story

What we may call the central Grail Myth has almost as many forms as there are texts that tell of it. Many do not agree on either the names of the characters, the sequence of events, or the places and times in which these took place. For this reason, we have compiled a basic outline of the story, synthesised from the medieval Arthurian romances that remain, to this day, the primary source for what we know about the Grail.[1]

*

The story begins with Joseph of Arimathea, a wealthy merchant said to be Jesus' uncle, into whose care Christ's body is given for burial. According to some accounts, at this time he also obtains the cup used by Christ to celebrate the Last Supper. While the body is being washed and prepared for the tomb, some blood flows from the wounds, which Joseph catches in this same vessel. After the Resurrection, Joseph is accused of stealing the body, and is thrown into prison and deprived of food. Here Christ appears to him in a blaze of light and entrusts the cup and its secrets to his care. He then instructs Joseph in the celebration of the Mass and mystery of the Incarnation, before vanishing. After this Joseph is miraculously kept alive by a dove that descends to his cell every day and deposits a holy wafer in the cup. He is finally released in AD 70, and joined by his sister and her husband Bron, goes into exile overseas with a small group of followers. A table called the First Table of the Grail is constructed, to represent the table of the Last Supper. Twelve may sit there, but a thirteenth seat remains empty, either in token of Christ's place, or that of Judas. When one of the Company attempts to sit in it, he is swallowed up and the seat is thereafter called the Perilous Seat.

Joseph next sails to Europe, and then to Britain, where he establishes the first Christian church in Glastonbury, dedicating it to the Mother of Christ. Here the Grail is housed and serves as a chalice in celebrations of the Mass in which the whole company participate, and which becomes known as the Mass of the Grail.

In other versions Joseph goes no further than Europe and the guardianship of the Grail passes to Bron, who becomes known as the Rich Fisherman after he miraculously feeds the entire company with a single fish. The company settles at a place called Avaron to await the coming of the third Grail keeper, Alain.

From here the Grail is taken to Muntsalvasche, the Mountain of Salvation, where a temple is built to house it and an order of Grail knights comes into being to serve and guard the vessel. They sit together at the Second Table of the Grail and partake of a feast provided by the sacred vessel. A form of Grail Mass once again takes place, in which the Grail keeper, now described as a king, serves as priest. Other stories relate the miraculous building of the temple and offer detailed descriptions of its appearance.

Shortly after this, the Grail King receives a mysterious wound, variously in the thighs or more specifically the generative organs, caused by a fiery spear. Thereafter the guardian is known as the Maimed or Wounded King and the countryside around the Grail Castle becomes barren and is called the Waste Land – a state explicitly connected with the Grail King's wound. The spear with which he is struck becomes identified with the Lance of Longinus, the Roman centurion who in Biblical tradition pierced the side of Christ on the Cross. From this time forward there are four objects in the castle: the cup itself, the spear, a sword with which John the Baptist was beheaded, and which is said to break at a crucial moment, and either a shallow dish or a stone. These are the Hallows, or sacred, hallowed things, four sacred treasures that must be sought, and wielded in a mysterious way, by those who seek the Grail.

By this time, we have reached the Age of Arthur, and the scene is set for the beginning of the great Quest. The Round Table is established by Merlin as the Third Table of the Grail (though the vessel is absent). In the new king's citadel of Camelot, a fellowship of knights, called the Knights of the Round Table, meet and establish a code of chivalry. At Pentecost the Grail makes an appearance, floating on a beam of light through the hall, and each and every person there receives the food he likes best, whereupon the knights all pledge themselves to seek the holy object.

There follows an extraordinary series of initiatory adventures, featuring five knights in particular: Gawain, Lancelot, Perceval, Galahad and Bors. Of these, and of the many knights who set out from Camelot, only three are destined to achieve the Quest. Lancelot, the best knight in the world, fails because of his love for Arthur's queen. Gawain, a splendid figure who may once have been the original Grail knight, is shown in the medieval texts as being too worldly – though he comes close to the heart of the mystery.

As for the rest, Galahad, the son of Lancelot and the Grail Princess, is destined from the beginning to sit in the Perilous Seat and to achieve the Quest. Perceval, like Gawain originally a successful candidate, is partially ousted by Galahad, so that while he is permitted to see the Grail – and to use the spear to heal the Wounded King – at the end of the Quest he returns to the Grail Castle where he apparently becomes its new guardian.

Bors, the last of the three knights to experience the Grail directly, is the humble, dogged, 'ordinary' man, who strives with all his being to reach towards the infinite, and who succeeds, voyaging with Galahad and Perceval to the Holy City of Sarras, far across the Western sea, where the mystery of the Grail is finally achieved. Of the three, Bors alone returns to Camelot to tell what has happened.

One other seeker, a woman named Dindrane, Perceval's sister, has a vision of the Grail before any of the knights, and in some versions of the story accompanies the Grail knights on their quest. Later, having given her life for another, she is carried to the city of the Grail and buried in splendour beside Galahad.

Once the Grail has been achieved in that time, and since it is fully achieved by one person only, the vessel is withdrawn – but not entirely, and not forever. Perceval takes up residence again in the empty castle to await the return of the Grail – which will thereafter be once again available for all true seekers.

*

Such is the story in its essentials. It took many hundreds of years for this myth to evolve to this point. Many different streams flowed into it, sometimes forcing the central river of the story to overflow its banks – forming new tributaries, some of which become dried up and lost, others that broadened out for a time, then shrank again to no more than a trickle. Here, we can only follow a few of these tributaries, along with the main river of the story itself. Many of these streams flow side by side, connected only by the presence of the Grail; but all flow onward, carrying with them a dream that seems to have been part of our consciousness for as long as history itself has existed.

We must travel a long way back in time for the oldest versions (for there are more than one) of what is today understood to be the Grail. Not for us the panoply of King Arthur and his Round Table Fellowship; we see no shining cup or radiant maiden bearing the holy relic through the hall of a medieval castle. Instead, we find an ancient cauldron, intricately carved, its rim set with pearls 'warmed', according to one text, 'by the breath of nine maidens'.[2] This cauldron has the power to grant life, to give forth rich foods, and to bestow upon its owner rare favours. Gods and goddesses possess it; it is stolen, recovered, and stolen again. Hidden and revealed, it lies at the centre of ancient British mysteries and is an important part of the foundation-myths of Christianity and Judaism. It is still sought after as a talisman of power, just as the Grail was to be in the time of Arthur.

It is thus to the mysterious realm of the Celtic imagination that we look first. This may seem to take us a long way from the broken remains of the Nanteos Cup, but each strand is part of the story of which it is a part, and these must be considered before we can begin to trace the journey taken by the story from Palestine to Wales.

The Cauldrons

It seems more than a little appropriate that an object associated with the Grail should turn up in Wales and the Borders, because some of the most striking aspects of the myth originate in the rich traditions of the Celtic peoples.

There, it is not a shining chalice, as most are used to think of it, or indeed as the broken wooden bowl of Nanteos, but a mysterious cauldron, once perhaps connected to a Goddess. One of the earliest of such vessels belonged to a wise woman named Ceridwen, who had a son named Avagddu, or 'utter darkness', who was of such terrible hideousness that no one could bear to look upon him. So Ceridwen decided to brew an elixir of pure wisdom and knowledge that would equip her offspring to fare

14

better in the world. She set out to gather the ingredients that would go into the brew, and she set her servants, an old blind man named Morda and a boy named Gwion, to boil her great cauldron.

The ingredients were gathered, and the cauldron heated. Then Ceridwen went out again, leaving Gwion to stir the mixture. While she was away however, three drops flew out of the cauldron and scalded Gwion's finger. Automatically, he thrust the finger into his mouth and thereby gained all knowledge – for the three drops were the distillation of Ceridwen's brew.

At once Gwion was aware that his mistress knew what had occurred, and that she was coming after him in anger. With his new-found powers he changed his shape to that of a hare and fled. Ceridwen changed her shape to that of a greyhound and gave chase. Through several more metamorphoses of animal, bird and fish, Gwion fled and Ceridwen pursued, until finally in desperation he became a grain of wheat in a heap of chaff. But Ceridwen took the form of a red-crested hen and swallowed the grain. Thereafter she bore a child in her womb and gave birth to a son nine months later.

Ceridwen would have killed the child, but she saw that he was beautiful beyond measure, and so she put him into a leather bag and cast him into the sea, where he floated for nine nights and nine days until the bag caught in the weir of the Chieftain Gwyddno Garanhir. There it was found by Gwyddno's son Elphin, an unlucky youth who had lost all his goods and had been awarded a fateful May-Eve catch of salmon that always came to his father's nets on that day. This time, however, the salmon were absent – yet another sign of Elphin's ill luck. But instead of the fish there was a leather bag that squirmed and wailed. When Elphin took it forth, bemoaning his fate, and opened it, he found the child within, and one of his men remarked at once on the beauty of the infant, and especially his broad white brow. Whereat the child spoke: 'Taliesin shall I be called,' for the name meant 'radiant brow'. From here he grew rapidly, and proved himself a mighty poet and magician, becoming in time the chief bard to King Arthur himself.

This is an ancient tale, and an even older theme.[3] It hides an ancient initiatory experience, in which the candidate was given a drink that put him into a visionary trance in which he saw past and future events and was put in touch with the *Awen*, or inspiration, becoming at once a poet and a prophet. The nature of the transformations, into bird, beast and fish, indicate the shamanic nature of the experience, since all shamans were taught to discover and identify with various totem animals who became their guides and helpers in the inner realms, whence they travelled to learn the secrets of creation.

The Cauldron of Bran

The second example of the Celtic fascination with Cauldrons – and one which brings us firmly into the realm of the Grail – is that of the demi-God Bran, whose title 'the Blessed' indicates in what degree of reverence he was held. The story comes, as does that of Taliesin, from the collection of Celtic wonder-tales gathered together under the title *Mabinogion*, which means literally 'tales of youth', or as we might say, 'tales of young heroes'. It contains some of the earliest references to Arthur and the Grail, as well as an astonishing collection of magical stories.[4]

In one of these, the story of *Branwen Daughter of Llyr*, we find the following account: Bran the Blessed was King of Britain, and he arranged for his sister Branwen to marry Matholwch, the King of Ireland. At the wedding feast one of his brothers, Efnissien, took slight at the Irish king and mutilated his horses. Strife seemed immanent, but Bran offered Matholwch the Cauldron of Rebirth, into which dead warriors were placed and came forth alive again. Matholwch already knew of the cauldron that came originally from Ireland and was owned by a giant and his wife, Llassar Llaes Gyfnewid and Cymideu Cymeinfoll, who gave birth to a fully armed warrior every six weeks. They had been driven out of Ireland because of this and had taken refuge with Bran.

Branwen now went to Ireland, where she bore Matholwch a son, but was so unpopular with the people that she was forbidden his bed and put to work in the kitchens. There she trained a starling to carry a message to her brother, who, once he heard of her ill treatment, came with all his warriors across the sea. Matholwch retreated and sued for peace – granted on condition that he abdicated in favour of Gwern, his son by Branwen.

At the feast that ensued, Efnissien again brought disaster by thrusting the child into the fire. Fighting broke out and the Irish were winning because they put their fallen warriors into the cauldron. Efnissien then crawled inside and stretching out, broke both the vessel and his own heart. Bran was wounded in the leg or foot by a poisoned spear and instructed his surviving followers, who numbered only seven, to cut off his head and bear it with them on a journey.

They travelled to an island named Gwales, where they were entertained by the head of Bran and the singing of the mystical Birds of Rhiannon for eighty-five years, during which time they knew no fear or hardship and forgot all that they had suffered. Then one of their number opened a forbidden door, and at once the enchantment ceased and they remembered everything. Bran's head then told them to carry it to London and bury it beneath the White Mount with its face towards France. The seven returned to Bran's country and found it under the power of a magician named Caswallawn. The remainder of the story is told in the next tale in the *Mabinogion* but does not concern us here.

Here the cauldron is shown to have definite other-worldly status. The gigantic man and woman, Llassar Llaes Gyfnewid and Cymideu Cymeinfoll, can persuasively be identified with Ceridwen and Tegid Foel, the parents of Taliesin. Both are said to come from a lake with an island in the centre, and both possess a wonder-working cauldron. We may perhaps go no further with this identification than to say that both couples seem to represent an earlier, more primitive tradition of the other-world, connected in some way to the race of aboriginal giants hinted at elsewhere in Celtic mythology. But it is worth remembering that the woman of the pair in 'Branwen' is said to give birth to fully armed warriors – which seems itself like another echo of the cauldron story, where it is seen as giving life to (previously dead) warriors.

The Cauldron Quest

Bran is seen as a type of the other-worldly host who feasts heroes in his magic hall, feeding them from an inexhaustible cauldron that 'will not boil the food of a coward'. We can see another example of this kind of vessel, and incidentally complete the connections of Bran and the various cauldrons with the Grail quest, by looking at another poem, *Prieddeu Annwn*, attributed to Taliesin (who, we should remember, was present at the Entertainment of the Noble Head, and is himself one of the Cauldron-Born, an initiate of the sacred vessel).

The poem begins:

Predestined was Gweir's captivity in Caer Sidi,
According to the tale of Pwyll and Pryderi.
None before him was sent into it,
Into the heavy blue chain which bound the youth.
From before the reeving of Annwfn he has groaned,
Until the ending of the world this prayer of poets:
Three shipburdens of Prydwen entered the Spiral City
Except seven, none returned from Caer Sidi.

Is not my song worthily to be heard
In the four-square Caer, four times revolving!
I draw my knowledge from the famous cauldron,
The breath of nine maidens keeps it boiling.
Is not the Head of Annwfn's cauldron so shaped:
Ridged with enamel, rimmed with pearl?
It will not boil the cowardly traitor's portion.
The sword of Lleawc flashed before it
And in the hand of Lleminawc was it wielded.
Before hell's gate the lights were lifted
When with Arthur we went to the harrowing.
Except seven none returned from Caer Feddwit.[5]

We are hearing of a raid on the other-world, led by Arthur, to steal the magical cauldron of Pen Annwn. Once again, the word *pen*, head, is important. In this case it refers to the other-worldly King Arawn, who possesses a cauldron of incalculable power. Clearly, also, as in the Grail quest, the task is not an easy one. Only seven men – the same number, we note, as returned with Bran from Ireland – come back with Arthur. One of them, again, is Taliesin, who tells the tale. And we may note that the description of the *caers* through which the heroes must pass in order to reach Arawn's hall are strikingly reminiscent of the island of Caer Siddi in Taliesin's song, and like the island of Gwales in

Branwen. Indeed, the voyage of Bran to Ireland seemed to have been modelled on the *Spoils of Annwn* and may at one time have contained only this story, before the account of Branwen's adventures were grafted onto it.

Keepers of the Hallows

All of this throws a new light on the idea of a long series of guardians of the Grail. They are a part of the legacy of Celtic tradition that helped – along with other strands borrowed from Hebrew tradition – to shape the future development of the Grail myths and which is recognizable throughout most of the medieval retelling that followed.

For almost 500 years, beginning in the eleventh and continuing to the middle of the fifteenth century, these and other stories continued to circulate, first in Britain and later in Europe. Eventually, they returned, Christianized and shaped anew, but with the same underlying elements still perceivable beneath the layers of new material that had been grafted upon them.

By the late twelfth century, the stage was already set for a new epiphany of the Grail. The Middle Ages had achieved their first flowering: a springing forth of new ideas and beliefs in minds freed at last from the sheer effort of survival. Art, architecture and literature were in their vernal aspect; Chartres Cathedral was still under construction, and complex webs of theology and mysticism were being unwound and rewound in both monastery and university. The relationship of mankind with creation, and with God, was the all-important question of the age.

Despite, or perhaps because of, the fact that literacy was a skill reserved almost exclusively for clerics, memory was correspondingly stronger than today. The ear, not the eye, was the gateway to the imagination; when it came to storytelling, there were always willing listeners to wonder-tales in which a semi-divine hero slew beasts and overcame implacable enemies in order to rescue and eventually marry archetypal maidens.

There was also a stronger sense of conceptual or symbolic understanding. Labourers were known by their implements of toil, religious by their habit, nobility by their rich apparel, knights by their mounts and weapons. Although the liturgy of the Mass was in Latin, except perhaps for the sermon, which may have been in the vernacular, this did not seem to matter; the actions of the priest at the altar were necessarily mysterious, emblematic of the way in which he mediated between heaven and earth on behalf of the congregation.

Factors such as these helped prepare the way for the return of the Grail in its heightened form, as did the political state of Europe at this time. Prior to the spread of Christianity, the whole of the Western world had been torn apart by war and insurrection; orphaned from its Classical roots by barbarians who eventually made the West their own homeland, Europe remained a tangle of petty kingdoms, each one battling for supremacy.

Each kingdom, however small, had its own capital. The archetype for these capitals was, religiously, Jerusalem, the city of the Divine King; mythically, it was Camelot, the stronghold of the Earthly King, Arthur of Britain. And indeed, the role of kingship within European society was a significant one: kingship sprang from a divine source as it had from the Goddess of Sovereignty in Celtic times, and kings were anointed with oil just as priests were – emphasising the priest-like nature of the office.

The mysteries of the Priest-Kings were embodied in the story of Prester John, a mysterious monarch who sent a letter to the heads of the Christian West, offering succour wherever and whenever it was needed, which was widely believed to offer proof of the existence of a Christian kingdom behind the threatening Islamic forces of the Middle East. The story of Prester John would eventually be proved no more than a myth, but a powerful one that became, in time, connected with the ever-expanding history of the Grail. Who better than this mysterious figure to be the guardian of the sacred vessel?[6]

The descent of kings from a divine source was of the greatest importance to medieval man. Europe was a wilderness of forest and trackless wastes, partitioned by rivers and lakes and still very much under the influence of tutelary gods and goddesses. Each tree, hill and well had its guardian spirit; standing stones, circles and sacred groves retained a sense of the numinous. Although only folk memory of these things survived, the king had to be a consort of the gods as well as the people if he was to wield any power.

It is this that makes the idea of the Wounded King such a powerful theme within the Grail cycle. The wounding of the king caused the wounding of the land because of the deep and indissoluble links between them. Its presence within the Arthurian stories demonstrates how thin the veneer of Christianity upon the original beliefs of the West was. The power of Rome had not yet assumed the extremes that resulted in reformation and counter reformation, but few had the strength to step outside its laws.

The further the influence of the Church spread through Europe, the more dogmatic and exoteric became its expression. Yet even within such strictures, the real message of Christ managed to survive; a body of mystical and esoteric teaching upheld by isolated people: mystics, solitary madmen who were either ignored, lauded as exemplary members of the Church, or if their doctrines attracted undue attention, summarily dismissed as heretics.

It is perhaps significant that there are no 'Grail Saints', no officially approved expositors of what might be termed the Grail 'school' of mysticism, any more than there is either specific recognition or denial of the Grail itself. Yet one of the earliest of the Grail romances – the thirteenth-century *Estoire de Saint Graal* (History of the Holy Grail)[7] – tells us of a sacred book that contains the mysteries of Christ's teaching: yet another image that the Grail would take in times to come. That other than these few references in non-canonical texts there is merely a deafening silence, in an age of relic hunting, is itself telling. All of this prepared the way for an absolute belief in a physical relic such as the Nanteos Cup.

The New Corpus

Almost the entire corpus of Grail literature was written between 1170 and 1225, appearing suddenly and ending almost as abruptly. We can only guess at the extent of oral tradition behind their composition. Certainly, the Arthurian canon had already been established well before the twelfth century, deriving its roots from Celtic and Hebrew sources. Storytellers such as the trouvères, wandering singers and poets who were able to cross all boundaries, both physical and religious, fused pagan and Christian ethe with chivalric achievement and folk-culture, forming an archetypal world which lived in the imaginations of all kinds of people.

Two authors who established the medieval story of the Grail were Chrétien de Troyes and Robert de Boron. Chrétien (1130–91) was already famed throughout Europe for his Arthurian poems, in which he had introduced such figures as Lancelot, Gawain and Geraint to a Norman French courtly society who were hungry for more. The Matter of Britain, as it was known, became all the rage, with countless new stories appearing all the time. Chrétien's last work, left unfinished at his death, was *The Conte del Graal* or *Story of the Grail*, in which he told of the adventures of a young, innocent youth named Perceval, who happened to catch sight of two knights – whom he mistook for angels – in the forest where he had been brought up in ignorance of manly pursuits. From this moment he desired only to follow them and to discover where and how they lived. He met many adventures on the way, but the strangest of all was that of the Grail.

Finding himself at the Castle of the Fisher King, Perceval witnesses a mysterious procession in which a vessel called the *Graal* is borne through the hall and is used in some way to sustain a wounded man. Perceval, both from misallied politeness and simple ignorance, fails to ask the meaning of these things, and finds himself outcast to wander in the wilderness of the Waste Land as a result. A hideous damsel chides him for his failure and tells him that had he asked the required question, the land and the king – actually his uncle – would have been restored. Thereafter the foolish youth has to suffer in the wilderness for some time before he finds his way back to the castle; but the outcome is never revealed since the poem breaks off before the mystery of the Grail is explained.[8]

The enigma of this story touched the imagination of the Western world, expressing feelings that were already latent within the consciousness of medieval man. A Swiss knight named Robert de Boron, whose exact dates are unknown but who was alive in the late twelfth to early thirteenth century, may have already been working on a Grail text of his own prior to Chrétien; but in any case he took the story back through time to the days when Christ walked the earth, telling how Joseph of Arimathea, who we remember gave up his own tomb to contain the body of the Messiah, had given into his keeping, by no lesser person than Jesus himself, the Cup of the Last Supper.[9]

Other writers, notably Wolfram von Eschenbach, whose *Parzival*[10] brought in ideas borrowed from the Orient, and the anonymous authors of *The Elucidation*,[11] the *Didot Perceval*[12] and the vast compilation known as the *Lancelot-Grail*, added to and strengthened both the Arthurian background and the mystical continuity of ancient belief.

The dangers of such rival interests were not lost upon the Church which, perhaps in the interest of survival, did its best to exclude troubadours and other storytellers from communion on the grounds that they were agents of the devil. Eventually, the Church itself took over the office of storyteller; texts such as *Perlesvaus*[13] and the *Lancelot-Grail* cycle were written down by monks who incorporated the uncanonical writings of earlier writers to produce a version which, though it suffers at times from a heavy moral underscoring, yet expresses one of the finest and most complete visions of the Grail to date.

The spate of texts continued unabated. Chrétien's *Story of the Grail* now boasted four continuations, by different hands, which extended the original by thousands of lines. Robert de Boron completed his trilogy: *Merlin, Joseph d'Arimathie* and *Perceval*,[14] adding both Christian and Jewish traditions. Versions of these stories began to appear throughout Europe, drawn now into the whirlpool of Arthurian literature. Descriptions of the Grail and of the mysterious procession, some based on Chrétien's original version, others displaying a knowledge of other sources, appeared in Germany, Italy, and Spain. The mighty *Lancelot-Grail* cycle – consisting of five volumes of myth, legend and theology – was begun; its authors, Cistercian monks, representing an intention to give a more authoritative Christian stamp to the material.

The Oldest Church

Yet another strand in the strange and wondrous history of the Grail was its part in the division between Rome and the so-called Celtic branch of Christianity. Robert de Boron had connected the Grail with Joseph of Arimathea and had brought his saintly hero to Britain along with the Grail. Here he was said to have founded the first Christian church in these islands, substantially before the Church of Rome and with the apparent warranty of both Christ and his mother. In more than one Church council, British bishops claimed the right to prior speech before those of other countries, solely on account of this early ascription of Christianity to Britain.

Celtic Christianity was discouraged and secretly considered heretical by Roman missionaries, who found it well established when they arrived in the first century. Even after the Synod of Whitby in AD 663, which established such matters as the tonsure of monks and the date of Easter, all was not as it might have been between the different professions. Monks and clerics of the Celtic rite were rarely considered for high office within the Church.

But it was within the boundaries of Celtic Christendom that many of the stories of the Grail first arose. We have only to look at the wonder voyages of monks like Brendan, written in Latin in the ninth century, to see the tendency among such Celtic monkish scribes. The *Navigato Sancti Brendani*[15] is rife with elements which might just as well have come from an Arthurian or Grail adventure: the bold adventurer who goes in search of God's mysteries, treasure, beautiful maidens, monsters, islands shimmering in the seas of the West – the Lands Adventurous indeed. A little-known but important text, the *Sone de Nansay*, echoed the voyage literature and depicted a visit to a mysterious island of the Grail.[16]

Such writings as these were the product of a solitary, hermetic existence, suited to an isolated earthen bothy rather than the community life as witnessed in Benedictine or Cistercian houses. It is perhaps significant that Pelagius, a fifth-century theologian and exegete whose doctrine was that man could take the initial step towards salvation by his own efforts, should also have originated in Britain. There has always been something sanguine in the British make-up which has not reacted well with the Augustinian doctrine of Original Sin, and we may see in the Grail Tradition this same yearning towards independent salvation – for the meaning of the Grail seems to have little to do with the established means to such an end.

The Reserved Body

Seen in this light the actions of the Grail are all the more unusual and lead us to consider another interesting practice. The consecrated bread was, from earliest times, reserved in a box called an aumbry. This happened not only within churches but in private houses as well, where the faithful would administer the sacrament to each other in default of priest or deacon, or during times of persecution. The reservation of the sacrament is an intrinsic part of the Grail legends and is mentioned specifically in a translation into medieval English of Robert de Boron's *Joseph*. In the episode in question, Sarracynte, the wife of Evelach of Sarras, one of the earliest Grail kings, relates how her mother kept the host in a box, being a Christian secretly in fear of her pagan husband. Each day she washed her hands and,

> *The box anon she opened there;*
> *Out of the box there issued anon*
> *Our Holy Saviour in flesh and bone*
> *In form of bread...*
> *... with many tears and sore sighing*
> *There received she that holy thing...*[17]

Shortly after this she died, charging her daughter to keep the box hidden safely. This is one of many examples of the way in which women seem to have been the bearers of the Grail, while the men were its guardians. It also showed how central the mystery of transubstantiation was to the medieval Christians. To the keepers of the Nanteos Cup this would have added significantly to their understanding of the ideas surrounding the vessel in their care.

The Mysteries of the Grail

These, then, were the sacramental mysteries around which the life of medieval Christendom revolved. Christ was present among men, not just in the reserved host on the altar, but also in each person who partook of the sacraments. This realization is an important one. People did not frequent the sacrament in order to be 'good' in some perfunctory manner, but in order to be at one with Christ – in communion. This was, and is, the ultimate aim of every Christian: to be at one with God in the person of Christ, whether on earth or in heaven. But the obstacles to this union must be overcome. Man suffers the effects of Original Sin, a loss of sanctifying grace, brought about through Adam's fall. Thus, the Grail knights had to struggle against overwhelming odds, always supported and aided by their faith and by the presence of the holy hermits who peopled the forest of adventure through which they rode in quest of the miraculous vessel.

The Redemption, whereby man is saved from sin and death, was seen in various ways. In the West, emphasis was given to the expiation of sins through the sacrificial death of Christ; while in the East, the Greek fathers were more concerned with the restoration of man to Divine life – an idea referred to by the term *theosis* or God-bearing. It is a delicate idea to comprehend, and one that the Western Church has understated again and again. Not so the Eastern Church, in which it remains an article of faith. For this reason, perhaps, we hear less of the Grail in Eastern orthodoxy than in the West.

The fact that the Grail is housed in the castle of Corbenic, which can be translated as meaning 'blessed or transfigured body', is not without significance. Did the Grail offer an alternative way to salvation? Is this the reason why the Grail knights embarked on a quest for something that could ostensibly be gained by worshipping daily at the sacrament of the altar?

Perhaps the answer is that the Grail legends symbolized man's personal search for perfection; not a narrowing of sights and a cramping of style, but a generous impulse which could not be contained within the straitened ways of orthodox belief. The Church had already begun to develop into an administrative organisation concerned with political, as much as religious, motivation. It had established an exoteric mode of expression.

But, when a received tradition begins to petrify in this way, losing its original cutting-edge of truth in a tangle of dogmas, it becomes time for an esoteric tradition to arise by which the great truths may not perish but be revivified and transmitted to further generations. When the established hierarchy fails in its duty, it is as though the angelic powers inspired humankind to produce those who will continue them. These are the people who stand in direct communication with the Will of God: the mystics, who interpret the inner workings of creation; the storytellers, who realise the truths in popular manner; and the heretics, who delve into forgotten or half-forgotten lore, and who formulate alternatives to established ways of belief.

Each of these categories can be seen to have influenced the growth of the Grail legends in one way or another, and many of them are paralleled in the developing story of the Nanteos Cup. They can be viewed as simple Christian allegory, as straightforward story, or as rank heresy, according to the prevailing tone of the time. Yet there were those who found no dichotomy in such matters, and it was they who kept the idea of the Grail alive throughout the Middle Ages. Without this, there could have been no such relic as the Nanteos Cup – belief in which must have worked at a profoundly deep level in the imaginations and traditions of those who encountered it.

A New Tide

The unique quality of European Christianity did not long remain isolated. Just as it had come to establish itself and was even beginning to seem tame, the rallying call went out through the Western world: '*Aidez le Saint Sepulchre*', save the Holy Sepulchre. The city of Jerusalem, long seen as an image of heaven on earth, demanded rescue from the Infidel. It was the beginning of a great and powerful movement, which swept up just about every able-bodied man in Europe and flung them headlong into a venture that was to take them into strange lands. Out of this emerged a new strand in the story of the Grail, which went with the Crusaders in their dreams and their literature, and returned, once again transformed, through their encounters with Oriental beliefs and traditions and the still active ghosts of the first Christians.

So far, we have dealt with the Christian and Celtic faces of the Grail Tradition. Now, like true Crusaders, we must venture into the realm of Islam.

The third of the so-called religions of the book – the others are Christianity and Judaism – Islam spread quickly throughout the Middle East from the middle of the seventh century onwards, eventually encompassing Egypt, Morocco, Spain, Persia and India. It brought with it a new culture as well as a new religion. In medicine, arithmetic, astronomy, geography and philosophy it led the world: Islamic scholars had access to major Greek writings long before the West; in fact, it taught the West.

The Holy City of Jerusalem had been in Islamic hands for a long time before the beginning of the Crusades. Pilgrimage to the Holy Land was possible, if hazardous, under the Abbasid caliphate; but towards the end of the eleventh century the balance of power changed – under the new Fatimid dynasty, permission to enter Palestine seemed doubtful. It was no accident that Pope Urban II should initiate the call for Crusade in 1095. His motivations may have been politically oriented – he desired above all to see an incipient split between Eastern and Western Christendom, Constantinople and Rome, healed – but he also expressed goodwill and a genuine concern that the Eastern Church should not suffer while the Western stood by and did nothing to help its brothers in Christ. He therefore proclaimed, at the Council of Clermont, that to those who fought to protect Eastern Christendom from pagan incursions, and to liberate the holy places, he would grant general absolution and remission of sins. To those who forsook their promise, he vowed excommunication.

Urban's clarion call opened the way for Christians to perform their duty in clear and unambiguous terms; he managed, albeit unknowingly, to call into being the greatest fighting force Europe was to see until the Second World War, and at the same time helped to solve the problem of unfocussed strength. Not long since, Christian armies had been persuaded not to fight with each other without good reason, and some areas of Europe still faced the problem of armies fighting across their fields.

The situation is readily paralleled by the Arthurian tradition. When Arthur came to the throne, he had first to prove his supremacy in battle over the rival kings of Britain. After he had done this, he engaged their services in policing the country. But when all the fighting is done, when there are no more bold, bad barons to discomfit, no more black knights hoving at fords, and when all the dragons are dead, then the famous Round Table Fellowship becomes lethargic and exhibits some of the traits they were once dedicated to overcoming. Then, as the whole court is teetering in the balance, and with the scandal of Lancelot's illicit passion for Arthur's queen about to break, the Grail appears, leading to renewal of enthusiasm and plenty of wondrous opportunities for personal growth and adventure.

So, too, the Crusades appeared at the right moment to harness the combined strengths of Christendom into a single spearhead of power. Unfortunately, the parallel holds good when we come to look at the course of the Crusades: great deeds were achieved, but great evils unloosed as well; those who approached the Grail quest unworthily may well have wreaked worse damage than if they had stayed at home. In the Arthurian Tradition, the appearance of the Grail heralds the ultimate break-up of the Round Table; we must view Urban's call to Christendom in the same way, for it undoubtedly set up a chain reaction that we still feel today. Ownership of the Holy Lands, the division between Catholic and Orthodox churches, and many other issues which still trouble us may be seen as originating with the Crusades.

The Crusader Cup

The chief object of the Crusader armies was to liberate the Holy Sepulchre, in the same way that the goal of the Quest knights was to seek the Grail. But a problem soon emerged: when the Crusaders finally beheld Jerusalem in 1099, there was not a dry eye in their ranks. Hardened killers wept at the sight of their God's tomb, which was, after all, merely the temporary resting place of Christ's body prior to the Resurrection. The dilemma had still not struck them. The tomb was empty, their victory hollow. It was not until the leaders of the First Crusade began supervising the removal of bodies from Jerusalem, whose streets had been purged of every last Moslem, Jew and, for that matter, some Christians sympathetic to Islam, that they began to wonder – what next?

Christendom retained its tenure in Jerusalem until 1187, when it once again fell into Moslem hands. But just as no one can appropriate heaven as a personal possession, neither could the Crusaders establish an earthly city as a heavenly enclave. It was not long before wrangling began; religious and secular leaders were chosen, after long dispute, and a kingdom of Jerusalem, known as Outremer, was formed. It remained a bone of contention as claimants came thick and fast on the death of any king careless enough to leave doubtful successors.

The Crusades brought many changes to Christendom. Coffers were emptied to send forth vast armies of men who returned to find themselves homeless. Disillusioned by fighting and religion, they roamed through Europe, begging for food or forming themselves into armed gangs who terrorized the land. The strengths of Christendom were found to have their weaknesses also; the holy images were blackened by smoke and slaughter. All save one: the Grail, which instead of being weakened by the souring of the great enterprise, seemed to be strengthened.

Chrétien de Troyes – whose *Le Conte del Graal* is the oldest text we have on record, though he was undoubtedly drawing upon much older sources – was himself in the service of one of the most renowned

Crusading families, that of Philip of Flanders, who Chrétien declared had given him the source for his poem from a book he had obtained in the Holy Land in 1177. This date certainly tallies with Philip's movements at the time, and even if he did not bring back an actual text, he could certainly have carried home an account of several sacred objects discovered by the Crusading armies.

Above all it was the *stories* that they returned with that continued to shape the Grail myth throughout the Middle Ages. Descriptions of ancient temples in the desert became adapted into temples of the Grail in Western epics like the thirteenth-century German *Der Jungere Titurel*, which took an actual building situated within lands belonging to the Persian Empire and used it to describe a magical home for the Grail. Interestingly, the occultist A. E. Waite, whose part in the story of the Nanteos Cup we shall return to later, was amongst the first to rediscover the story of the Grail's journey to the great city of Edessa, as described in the *Titurel*.[18]

Another thirteenth-century poet, Wolfram von Eschenbach, crafted his great work *Parzifal* based in part upon Chrétien's tale but elaborated by stories and lore from the East into something even more mysterious and mystical.[19] Chrétien himself had almost certainly borrowed from Jewish lore and legend, shaping them into a mysterious tale of a relic too precious to be kept in the open, but instead hidden away, subject to a long quest that involved its seekers on a journey that changed their lives forever.

All of this paved the way for the appearance of a mysterious relic, with its own persuasive history, in the misty lands of Wales. What is interesting about this is just how at variance it is with the history of the Grail as traced above. The Celtic connection, made via the various magical tales and poems written by early medieval Welsh scribes, is in fact a distinct and probably late development in what was a far older tradition originating in the East rather than the West. The existence of the Nanteos legend is much at variance with this but demonstrates the powerful effect of the Grail story wherever it appears.

There is no hard evidence for the story of the monks of Strata Florida and their guardianship of the relic that became known as the Nanteos Cup, yet the story persisted – as it does to this day – and within it is just enough of reality to give one pause for thought. If a cup or dish, a mazer bowl or a Seder vessel from Hebrew tradition, was brought back to Britain from the Holy Land by a Crusader knight, it could have been seen, because of its place of origin, as somehow imbued with divine presence. It needed only one person (who had already heard tell of the mysterious Grail) to suggest that it might have been used at the Last Supper, and the rest would have followed inevitably. There is no reason to suppose that the monks were lying, or that anyone made up the story. It is enough that they arrived at this idea, from whatever source, and that they believed in it. This is the nature of myth, which envelops a seed of reality within a shell of dreamlike story.

To understand this more fully, it is time to look at what is known of the monastic settlement of Strata Florida, so that we can better understand how the story began and how it was shaped. After that, the path is clear, and we can follow the journey of the Nanteos Cup to the present day. For the next part of the story we need to keep an open mind and reach our own conclusions as to its reality or otherwise, based upon what can be reconstructed from the few fragmentary accounts that remain.

2

Strata Florida, the Mazers and a Prince of Arabia

The lack of connected evidence for the antiquity of the Nanteos Cup has been one of the greatest stumbling blocks for those seeking to trace its origin and early history. The most widely related account of the way it arrived at Nanteos House has remained largely unchanged since it first appeared in the early nineteenth century. Essentially, we are told that monks of Glastonbury Abbey, fled – fearing the inevitable visitations of Henry VIII's chief inquisitor Thomas Cromwell – taking with them the priceless relic known as the Holy Grail. They went north to Strata Florida (Ystrad Fflur) in Cardiganshire, where they were welcomed by the Cistercians who maintained the abbey. Soon, however, the shadow of Cromwell's men grew near again, and seven of the monks took their precious burden to the nearby home of the Stedman family, who were sympathetic to the Catholic cause, and took in both the monks and their charge. Here the relic remained – and following the death of the last of the seven monks, passed into the keeping of the Stedmans, and later, through marriage, to the Powells. There it has remained ever since.

Such is the story, as told and retold throughout the nineteenth and twentieth centuries into our own time. It has been modified several times, with certain details being added and others removed, but the essence of the tale is as given here. From its first appearance in 1828 we can trace virtually every detail of the story, which evolved, as did the relic itself, into something that has proved irresistible to generations of Grail seekers. Yet, before the beginning of the nineteenth century, there has been no hard evidence to support the story of its medieval – or even older – origin. Given that the connections of the Grail and King Arthur with Glastonbury are themselves doubtful, with no real evidence ever produced to support them, the whole story begins on shaky ground. But if we set aside, for the moment, this part of the story, then our attention is directed towards Strata Florida and the Stedman family. Can we see anything in the history of this great abbey, or the family, that might have given rise to the legend of the Nanteos Cup? We think we can.

We have already seen that the period of the Middle Ages was wide open to the appearance of the Grail story. Though the vast collection of romances, written between the twelfth and fifteenth centuries, retold, embellished, altered and recast the story many times over, the heart of it remained the same – that there existed a relic indissolubly tied to the life of Christ and to the development of the early Christian church.

In this chapter we will examine some of the possible origins of the Nanteos Cup, as a relic, as a survival from the period of the Reformation curated by two families, its use in a medieval Catholic context, and its probable identity as a kind of vessel known as a mazer.

Hewn from Sacred Wood

Some of the beliefs and ideas concerning the cup are clearly very old, but more motifs and traditions would be added to the mix as it began to evolve into the symbol we recognize today. How this came about is a fascinating story, and one that is full of surprises.

One of the earliest theories concerning the origin of the cup was that it was made from the 'True Cross' – the very cross on which Jesus Christ was crucified. The earliest written references to this tradition that we know of – and of its connection to the Nanteos Cup – come from articles in the Welsh language journal *Lleuad yr Oes* for the year 1828, which we shall return to in more detail in Chapter 3. After this, in 1878, the tradition was mentioned again by the Bishop of Saint Davids, Basil Jones, when he gave an address to the Cambrian Archaeological Association, on the occasion when the Nanteos Cup was being publicly exhibited for the first time:

> It is supposed to have been a possession of the abbey of Strata Florida, and to have passed with that demesne from the Stedmans to the Powells... The source of its alleged virtues were supposed to lie in its having formed a portion of the True Cross. I think there can be little doubt that so much of its pedigree is true as traces it to the possession of the Cistercians at Strata Florida. Nothing is more probable than that it was preserved in their church as a relic to which thaumaturgic powers were ascribed.[1]

The bishop here neatly avoids coming down on one side or the other. He obviously likes the idea of the cup's healing power, and his mention of the True Cross looks towards a well-established tradition, but words like 'supposed to' offer a shading of uncertainty. The legend itself clearly retains its fascination.

In the early fourth century, some ancient timber was discovered at Jerusalem and it was believed that this wood was the remains of the True Cross. It became greatly revered throughout Christendom; many cures and miracles were attributed to it.[2] Eventually, legends sprung up around it, most notably that it had been discovered by Helena, the mother of Constantine the Great.

According to this story, Helena, acting under divine instruction, undertook a journey to Jerusalem, where she discovered from local people the place where Christ had been crucified. This place had been largely forgotten about because a temple to Venus (some say Jupiter) had been constructed over the location of the crucifixion; nevertheless, the location of the holy site was found, thanks to divine intervention.

Helena ordered that the pagan temple should be torn down and eventually three crosses were found, lying buried beneath the place where the temple had stood. The board that Pontius Pilate had made for the cross of Jesus was also found, but they still did not know which of the three crosses belonged to Jesus. Helena prayed for guidance, so that the identity of the True Cross should be made known to them; she then ordered that a corpse be laid on each of the crosses in turn. When the corpse was laid on the third cross, the body sprang back to life, thereby revealing that this was the True Cross of Jesus.

The likelihood is that there is no truth in *any* of this, let alone the resurrection. Piety and belief mingled equally with superstition at this time, and it has been noticed more than once that if every sliver of the True Cross proudly displayed in churches across the medieval world were put together, we should have a small stretch of woodland!

Fragments of the True Cross were certainly widely distributed. That such a holy relic should have been treated in this way seems rather shocking from a modern perspective. It is clear that believers respected the sanctity and power of the cross but had no strong desire to preserve it. One early commentator noted:

And it is said that one time a person fixed his teeth in it, and so stole a piece of the holy wood, it is now guarded by the deacons standing round, so that no one who comes may dare to do such a thing again.[3]

This text is attributed to a fourth-century nun, sometimes referred to as Sylvia, or more recently, Egeria. The manuscript referred to is the *Itinerarium Egeriae*, and the only copy of her work that survives today was transcribed in the eleventh century.[4] The manuscript then vanished for 700 years until the year 1884. It was translated into English in 1891.[5] It might be tempting to suppose that the story about the Nanteos Cup being nibbled by its borrowers could be connected with the rediscovery and translation of the *Itinerarium Egeriae*, but in truth the nibbling patients had already been mentioned by Bishop Basil Jones in 1878, some years before the Egeria MS was rediscovered:

The patient had to drink wine, or some liquor out of it. Not content with this, he sometimes nibbled a piece from its edge: hence its present unshapely condition.[6]

Nevertheless, it is interesting to note that the tradition of biting or nibbling the True Cross goes back centuries. The Venerable

Bede, commenting on another wooden cross set up by the seventh-century Northumbrian King, Oswald, noted:

> ... for even to this day, many are wont to cut off small chips from the wood of the holy cross, which being put into water, men or cattle drinking thereof, or sprinkled with that water, are immediately restored to health.[7]

It should not be forgotten that it was necessary for any altar stone on which the mass was celebrated should have relics embedded beneath it, and every new church required the same. Tiny fragments of martyrs' bones or hair were thus in great demand, and the trade in stolen or fake relics was considerable. Several of the finger bones of the deceased Saint Theresa of Avila were bitten off in this manner.

Possibly one of most historically significant relics derived from the True Cross was the Cross of Gneith or *Croes Naid*. According to legend, a priest by the name of Neotus brought a fragment of the True Cross from the Holy Land to Wales. It is depicted on a roof-boss in St George's Chapel, Windsor, as a beautiful jewel-encrusted Celtic cross, standing on a mound. It was kept at Aberconway and was the treasured possession of the Welsh Princes. When the last Welsh Prince, Llewelyn, was slain in 1282, it was captured by the English King, Edward I (known as 'Long Shanks'), who took it with him on his military campaigns to Scotland. Nothing remains of the Cross of Gneith today.[8] Edward, indeed, had a great hunger for relics of many kinds, at one time supposedly possessing the crown of King Arthur, so his desire to own the *Croes* is no surprise. Despite the curiously similar name of the priest Neotus and the house of Nanteos, this seems to be no more than a coincidence.

Another relic of the True Cross came to Dore Abbey, Herefordshire, in 1321. Again, it was decorated with gold and layered with precious gems. It came to Dore by way of William de Grandison, who handed it over to the monastery as recompense for a debt owed to the abbot, Richard de Straddel.[9] Margam Abbey in South Wales also possessed a similar relic. A Welsh lord named Leisan Morgan granted lands to the abbey and the document records that it was sworn on the relics kept at Margam, including their piece of the True Cross.[10] Strata Marcella Abbey in North Wales may also have had a sliver of the True Cross.[11]

Could the Nanteos Cup have been made from this wood? To us this seems unlikely, if only for the simple reason that a cup used at the Last Supper could hardly be made from the wood of the Crucifixion, since the latter took place after the former, and that the use of wooden vessels for a ritual meal was forbidden. However, the tradition may be as old as the cup itself and it certainly added a dimension of wonder and sacredness to the story.

Healing and the Early Church

If we look more closely at some of the elements of the Nanteos story, we find several interesting details. Take, for example, the central fact of all – that the cup performed miraculous healings. Was this simply a matter of faith, or did the cup actually possess a miraculous nature? This aspect was emphasised from the start, so we should look to the understanding and nature of such events in the Christian church.

One of the most important early Christian thinkers was the North African Bishop Augustine of Hippo (354–430), whose writings, especially his *Confessions* and *The City of God*, were to have an influential and lasting effect on the course of Christianity, especially in the West. In *The City of God*, Augustine endeavoured to explain why the miracles of the early years of Christianity and of Christ's own ministry were no longer being performed.

> Why, they say, are those miracles, which you affirm were wrought formerly, wrought no longer? I might indeed, reply that miracles were necessary before the world believed, in order that it might believe.[12]

Thus, according to Augustine's argument, the Christian faith, having established itself, no longer required miracles to occur with such great frequency. The miracles were directly linked to Christ's bodily ascension into Heaven, which Augustine believed was the greatest miracle of all:

> But we cannot deny that many miracles were wrought to confirm that one grand and health-giving miracle of Christ's ascension to heaven with the flesh in which He rose.[13]

Having previously explained why miracles were diminished in number, he nevertheless asserted that they were still being performed in his own time:

> For even now miracles are wrought in the name of Christ, whether by His sacraments or by the prayers or relics of His saints; but they are not so brilliant and conspicuous as to cause them to be published with such glory as accompanied the former miracles.[14]

Augustine linked miraculous events with relics and also with the Eucharist; there are also hints from very early records that the Eucharist was linked with healing. In the third-century account known as *The Apocryphal Acts of Thomas* there is a story of a man who had committed a crime of passion and then partaken of the Eucharist, only to have his hands wither away. He is brought before a priest who says:

> Tell me, my son, and be not afraid, what thou hast done, ere thou camest hither. For the Eucharist of the Lord has convicted thee... For this gift, by permeating them, **brings healing to many**, especially to those who come in faith and love; but thee it has withered away, and what has happened has happened not without some cause...[15] [Authors' emphasis]

The above passage seems to imply that partaking in the Eucharist might result in healing, but could also have a negative, baleful effect on the participant if he or she was in a sinful or impure state. We find a similar idea in late medieval times, when menstruating women refrained from taking communion.[16] The communion host could be subject to abuse and even used for magical purposes if it fell into the wrong hands. Saint Bernard of Clairvaux was said to have cured a man of bewitchment by hovering a *ciborium*, a metal cup with a lid, used for holding the consecrated Eucharistic bread, over the man's head.[17]

In ancient accounts of healing, the notion of touch is very prevalent; this extends to contact not just with the healer, but something connected to him. We see this in Biblical accounts of Jesus' own healing ministry when a woman is cured of a haemorrhage simply by touching his clothes (Mark 5:25-30).

Jesus notices that someone has made contact with his robe because he senses healing energy flowing from him (Mark 5:30). In another concept, *brandea*, we have a similar idea: the notion being that a piece of cloth touched against a holy object, or taken to a holy place, thus becomes imbued with holiness. This explains the desire amongst believers to get physically close to holy objects such as relics of the True Cross. In the case of the Nanteos Cup there was a belief that a handkerchief tied to the cup for a day would result in the curative powers of the vessel being transferred to the cloth. According to the Revd G. Hartwell Jones, this was 'precisely the same process as may be witnessed at any Continental shrine or at Westminster Abbey'.[18]

The story of the Grail itself, in its most widely accepted sense, is linked both to the Eucharist and to healing. The Grail is responsible for keeping the wounded Fisher King alive, extending his life for many years, and there are other instances within the prolix accounts of the *Lancelot-Grail*, in which just being in the presence of the sacred vessel could bring about miraculous cures.

Houses of Prayer and Healing

Medieval abbeys, such as those described in the accounts of the medieval history of the cup, were largely independent communities, ruled over by an abbot and following the specific rule of their denomination: Cistercian, Benedictine, Carthusian, and Franciscan. Their days were divided into periods of devotion known as 'Canonical Hours', which marked out the celebration of the Divine Liturgy as it was celebrated seven times daily throughout the Christian world from the earliest times.

Their days filled with prayer and contemplation, the monks were also known for their skills in medicine, farming and the collection and preservation of knowledge. Some of the most important works that preserved the history of medieval England were collected and written down in these great buildings, most of which included a scriptorium where skilled monks laboured to produce copies of the Gospels and histories of the area and the country as a whole.

The abbey of Strata Florida was one of the larger foundations, founded in *c.* 1164 by the Cambro-Norman knight Robert FitzStephen (*c.* 1123–83) under the patronage of Rhys ap Gruffudd, who issued a charter affirming it as a monastery in 1184. The abbey church was consecrated in 1201, and from this point onwards it became a centre of learning and teaching which lasted, with a brief interruption during the period of the Owain Glyndŵr rebellion in 1401, until 1539, when the monastery, along with others across England and Wales, including Glastonbury, was dissolved by Henry VIII as part of his establishment of the Church of England.[19]

One of the most important ways in which the abbey served the surrounding community was the establishment of an infirmary, which offered healing and palliative care for the sick, not only among the monks themselves but for the local villages. The infirmarer (or server of the sick) oversaw the care of the sick and those recuperating after bloodletting, as well as any elderly members of the community who were unable to observe the full rigours of the monastic life. The infirmarer's office was an important and prestigious post; his duties including making sure that the fire was lit, lighting the candles for Matins, cleaning the bowls that had been used at bloodletting and disposing of the blood. On Saturdays he washed the feet of those who resided in the infirmary – if they so wished – and shook their clothing.

Whenever one of the monks was received in the infirmary it was the infirmarer's responsibility to transfer his utensils from the refectory and his bedding from the dormitory – which he then replaced when the monk returned to choir – and to fetch the sick man's allowance of food and drink from the cellarer each day. The infirmarer borrowed books required for services in the infirmary chapel from the abbey church and ensured that these, along with any other books, were returned safely. He notified the sick of any matters of importance that had been raised at the daily chapter meeting and alerted the community of any inmates who were about to die, so that the brethren could make appropriate provision for his soul.

Whenever one of the inmates of the infirmary was ready to rejoin the community, the infirmarer sought authorization from the Abbot for his return to the cloister. The infirmarer was thus responsible for the overall management of the whole process of illness, death and burial. He alone was allowed to speak to the inmates, in an otherwise silent community; but was to do so quietly and only in designated areas.

The twelfth-century Customary of the Cistercian Order (*Ecclesiastica Officia*)[20] discusses the infirmarer's managerial duties in some detail but says little of his medical knowledge. However, it is likely that he – and no doubt others in the community – was well versed in herbal remedies and administered herbs grown at the abbey. The infirmarer may well have had access to written medical works. Surviving manuscripts and library catalogues suggest that the Cistercians in England owned works by ancient and contemporary medical authorities, as well as more traditional works such as herbals. For example, a thirteenth-century manuscript from Kirkstall Abbey contains a copy of the *Medulla Philosophorum*, a miscellany of tracts that includes explanations of various herbs and plants, as well as passages on digestion and blood.[21]

It is easy to accept the idea that if one of the infirmarers, skilled in the use of herbs and either medicines, used a particular vessel to treat his patients, and if one of the sick became unexpectedly restored to health, the vessel used could have been regarded with a sense of awe, rapidly turning to a belief in its 'miraculous' properties.

Beyond any such events, Strata Florida was important for a number of other reasons – notable for the fact that one of the primary sources for the history of Wales was compiled there. The *Brut Y Tywysogion*,[22] which traced the evolution of the country from its mythical founding by Brutus of Troy to the coming of the Normans, remains an important document, and though it contains no references to the Grail, its inclusion of a number of legendary tales suggests that the monks had access to documents other than the historical records of Britain. According to the Welsh writer Saunders Lewis, there is even a possibility that the great collection of Mythic tales collected under the title of the *Mabinogion* may have been first written down here.[23] If so, these would have included 'Peredur', a Celtic version of the Grail story which may have been composed before Chrétien de Troyes' version in 1181.

We have no exact information relating to the number of monks who lived in the community. These could vary anywhere between fifty and 200, and the foundation itself owned large areas of land and often ran several farms which provided food for the community, shared also with the inhabitants of the surrounding area. What we do know is that shortly before the final dissolution of the abbey, under its last abbot, Richard Talley, only six monks remained at Strata Florida, one of whom was to stand trial on the charge of coining money.

By this time the old medieval economy was breaking down, and lands and pastures were being let out on long leases to the monastery's lay tenants. The infirmary was in ruins, and an alehouse had been built within the abbey grounds. However, some of the abbey's lay tenants had already begun to transform the holdings into farmland.

The administration of the dissolution of Strata Florida Abbey was carried out by Thomas Cromwell's agents. A commission of four was appointed for Wales in 1535, to make inventories of the possessions of religious houses, and to enquire into alleged abuses and excesses. These visitors included Richard Ingworth, Bishop of Dover. The report of the commissioners was destroyed during Queen Mary Tudor's reign, and no Surrender Deed for any Welsh Cistercian monastery seems to have survived. The investigators and their agents spent nine months in their visitations, and it is evident that no significant item escaped their attention.

Richard Ingworth seems to have carried out his task with great enthusiasm, for in a letter to Thomas Cromwell he reported that he had 'too cumbrous a collection' to send to London. He did send one, however, an image – 'the holiest relic in all North Wales' – taken from the Black friars of Bangor. It seems possible that the Strata Florida Cup might have passed unnoticed as a sacred relic if it had been removed from the elaborate reliquary in which it was most probably kept, or may have been simply overlooked because of its ordinary appearance.[24]

Henry's commissioners systematically visited and listed the possessions of all Welsh churches and monasteries in 1535. Their procedures were expert and thorough. Eight monks are recorded as having been promised pensions at Strata Florida in 1539 and five were still receiving them in 1558. It is likely that one of these monks, John Yorke, was restored to his earlier position as bailiff of the abbey grange of Mevenyth by the Crown lessee.

The eleven years of Abbot Talley's rule were stormy: there had been disorders at Strata Florida. A monk was tried for coining money in his cell, though his name appears on the pension list. Talley was a considerable landowner and returned to Ystrad to devote himself to increasing his fortune for his son. He had been involved in a dispute with another monk over the abbacy, and two letters of the period refer to his improper holding of a relic belonging to another Welsh abbey. After the Dissolution it was discovered that Talley had awarded the grange of Aberdehonowe to its tenants, under a counterfeit lease, for his own gain. The portrait of the venerable prior and his devout monks is somewhat tarnished in the harsh light of such historical facts.

The historian Stephen Williams records a tradition of the area that the church was used for divine service until the time of the Commonwealth, and this certainly happened in other places. He also tells of another tradition – that the monks lived on in the area in poverty and destitution and continued to occupy some portion of the conventual buildings, dependent upon the charity of local farmers and peasants.[25]

Was there a cup at Strata Florida that was the object of pilgrimage from early times? And if so, what happened to it and to the monks who protected it? And to whom did this precious relic pass? According to an article by D. and A. Matthew in *The Dublin Review* for January 1929,[26] monks of the more remote Welsh monasteries (which could have included Strata Florida) went to live in the mountain woodlands. There they were supported by the common people and by the robber bands, several of which were known to have kept Catholic chaplains. This situation was unique in the British Isles, made possible by the mountainous terrain and the lawlessness of the country at that time.

These same writers claim that the great relic of Strata Florida, the Holy Grail itself, was hidden when the monks disappeared into the mountains beyond Plynlimon, into an area controlled by local nobles who made a scanty livelihood from the few travellers to the sea. To this place had been brought the crozier of St Paternus from Llanbadarn Church, along with the miraculous arm of St Cyricius of Iconium. The monks seem to have followed their rule until all the survivors were dead, for there are references to 'the sacred fire at Llys Celyddon' and that 'Arwystli enjoyed the protection of saints'. None of this seems to stand up to close scrutiny.

The Inheritors
As we saw, when the abbey was dissolved in 1539, the church and its attached buildings were demolished, and the contents valued and sold off (those which had not already been hidden away or removed). The abbey church itself may have continued to be used

for parochial purposes until the seventeenth century, after which it became a total ruin. Stones from the fallen walls were reused to build houses, one of which, known as *Ty Abaty* (Abbey House), became the home of the Stedman family, who were certainly living there, according to local records, in 1567, just a few years after the dissolution of the abbey.[27]

The family claimed a somewhat romantic ancestry from a certain Galearbus, a 'Duke of Arabia', which has generally been dismissed as invention. However, in Book V of *The British Genealogist*, compiled by Edward Llwyd, keeper of the Ashmolean Museum in Oxford in 1693 and added to later by Samuel Meyrick, we find the following:

> Galearbus, a Duke of Arabia, was through the tyranny of the King of that country banished thence and coming with his son Stedman and daughter Clarissa toward the holy land died ere he arrived there; but his son came to Jerusalem and being a gallant person was by King Richard the 1st of England very much esteemed, he was made [a] knight of the Sepulchre and had for arms a cross fleury vert in a field or. He came over to England Anno Domini 1191 and had given him in marriage by the said King, Joan daughter and heir to Sir John Tatsall or Tatshall, knight brother to Robert Lord Tatshall.[28]

Galearbus, or perhaps Galeribus, is a curious name. It sounds more Roman than Arabic, but the fact that his son is made 'a Knight of the Sepulchre' is striking. It may also imply that Galearbus, if he was of Middle Eastern origin, may have converted to Christianity, rather as the Knight Sir Palomides does in the Arthurian legends. The Order itself was founded as the *Milites Sancti Sepulcri* in 1113 by order of Pope Paschal II and later ratified by Pope Calixtus II in 1122. It traces its roots even earlier to *c.* 1099 under the leadership of Godfrey of Bouillon (1060–1100), one of the most important leaders of the First Crusade and the first ruler of the newly created Kingdom of Jerusalem, whose title was 'Defender of the Holy Sepulchre'.[29] Godfrey was accorded the status of a hero of almost mystical standing, and in more recent times has been associated with the notorious Priory de Sion, the Templars, as well as other currently unproven connections. He was, however, counted as one of the Nine Worthies: powerful figures – some historical, others mythical – said to be sleeping beneath Mount Etna until 'a time of need'. King Arthur was numbered amongst them, and if someone was indeed looking to establish a link between the Stedman family and the Holy Grail, it is easy to see how a knight of the Order of the Sepulchre could have come by such a sacred relic, and to have brought it home with him to Britain.

A slightly different version, including a variant name, is found in *The History and Antiquities of the County of Cardigan* written by the redoubtable and well-respected historian of chivalry and medieval heraldry, Samuel Rush Meyrick, who had previously collaborated with Edward Llwyd. In an entry on Stedman of Dolygaer (in Powys, Wales) we find the ancestor called 'Calcarbus or Calcarba, duke of Arabia, who was exiled with his son Stedman and [daughter] Clarisia by the tyranny of the king of the country'. The rest of the entry reads:

> ...the son, following the fortunes of that monarch, was made knight of the sepulchre, and imprisoned with him on his return home. Part of this tale may be true: Stedman, without the affectation or punning, may have received this appellation from his steadiness and fidelity to his sovereign, and may have been an Asiatic, and the domestic of the enthusiastic Richard, during his captivity. If so, I trust that the name of Stedman will be substituted in the drama of Coeur de Lion instead of Blondel. Richard, it is said, gave his faithful adherent for a wife, Joan, daughter of Sir John Tatsall, knight...[30]

Again, the names are European rather than Arabic, and though we hear no more of Clarissa, her presence brings a note of authenticity to the story.

Sir John Tatsall, or Tatshall, was the brother of Sir Robert Tatshall, Sheriff of Lincolnshire, part of a family that came to England with the Conqueror and was descended from a Breton knight named Eudo son of Spirewic. Their holdings are well attested to in the Domesday Book. A cadet branch of the Strata Florida Stedmans bore the Tatshall arms as a quartering, while those coming from Shropshire bore 'the cross moline on a chevron between three boars' heads'. Major Stedman Farmer, of this branch, possesses what is claimed to be the first Stedman's crusader ring, a large gold hoop on which a cross moline is engraved. It is worn on the thumb and used as a seal.

Looking further, we found in a book entitled *Annals and Antiquities of the Counties and Country Families of Wales* vol I, published in 1872 by Thomas Nicholas, under the heading 'the Stedmans of Strata Florida', a longer entry which once again repeated the Duke of Arabia story, but included reference to a Welsh genealogist named Lewys Dwnn (*c.* 1550–1616), which included the following entry: 'Y Syr John Ysteidmon yna oedd vab y Dawk Arabia, henw y Dawk oedd Galabia.'[31]

Nicholas also mentions 'The Dale Castle manuscript', presumably a genealogy, most likely of the Phillips family who owned Dale Castle (in Pembrokeshire). According to Nicholas, the tenth generation from the 'Arabian' Stedman (son of a second son) married Anne, natural daughter of William Phillips of Pentre Parte. The last Richard Stedman, born in 1693, was added (in a different hand) to the Dale Castle MS:

> ...married Anne, second daughter of William Powel of Nanteos, Esq. He left no issue, but was prevailed upon to disinherit his sister's issue, and to give his estate to his wife's brother and his heirs.

Nicholas dryly remarks of all this: 'So Strata Florida came to Nanteos. This was the end of the Stedmans of Ystrad-Fflur.'

What, if any, reliance can be placed on this is doubtful, and remains purely speculative; however, it certainly establishes the importance of the family and is in keeping with their subsequent history.

'Prince of Arabia' does not necessarily imply someone of Arabic descent. Given the time and situation, this could simply mean that Galearbus was a faithful follower of Richard I, who was rewarded by a title and lands subsequently inherited by his son. We cannot know this for certain, but it does fit the setting of the time. The fact that there are two different accounts of the origin story is significant. If it had simply been an invention by a later member of the family, retrospectively desiring to give more significance to the Stedmans, it seems unlikely that there would be variant versions.

Strata Florida and the Stedmans

In 1539 Richard Devereux, Sir Walter's son, was appointed Receiver-General of all the possessions of the abbey, and Lord Ferrers was appointed King's Steward of the Crown and manors of the Court of the Abbots of Strata Florida. A valuation was made in 1543 of the estates, rents and profits issuing from every part of the granges, farms and lands of the abbey, but nothing was said of the church itself or the graveyard. In March 1547 the first lease of the house and site of the 'late monastery' was granted to Richard Devereux, but again, no mention is made of the church itself. This is unusual in such a carefully drawn-up legal document of the period.[32] If the monks from Glastonbury existed and reached Strata Florida, they must have had a shock. The stewardship and the Court of the Abbey were in lay hands even before its dissolution in 1539. John Stedman was agent and bailiff of the Devereux family, Earls of Essex, who held the first lease. Later he purchased the abbey and its lands himself, but he claimed in a legal case that Richard Talley, the wily Abbot, had leased lands to his family as early as 1533. The Stedmans lived in part of the converted buildings before Abbey House was built. If the cup was handed over to anyone it would be John Stedman, for the Powells did not move to Nanteos for another 150 years. Stephen Williams, the historian of Strata Florida, records a tradition of the area that the church was used for divine service until the time of the Commonwealth. He also tells of another tradition – that the monks lived on in the area in poverty and destitution and continued to occupy some portion of the conventual buildings, depending upon the charity of local farmers and peasants, as mentioned earlier.

The Stedmans could have obtained the cup from the monks themselves or from the Devereux family, perhaps as a mere curiosity. As sheriffs and justices of the peace, it is difficult to believe that they would have allowed Catholic services to continue in the abbey precincts upon which their own house stood and the Devereux were positively Protestant in their outlook by that time. Whether the Stedmans had 'some belief', as stated by Bishop Basil Jones, can only be surmised, but they may have allowed borrowing of the cup for requests from the simple, superstitious local people, bereft of the medical support that the monks had given them – a bowl such as they were familiar with and associated in their memories with the healing potions of the monks' infirmary.

Sir Richard died in 1547 and the lease was held by his widow, Lady Dorothy, and renewed by his son, Walter, Viscount Hereford, 1st Earl of Essex, in 1564. In 1571 Devereux sold the site, its demesne lands and tenements to John Stedman, who was described as of 'Stratflour' in earlier documents dated 1564. This family held the lands until 1742 when Richard Stedman died without issue and the estate passed to his brother-in-law, Thomas Powell Esq. of Nanteos. Samuel and Nathaniel Buck's engraving of 'The West View of Stratflour Abby', made in 1741, shows the Abbey House standing within the monastery grounds and bears the combined arms of Richard Stedman and his wife, Anne Powell. The Stedman arms are 'or, a cross Moline, vert'; the Powell arms are 'a cross Flory engrailed sable between four Cornish choughs proper'. (The chough is King Arthur's bird in folklore.) The crest is a virgin holding a cross in her right hand. These are fitting arms for the guardians of the Cup of the Holy Cross.

In the early seventeenth century, Robert Devereux, Earl of Essex, brought Exchequer proceedings against James Stedman, for wrongful intrusion and non-payment of dues as his bailiff. The action was not allowed but the defence is interesting. James Stedman did not claim that his family had bought the land in 1571 but that the late abbot had demised the abbey lands to his family for ninety-nine years in 1533, before the Dissolution. It seems certain that the Stedmans were at the abbey very early, perhaps as agents of the commissioners, most probably as stewards for Lady Dorothy Devereux during her son Walter's minority.

The last of the line, Richard Stedman, married Anne, the second daughter of William Powell of Nanteos. Their two daughters died young and were buried in the church of Strata Florida. Richard himself died intestate and administration of his goods was granted to Thomas Powell, his principal creditor, in 1747. His widow later married Sir Herbert Lloyd of Peterwell, but she continued to reside at Voelallt until her death in 1778 at the age of seventy-six. Strata Florida then passed to the Powells and became part of the Sunny Hill Estate. Secondary branches of the family continue into our own time, and include our own late colleague Fred Stedman-Jones (1932–2016).

During his research into the Stedman lineage Fred Stedman-Jones came across a curious echo of the family's connection to

Strata Florida. There, as we have seen, the Stedmans built a manor house on Cistercian abbey lands where a cup of unknown origin was located. In Somerset, from where the stone facing for the Welsh abbey was probably mined, another Stedman family lived on the Fosse Way, at Downside. Their lands were sold in the early nineteenth century when the direct male line ended, and the Benedictine abbey of Downside now occupies their land, incorporating 'The Squire's House', as it has long been known. The original manor and estate were known as Mount Pleasant. In the 1900s an Iron Age sword was found in a quarry on the estate and this was described by Dr Bulleid, the discoverer of the Glastonbury lake village, as the finest in England. Curiously, until the 1980s, when they appear to have disappeared, Downside kept the papers relating to the discovery of the famous 'Blue Bowl' of Glastonbury, still believed by many to be the Grail.[33]

Downside's own monastic community fled from Flanders during the French Revolution, in a similar fashion to the monks in the time of Henry VIII, and were expelled from the country in 1795. They settled for twenty years as guests of Sir Edward Smythe at Acton Burnell in Shropshire before moving to Mount Pleasant, Downside, in 1814. It is possible that they were given the land and buildings by one of the Somerset Stedmans.[34]

Excavations at Strata Florida Abbey

For over a century there has been speculation that the Nanteos Cup might simply have been found by accident in the vicinity of Strata Florida.[35] It is true enough to say that some chance finds have sometimes been made there; for example, in 1800, a fine silver abbot's seal was discovered on land close to Strata Florida by a boy engaged in ploughing. However, to suggest that the Nanteos Cup was discovered in this way would be to indulge in speculation, as there are no records to suggest this – and wood, in any case, does not survive well when buried. There are, however, alternative suggestions, which we shall explore below.

The first attempt at archaeological excavation at Strata Florida occurred in September 1847, with permission of Colonel Powell of Nanteos. Three days before the archaeologists arrived at the site, some hired labourers, working under supervision of members of the Cambrian Archaeological Association, had excavated selected areas in advance. The archaeologists, led by the Dean of Hereford Cathedral, arrived to inspect what the labourers had excavated, in what was described as a 'cursory visit'. Although some finds were made, such as tiles, masonry, a skeleton, etc., there is no record of anything resembling a bowl or cup having been found.[36]

There were no further excavations at Strata Florida for another forty years, until Stephen W. Williams (1837–99) was eventually given the task. Williams was a surveyor, church builder and restorer, volunteer soldier, architect and engineer who settled in Penralley, Rhayader, in around 1861. He was a member of the Royal Institute of British Architects, the Surveyors Institution, the Honourable Society of Cymmrodorion and the Cambrian Archaeological Association. In spite of his interests, he had no professional qualifications as an historian or archaeologist.[37]

In June 1887, Williams, aided by a small group of labourers, was able to excavate the abbey of Strata Florida over the duration of two weeks, resulting in the general outline of the monastery and some conventual buildings being revealed; a plan was drawn up and drawings were made.[38] Williams gave a report to the Cambrian Archaeological Association in August of that year.[39] In what was a rather unfortunate episode, the quality of Williams' work was criticized by a member of the Society of Antiquaries, a Mr J. W. Willis Bund: 'So far but little has been done, and the excavations have been undertaken more for the purpose of making finds than in any systematic manner.'[40]

Willis Bund even tried to persuade William St John Hope (a noted member of the Society of Antiquaries who was also an expert on mazers) to intervene and supervise future excavations at Strata Florida himself. However, the differences between Williams and Willis Bund were eventually resolved and it was Williams who superintended excavations when work resumed the following year. The 1888 excavations ran from the end of May to the beginning of August, with St John Hope making what Williams described as a 'flying visit' over two days towards the end of the excavation period.[41] Williams presented another report to the Cambrian Archaeologists[42] the following year and subsequently, over a four-month winter period, collated a great deal of material into a substantial book entitled *The Cistercian Abbey of Strata Florida*.[43] In Williams' own words:

It has indeed been a somewhat heavy task, and one that when I commenced upon it four months ago, I little thought would prove so laborious. The Book grew in size as I progressed and each new authority I consulted opened a wider field of research.[44]

Williams fully deserved the praise he received for his work and it will be noted that Mr Willis Bund's name appears in the list of subscribers; Williams was elected a Fellow of the Society of Antiquaries[45] in 1892. Copies of his book were received by Queen Victoria and the House of Commons library.[46] In the summer of 1888, visitors paid admission fees to see the excavated ruins.[47]

Williams' book was widely read and reviewed. One reviewer, writing in the Roman Catholic *Tablet* noted:

Few Cistercian Abbeys in England have such an enthusiastic and able historian as the author of this goodly volume with its copious illustrations and wealth of historic and descriptive detail... Each step in the direction taken by our author in his labours is one more step towards the undoing of the unholy work of the sacrilegious destroyers of the ancient faith of England.[48]

A writer by the name of J. F. Tout, in the *Archaeological Review*, praised Williams' excavation work, but was more critical about his history:

It is no discredit to him that he is not a trained student of history and archaeology. But he has chosen to write upon these subjects, and candor compels me to say that he has not written well.[49]

Williams' book and related reports are extensively illustrated by drawings and diagrams by Telfer Smith and there are exquisite drawings of the west front arch and ancient grave-slabs by Worthington Smith. Smith also produced a famous drawing of the Nanteos Cup, which appeared in *Archaeologia Cambrensis*[50] and Williams' own book on Strata Florida.[51] Williams had actually commented on the Nanteos Cup in 1888:

I was staying at Nanteos for a few days last year [1887], and heard a good deal about the celebrated cup which is continually in use throughout the district by people who have faith in its healing powers... I did not see the cup, but I am told it is of dark wood, much worn. The tradition is that it came from Strata Florida Abbey, and it was probably a mazer cup. The belief in its curative virtues extends over a wide district of Carmarthenshire and Cardiganshire, and numbers of instances of cures supposed to have been effected by taking food and medicine out of the cup are related and believed implicitly by the small farmers and peasantry.[52]

This is the earliest known occasion that the Nanteos Cup was referred to in print as a mazer bowl – a conclusion with which we concur. It should be clear from his words that Stephen Williams did not excavate the Nanteos Cup from the ruins of Strata Florida abbey; neither had it been unearthed during the excavations of 1847. The earliest references to the Nanteos Cup, in *Lleuad yr Oes*, pre-date Williams' excavations by nearly sixty years and also pre-date the earlier 1847 excavations by nearly twenty years.[53]

It is plausible that Williams' description of the cup as a 'mazer bowl' was influenced by William St John Hope, who in 1887 had published an extensive article on mazers[54] – though not, unfortunately, including the Nanteos Cup amongst the extended list of medieval mazers discussed.

Amazing Mazers

From Williams' reference in 1888 onwards, the cup has regularly been described as a mazer – at least by the more serious enquirers into the history of the Nanteos vessel. Although we have, to date, no clear historical reference from the medieval period for the existence of a cup associated with the Last Supper and the Resurrection of Christ present in England (other than those found in the romances of the Grail), there are certainly many references to mazer bowls and cups, which later writers would identify as being close if not identical to the Nanteos Cup, and which were clearly regarded as important within the monastic communities.

Mazers are wooden bowls of various sizes, widely used both as everyday drinking vessels and, with increasing frequency through the Middle Ages, as Communion cups. They were often augmented with elaborate stands and decorations, including a persistently repeated silver band around the rim, which seems to have been added to make the bowls more cup-shaped and capable of holding more. The Nanteos Cup at one time possessed such a band, which seems to have been added to strengthen it, and was later removed when it was found to 'block' the cup's healing powers. In addition, another aspect of the mazer was the inclusion of a 'boss', usually cast in silver, which sat in the base of the cup. This could include both symbolic images and spiritual phrases. For example, we have seen one showing Saint George killing a dragon, the Virgin and Child, and the letters IHS.[55] An examination of the Nanteos Cup shows indications of a circular mark, this making its point of origin in the Middle Ages more likely.

Inscriptions on many of the surviving bowls – other than those which are simply the name of a donor or the abbey to which they belonged – indicate just how important mazers were, and the level of symbolic resonance they possessed. For example, a mazer belonging to St Margaret Pattens, of London, dated to 1479, reads:

Of goddes hande blissed be he
That taketh this Cuppe and drinketh to Me

And on the inside of the same vessel, we find:

God that suteth in Trynyte
Send us peace and unyte.[56]

One of the facts that have always made it difficult to accept the Nanteos Cup as a sacred drinking vessel is the early prohibition concerning the use of porous vessels for the celebration of the Eucharist. This was because it was felt that some of the transubstantiated blood would soak into the wood and become trapped there, allowing it to be misused in heretical ceremonies. Earlier still, in the eighth century, glass was also forbidden because of its delicacy and the fact that broken fragments might be used in magical rituals.[57]

At the Council of Rheims at the beginning of the tenth century it was ordered that no one could say mass with a wooden chalice. According to David Thomas, the nineteenth-century Archdeacon of Monmouthshire, in Britain in 1071 Archbishop Lanfranc forbade the use of chalices 'of wood or wax'. These instructions were beginning to be relaxed by the end of the fifteenth century, which suggests that if a wooden cup was indeed being seen as possessing miraculous powers at this time, it is unlikely to have been connected either to the Grail or other Eucharistic beliefs before that time. However, the fact that the Nanteos Cup is almost certainly a mazer opens a secondary line of thought.

The origin of the word *mazer* is itself something of a mystery. Depending on which authority or dictionary one consults it may derive from the Old Norse word for ash, *mase*, though since most mazers appear to have been made from maple wood this is unlikely. In German, *maserung* means 'wood grain', with the *maser* part of the word referring to the grain itself (either wood or wheat); while we also have *maserkopf* – a wooden cup. Old Welsh *masarn* means maple tree, which seems closer. Another suggestion, quoted by Saint John Hope, has the Old High German *másá*, meaning 'a spot'.[58] This is seen to refer to the fact that woodcarvers preferred a kind of maple called 'birds' eye', which is taken from a part of the tree where the branches grow from the trunk, and which gives a spotted appearance to the wood. This would give us a bowl of 'spotted wood'. In Old French this becomes *madre*, which refers to wood the grain of which is crooked or streaky.

Another early commentator, the antiquarian William Somner (1598–1669), who compiled the first dictionary of the Anglo-Saxon language, believed that mazers were a type of vessel that had previously been called *myrrhine* in the classical era.[59] Curiously, this refers to the myrtle plant, which symbolically inferred an act of sacrifice – an interesting point of origin for vessels later used in the Eucharist. The connection probably came from the fact that in the oldest property listings to include mazers, they were often called *murrae* or *murreus*. The eleventh-century philologist Johannes de Garlandia (*c.* 1190–*c.* 1270) ascribed this to a tree mentioned by the Roman writer Lucan in his *Pharsalia*, as *auro murraque bibunt* ('they drink from gold and the myrrh tree' – presumably referring to the wood from which the cups were made).[60]

Whichever of these origins one chooses, all refer very clearly to specific types of wood, several of which, especially maple, were used to carve mazers of the medieval period from the thirteenth to sixteenth centuries and beyond.

The sheer number of mazers that have survived – well into the hundreds – indicate how important they were. People also seem to have liked to give them names, implying that they were perceived as individually crafted objects. Amongst the 182 mazers listed at Canterbury in 1328, we find 'Solomon', 'Austin', 'Broke', 'Hare', 'Pylgrim', 'Fenix' and 'Bigge', suggesting a degree of personalisation; others were named 'Spang', 'Cossyn' and 'Crumpuldud'. That the monks of the various abbeys and churches which include mazers amongst their meagre possessions seem to have 'owned' individual vessels is evidenced by their listing in various personal wills.[61]

Edmund Spenser in his seasonal poem *The Shepheardes Calendar*, for the month of August, writes:

A mazer ywrought of the maple wood
Whereon is enchased many a fair sight
Of bears and tigers that make fierce war.[62]

Medievalist Roberta Gilchrist notes that between two inventories dated, respectively, 1290 and 1328,

The mazers are listed according to both their physical properties of decoration and their ownership or name. Private property was prohibited in monasteries and it is therefore surprising to find a collection of personalized drinking vessels for the common table. The second inventory confirms that many of the same mazers were still in use a generation later, long after the deaths of those whose names they bore.[63]

According to the inventory of 1290, the monks of the great priory of Christ Church, Canterbury, had as many as 182 mazers. Other inventories name thirty-two mazers at Battle Abbey in Sussex, forty at Westminster and forty-nine at Durham. Amongst these were several mazers that had even greater significance.

At Durham, the dining area was known as the 'loft', situated at the west end of a larger hall entered from the southern alley of the cloister called the 'frater-house'. In this hall 'the great feast of Saint Cuthbert's day in Lent was held'. And there, according to the author of the *Rites of Durham*, dating from 1593, 'In an aumbry in the wainscot, on the left-hand of the door', was kept a great mazer, called the Grace-Cup, 'which did service to the monks every day, after grace was said, to drink in round the table'. The cup was

> ...finely edged about with Silver, and double Gilt. In the same place were kept many large and great Mazers of the same sort, among which was one called Judas' Cup. Every Monk had his Mazer severally by himself to drink in, and had all other things that served the whole Convent, and the Frater-house in their daily Service, at their Diet, and at their Table.[64]

As a recent commentator noted:[65]

> It is apparent that in some abbeys each monk had a mazer of his own and these were often prized after their owners had died and were shown to novice monks as memorials of those who had been held in high regard in their religious community.

Sheila Sweetinburgh, a widely recognized expert in the field of medieval medicine and hospitals, in her book *The Role of the Hospital in Medieval England: Gift-Giving and the Spiritual Economy,* argues that

> mazers marked the entry ceremony of novices and were therefore impressed with the new identity of the individual monk. Deceased monks were venerated at mealtimes when the collection of mazers could be viewed; it was common monastic practice for the monks to process to the cemetery after dinner in order to commemorate the dead at their gravesites. These material practices embedded 'sensory memory', engaging embodiment with the evocation of past generations of the spiritual community. The maple wood bowls were viewed, touched and linked perpetually with the graves of the dead. For the monks of Canterbury Priory, mazers were 'good to remember with'.[66]

'Sensory memory' seems an excellent way of describing the power recognized as present within the Nanteos Cup.

The fact that one of the mazers kept at Durham was referred to as the Judas Cup shows there is clearly a precedent for the existence of vessels with connections to the story of Jesus, above and beyond the central Eucharistic event. The rite involving the Judas Cup gives us an insight into the kind of use to which a mazer of this kind was put.

Throughout the fourteenth and possibly fifteenth centuries, a ritual constituted a part of the Maundy Thursday liturgy. Following Holy Communion, the mazer was placed before the monks. As Professor James Douglas Davies, a current authority on medieval theology at Durham University, explains: 'it was ... called the Judas cup because the face of Judas was worked into its bowl so that when the monks drank from it they could see, as it were, the face of Judas looking at them and, in a sense, mirroring their own face' – a reference to the sharing of the cup of the Last Supper on the night when Judas would betray his master.[67]

The Grace Cup, also from Durham, was used in the celebration of Maundy Thursday as well, the day before Good Friday in the Easter liturgy, which specifically celebrated the Last Supper. The word 'Maundy' derives from the Latin *mandatum*, 'commandment', and recalled Jesus' words to his disciples that on this night he would give them 'a new commandment – that you love one another'. (New Testament: St John 13, 34-5)

In the rite celebrated at Durham, the Grace Cup was passed ceremoniously from person to person, each of whom drank from it in emulation of the original Last Supper. To an outside observer this would have recalled the scene from the Arthurian Grail legends in which King Arthur and his knights drank from the Grail and received both 'the food of their desire' and the gift of seeing into each other's heart.

Could this have added to the thinking of whoever first connected a mazer bowl from Strata Florida, or later on from Nanteos, with the Holy Grail? Since the Christian Grail was deeply associated with the love feast celebrated by Jesus and his disciples, it would not have required a great leap of imagination to make this connection. It would also explain why the Nanteos Cup does not seem to have been named individually until the nineteenth century. It could be that a mazer that came, for whatever reason, to be associated with miraculous healing was seen as standing out from the rest of Strata Florida's undoubted collection of mazers (or even those kept at Glastonbury, if we allow for a moment that the story of its journey from there is true).

A number of 'sacred' wooden vessels are listed amongst the churches of Wales. One such, discovered during drainage work at Caergwrle *c.* 1820, was, according to David Thomas, the nineteenth-century Archdeacon of Monmouth, later exhibited at a meeting of the Society of Antiquaries at which it was even suggested that it might be 'the Holy Grail'.[68] From this we can see that it would be easy for a similar wooden bowl from Strata Florida, to which had been ascribed miraculous properties, to have been seen as a Grail.

Another means by which a particularly valuable mazer could have passed from Strata Florida to the Stedman family avoids the need of any story of noble monks carrying their precious cargo to safety. In the aftermath of the Reformation, vast caches of church plate, removed at the instigation of Henry VIII, were sold off to local bodies, such as town guilds or landowners. Thus, mazers began to be listed in the wills of notable families. It is very possible that the Nanteos Cup, long before its first recorded cures, could have been sold to the Stedman family, from where it passed through marriage to the Powells. Such can only be speculation, but given the number of similar mazers that can be traced back to churches and abbeys sacked by Cromwell's men, there is a good possibility of this happening.

However, if, as we may suppose, the Strata Florida mazer was already imbued with mystical properties, it is more likely that the story of its being smuggled to safety is a more believable supposition. Any such relic, as the Nanteos Cup later came to be regarded, would have been more likely to be destroyed by the zealots of the Reformation.

It is not a proven fact that *all* mazers were made of maple wood; the form of these vessels is more important than the limiting of them to one type of wood. Could the Nanteos Cup have been handed down as such a vessel? The Stedman *Plas* (their home and latterly a farmhouse) was built on the site of the abbey's refectory. Did they just find it among the abbey's possessions when they took up residence there? Were they given it by the monk who was appointed priest to the new Protestant parish church at Strata Florida? His name was John Yorke and both he and John Stedman are known to have been bailiffs of the abbey's granges before the final closure of the abbey. Was this a special mazer bowl, prized as the possession of one of the abbots or a revered monk, or of one of the noble corrodians – elderly lay-people living in the security of the Founder's household – who had retired to the abbey and lived out his final days simply with the brothers, finally buried in a monk's habit there?

At least one possibility exists. The first recorded burial at the abbey is that of Cadell, brother of Rhys ap Gruffydd, the Lord Rhys. This prince was buried during the construction of the new building, probably in 1178. Cadell seems to have been a brave and gallant soldier who was fond of field sports. Hunting near Pendine, he was attacked by Flemings and very badly injured. For a long time he lay gravely ill and only partially recovered. He entrusted his affairs to his brothers and made a pilgrimage to the East.[69]

According to the early twelfth-century chronicle the *Annals Cambriae*, he visited Rome in 1175 and eventually became a monk in the abbey of Strata Florida, where he died and was buried. The work of erecting the abbey was proceeding rapidly at that date and Stephen Williams describes a series of 'monks' graves' on the eastern side of the south transept. Several of the headstones are carved with interlaced Celtic ropework patterns, and he claims that they are of very early date. He proposes that one with a cross may be Prince Cadell's grave.[70] It seems quite probable that this gallant Christian prince might have acquired a relic on his visit to Rome (perhaps even further east), which he bestowed upon the abbey in which he was to spend his last years in the vestments of a holy brother and of which he and his brothers were patrons.

Certainly, all that needed to happen was for a single instance of a sick person getting well after drinking from the cup to further this notion. Of all the possible origins for the seed from which the story of the Nanteos Cup grew, this seems to us the most likely.

Despite the fact that, as far as we know, the Nanteos Cup has never been tested or its period established, its design makes it almost certainly a medieval vessel. The many mazers listed by such experts as Wilfred Josephs Cripps, in his seminal account, *Old English Plate*, are very often vessels virtually identical to the Nanteos Cup.[71]

Although much has been made of the 'plainness' and 'simplicity' of the cup, at one time it would almost certainly have been set into a foot made of precious metal, and possessed a rim of the same material, along with a small circular boss in the centre of the inner surface. That none of these details remains, other than the references to the addition and later removal of such a rim, again speaks of the antiquity of the vessel. However, we must not forget that the existence of a faint mark in the base of the cup does suggest that at one time it did indeed possess a boss.

Summing up, it must be said that while there is little hard evidence for the cup's medieval origin, and none at all for a more ancient point of origin, every detail of its appearance, and even its history (stripped of the more colourful details) points to its being a medieval drinking vessel, which at some point, either in the period before the Dissolution of the Monasteries or soon after, acquired a mystical presence which led, in time, to its comparison or identification with the Grail. It was only later that it began to be acknowledged as a marvellous relic – one even touched by Christ – and which then acquired the patina of the miraculous which it still possesses to this day. It is time to look at the way in which this story developed, and how the evolution of the relic took place.

3

The Legend Begins

Nanteos and the Powells

The site that we refer to as 'Nanteos' was not always called by that name; neither did the Powells originally own it. The house was previously occupied by the Jones family, descended from the Royal Welsh tribe of Elystan Glodrydd.[1] In earlier times, the mansion had been called 'Llawdden'[2] but at least by 1665, if not before, it had been renamed 'Nant Eos' ('the brook of the nightingale'). One of the more notable of the previous occupants was Colonel John Jones (d. 1666) who, in spite of being ostensibly a Royalist, in 1646 laid siege to Aberystwyth Castle with Colonel Whitley on the side of the Parliamentarians.[3] Around two years earlier, Jones had raised a militia or 'regiment of foot' for the king.[4]

Colonel Jones was married to Mary Cornelius and had three daughters: Mary, Elinor and Anne. It was Anne who married Cornelius le Brun, a German-born engineer and mine-owner. Cornelius and Anne only had one child: a daughter by the name of Avarina.

As she was the only child, Avarina became heir to the Nanteos estate. In 1690 she married William Powell (1658–1738) of Llechwedd Dyrys – another mansion that once stood on the opposite side of the valley.

Before the marriage between William and Avarina took place, long and complex legal documents were drawn up which set out the marriage settlement, as a part of which money and property changed hands. Here is an extract from one of the documents:

> ...the summe of one thousand and fifty pounds paid and served to be paid by the said Cornelius Le Brun, to the said Sir Thomas Powell for the portion of the said Avarina in her preferment to the said marriage and for and in consideration that the said Cornelius and Anne have conveyed and assured the inheritance of diverse Mannors, messuages, mills, lands tenements and hereditaments to the use of the said William Powell and the said Avarina for the benefit of them and their posterities.[5]

This shows that the inheritance of the mansion by William and Anne's heirs was guaranteed by the marriage contract and the bridegroom was also rewarded with land and money. The amount mentioned in the above quotation is the equivalent to around £92,000 in today's money (or approximately $140,000).

In 1738 William died and his son Thomas inherited the estate. Soon thereafter, Thomas began building the new mansion on the site of the old. The cellar of the old mansion still lies beneath Nanteos and according to one legend the last seven monks from Strata Florida abbey lie buried in this cellar – a story to which we shall return later.

An elaborate plan of the estate was drawn up by John Davenport,[6] showing work intended to be carried out. Certain features were highlighted in red, such as the mansion, the stables and farmyard, ruins, a tower and dog kennels. Ultimately, John Davenport's plans were not executed, but the reasons are unknown.

Thomas Powell's sister, Anne Powell, married Richard Stedman of Abbey House, Strata Florida. Richard was the last of his line and when he died (intestate, in 1740) his brother-in-law Thomas Powell came into ownership of his estates and possessions. If the cup indeed passed from the Stedmans to the Powells, this is one way in which it could have happened.

The Powell line is said to be derived from a North Wales nobleman by the name of Edwin ap Grono, who was Lord of Tegaingl in Flintshire.[7] After the marriage between William and Avarina, nine generations of Powells lived at Nanteos and Llechwedd Dyrys was abandoned and eventually became a ruin. Many of the Powells held positions of social status or high military rank. The first of the nineteenth-century lords of Nanteos was William Edward Powell (1788–1854) who took charge of the mansion in 1809 and quickly became High Sheriff of Cardiganshire and Lord Lieutenant soon after. He was also Colonel of the Cardiganshire Militia. It was this William Edward Powell who first allowed archaeological excavations to take place at Strata Florida. It was also during William's time as Lord of Nanteos that we discover what may be one of the earliest references to the cup. The Revd J. T. Evans, writing in *The Church Plate of Cardiganshire*, tells us:

> Sir S. R. Meyrick does not mention [the Cup] in his History of Cardiganshire (1810), nor as far as I am aware, do any of the innumerable English tourists, but extraordinary tales have been told (since about 1836) of the healing powers supposed to be possessed by this fragment of what is probably an ancient Mazer Bowl.[8]

This early date of 1836 seems to us like guesswork; what we needed was solid evidence for this early reference, and eventually we found it in a Welsh journal called *Lleuad yr Oes*, which is discussed below. Samuel Rush Meyrick (1783–48), interestingly, was one of the earliest modern writers to study medieval arms and armour. He penned a book, *Medieval Knights and Armour*, which is still in print at the time of writing. He also wrote, as we saw in the previous chapter, about the origins of various Welsh families, including the Stedmans.

William Edward Powell's son, William Thomas Rowland Powell (1815–78), inherited the estate after his father's death and became a Conservative Member of Parliament for Cardiganshire and a Colonel in his own right. W. T. R. Powell and his father accumulated a large number of books for the Nanteos library, many of which were novels. These books were loaned out to local people and bore a printed label reminding borrowers to return them to Nanteos; they also bore the Powell coat of arms as a bookplate.

In the post-Powell era, the library was gradually broken up and many of the books were sold. An American collector by the name of Professor Robert Lee Wolff (1915–80) collected more than 200 Victorian-era novels from Nanteos; numbered amongst these, one of his most prized items was a first edition copy of the Gothic thriller *Uncle Silas* by Sheridan Le Fanu.[9] After the death of Professor Wolff, his entire collection was purchased by the University of Texas.[10]

The next Powell in line to inherit the mansion was also the most notorious. George Ernest John Powell (1842–82) was more interested in poetry than hunting and shooting. There is a story that when he was a teenager, his father tried to curb what he saw as his effete and possibly homosexual tendencies by persuading him to engage in more 'manly' pastimes. W. T. R. Powell instructed his son to take his father's gun out onto the estate and kill the first animal he came across. George obeyed his father's instructions to the letter by shooting his father's prize bullock.

This did nothing to calm what was becoming a very strained relationship! George loved literature, especially the writings of the Marquis de Sade. He also had a very close friendship with the notorious bisexual poet Algernon Charles Swinburne, known later as the author of several Arthurian poems, including the epic *Tristram of Lyonesse*.[11] The two of them met in 1866 when Swinburne visited Aberystwyth. During his stay, Swinburne and Powell were spotted on the beach. The eyewitness was a local antiquarian, George Eyre Evans, whom we shall encounter again. A correspondent (Thomas Witton Davies) reminded Evans of the occasion: 'I think you told me you remember seeing Powell & Swinburne on the sands of Aberystwyth with fleshly girls, not always the same girls.'[12]

However the pair were engaged that summer, Swinburne's reputation was enough for W. T. R. Powell to banish him from the grounds of Nanteos. The relationship between George and his father had in any case broken down beyond repair. In a letter later that year, Swinburne advised Powell:

P.S. As to your father, forget his existence especially during an English November. It is clear to me that Uncle Silas was a comparatively desirable relative, certainly during his too long life. I think in your place, I would not set foot in grounds which are his [Nanteos] until they become yours and regain their native attraction.[13]

Swinburne's comparison of W. T. R. Powell with the fictional Uncle Silas, featured in the novel by Sheridan Le Fanu, a first edition copy of which was found in the Nanteos library, was hardly flattering, but George would not have minded at all. It was not long after this time that George and his father were involved in a legal dispute over the Colonel's cutting down and sale of timber on the Nanteos estate.[14]

George seems to have followed Swinburne's advice and stayed away from Nanteos. He spent much of his time travelling abroad. Two particularly well-known incidents relate to his time in Etretat in north-western France.

The year was 1868. George Powell had bought (or rented) a small cottage in Etretat which he Christened *Chaumière Dolmancé*, named for the 'hero' of *La Philosophie dans le Boudoir* by the Marquis de Sade – much to the dismay of the locals. He invited Swinburne to come and visit him, to which Swinburne enthusiastically responded:

> Then – oh! shan't I be glad to accept your invitation! 1) to see you and cheer and be cheered if ill or worried 2) to satiate my craving (ultra-Sapphic and plusquàm-Sadic) lust after the sea.[15]

However, Swinburne's 'lust' for the sea nearly caused him to drown. George Powell himself related the story:

> During one of Mr. Swinburne's visits to me at Etretat, he was, whilst bathing, carried out to sea through a rocky archway, and entirely out of my sight, by one of the treacherous under-currents so prevalent and so dreaded on that dangerous coast. After I had lost sight of him for about 10 minutes, I heard shouts on the cliffs above me, to the effect that 'a man was drowning'. Guessing what had occurred, I gathered up Mr. Swinburne's clothes by which I had been sitting and running with them through the ankle-deep shingle to where some boats lay, sent them off to the rescue. In but a few minutes however, a boat coming from the point at which I feared a catastrophe had taken place, brought us the welcome news that my friend had been picked up by a fishing smack, bound for Yport, a few miles distant. I therefore took a carriage and galloped off at fullest speed, with the clothes of

the rescued man to the village of Yport, whence we returned to Etretat, in the smack which had picked up Mr. Swinburne, he declining to use the carriage.[16]

The second Etretat episode began the following day when the pair invited the famous writer Guy de Maupassant around for lunch. De Maupassant is remembered as a master of short stories and documented the episode himself in a story called 'L'Anglais d'Entretat' published in *Gaulois*, 29 November 1882. The story of what happened during Maupassant's visit has grown and there are different accounts, some contradictory, all of them eye-popping.

Chaumière Dolmancé was filled with ghoulish relics and curios, including human bones and a flayed, severed hand of a parricide, its bones still clothed in sinews, flesh and blood. There were many portraits, some beautiful, others gaudy and nightmarish. The Englishmen's minds were overbrimming with fantastic, macabre learning.[17] As a pet, Powell had a large monkey by the name of Nip, who would make a nuisance of itself and attempted to push Maupassant's head into his glass while he was drinking. Maupassant was plied with alcohol and shown photographs and drawings, including homoerotic pornography. Powell was often seen to nibble on the severed hand.

There was a servant present who took an intense dislike to Nip the monkey. On a later visit by Maupassant, the animal had been hanged, apparently by the servant; in his rage Powell chased the servant out of the house, firing his revolver – in other accounts the servant drowned himself.[18] Nip was buried in the garden and a tombstone erected to his memory. On yet another visit not long afterwards, Maupassant was served monkey flesh by the two Englishmen.[19] It has even been suggested that the monkey served for lunch that day was none other than poor Nip.[20]

It is widely believed that George Powell was an avid devotee of the music of Richard Wagner; however, Edmund Gosse, who knew about the Etretat episode, tells us:

...it is to be doubted whether either of them [Swinburne or Powell] had heard any of the compositions of these musicians performed in public or in private. It was the attitude of Wagner which attracted and delighted them...[21]

George Powell was a keen collector of books, paintings and other curiosities and intended to donate his collections to Aberystwyth, provided a museum could be opened to house them. When the plan fell through, he donated them instead to Aberystwyth University, where they remain to this day.[22]

William Thomas Rowland Powell died in London on Monday 13 May 1878. His funeral took place the following Saturday and his son George came home briefly before returning again to London. By the end of the month, he had still not returned to Nanteos to take his place as the new lord of the manor, leaving some doubt as to whether or not he would ever come back. According to a local newspaper report:

> NANTEOS – All kinds of rumours are current respecting Nanteos and the arrangements for the future. The fact is that nothing has been settled, and nothing is known. If Mr. George Powell should come and reside at the family mansion, the tenants and everybody in Aberystwyth will be glad, but nobody can say more than that people who speak with great confidence know nothing.[23]

The tenants of Nanteos need not have worried; George returned no later than the middle of June and very shortly took on the patronage of a church bazaar.[24] Soon after his return to Nanteos in June, it was noted that the cup was missing. This is the first time it is mentioned as being present amongst the papers that have so far come to light. It is clear from this reference that the cup had apparently been installed at Nanteos before this – evidently for some time, as the mention is so matter-of-fact.

Anna Maria Powell later related the tale to George Eyre Evans:

> When the late Geo. Ernest John Powell succeeded to the estate, he at once found that the cup was missing. High & low search was made for it but nowhere was it in Nanteos. On appealing to the old coachman for any knowledge of it, he remembered that a while before the death of the last master (Col. Powell) the Cup had gone to a sick bedside away into Radnorshire & had not been returned. At once Mr. Powell sent a mounted messenger to find it, with strict orders to lose not a moment, & not to return until he had found the 'Healing Cup'. Within four days the man

returned bearing the precious cup, which had been carefully put away on the recovery of the patient in a mountain farm, & its return had been overlooked.[25]

However, once it had been returned it was thanks to George Powell that the Nanteos Cup was first exhibited in public, at the Lampeter meeting of the Cambrian Archaeological Association. This took place on 20 August 1878, around two months after George's return.[26] The meeting must have been planned well in advance, so George's desire to retrieve the cup from Radnorshire probably had more to do with his plan to loan it to the archaeologists than any personal love he might have had for the vessel. In spite of his credentials as a romanticist, George Powell had precious little to do with the Nanteos Cup, and neither he nor his friend Swinburne wrote anything about it.

George Powell was made High Sheriff of Cardiganshire in 1880 and in 1881 married Dinah Harries of Goodwick, Fishguard. He died tragically at the relatively young age of forty in 1882 and was succeeded by his cousin, William Beauclerk Powell, who features in the next chapter.

Lleuad yr Oes – *Early Murmurings*
To date, the earliest writings we have been able to find concerning the Nanteos Cup by that name are to be found in a little Welsh language journal called *Lleuad yr Oes*. The first occurrence is in the February edition for 1828. A correspondent known as 'Ieuan' wrote in asking about the cup. Here is our own translation of the passage:

> MR. EDITOR. ... It is known to most of the residents in the neighbourhood of Aberystwyth, that some cup of remarkable medicinal capacity, in Nanteos (home to W. E. Powel, YSW. A.S.) that it is said, they say, can only improve the disease called flux, or disease of the blood, by drinking water from it. If there is such to be found, something [must be] known of from whence it came, and by what means is such merit in it, if so. It is declared by some that the cross of our Lord Jesus Christ was used to make it; others say some pious queen had prayed for it to be an effective cure for this bad disease: but I think that smells too much of Catholicism

on that. It is also said of this Cup that it split by some means or another, and it was sent to London to put a silver ring around it, and because of that the medicinal virtue failed; as a result the silver ring was removed, and it was given a ring of tin (elydn), and now they are declaring that it is as virtuous as ever. Some of the history of this remarkable Cup and certainly more, besides.[27]

It should be immediately obvious from this passage that many of the traditions concerning the Nanteos Cup were already in place well before the reign of Queen Victoria. These stories were not (as has been suggested by some) the inventions of a late nineteenth-century romanticist like George Powell. Indeed, George Powell was not even born when the above passage was penned. The early date also makes it far less likely that the cup was unearthed in the ground at Strata Florida Abbey. The only records we have concerning archaeological excavations and related clearing work date to a much later time. It is of course possible that a chance find was made, but there is nothing by way of real evidence to suggest that it was.

The editor of *Lleuad yr Oes* at the time was a man called David Owen (1795–1866), known by the pen name of 'Brutus'. He was a teacher, satirist and a Baptist minister and he had some medical training. Thus, he was scornful of anything that smacked of quackery. We translate his response to the above passage by Ieuan as follows:

WINE is the reason the above cup has cracked (in relation to this we saw a piece of it, it had been borrowed from Nanteos, for the aforementioned reason, in a neighbour's house last week), but whether it is true or false that it was given a ring some time ago of silver or tin we don't know; but we can confirm that not one type of indication of circling on it is present. - EDITOR.[28]

Owen's satirical humour is instantly apparent here: by 'wine' he surely means that some drunken episode leading to the cup becoming cracked! He confirms that the tradition of loaning the cup to the sick was already in place. We are also told that by that time the cup was already cracked and had already been taken to London for repair. As far as we know, no one would link the cup to the Holy Grail for another half century, but Ieuan confirms that the cup was at that time believed to have been made from the wood of Christ's cross.

In April 1828, David Owen offered more of his thoughts on the cup:

> IN relation to the comment made in the LLEUAD in February, relating to the query of Ieuan concerning the **phiol y groes** [Cup of the Cross], it can be added, it was with the greatest surprise, not rejected in the Principality henceforth with all superstitions, and flowing through the antichrist, and on whose back rode the great whore kings once believed. And if there be one who has received benefit through drinking from the aforementioned scoop, he must attribute his cure to his own imagination, and not to the virtue of the cup. And only for those whom believe, receiving the same benefit if undertaking the same thing from a pig trough. Undoubtedly, Christ Jesus is the saviour of the soul; but from his cross, if it could be proved that the phiol [cup] is fashioned from it or part of it, it afterwards remains to be proven, that it is a saviour to the body. And the best advice we can give to the gentleman in possession of it, is to put it on the fire, or make a gift of it to the Pope, in order to pour over the pile of relics, and so that it may deliver the destruction by assault and subversion, the throne of the gentleman from Rome.[29]

Through a sentiment that is as anti-superstition as it is anti-papist, the Baptist preacher 'Brutus' vents his bile and scorn on the poor Nanteos Cup! Ironically, three quarters of a century later, as we shall see, it was Baptists who were responsible for popularizing the cup as the Holy Grail.

Loaning out the Cup

The cup was clearly in the possession of the Powells by the early nineteenth century or before; at some point it became their custom to loan it out to people who believed in its curative properties. In order to keep track of the whereabouts of the relic, small, handwritten receipts were kept which recorded the name and address of the borrower, the person requiring the cup, the nature of the token left as a surety of its return and the dates borrowed and returned. In addition, many of the notes are marked 'Cured'.

The earliest of the receipts that are still extant dates to 1857. However, elsewhere it is recorded that there were receipts attesting to the cup's healing powers, which dated back to at least as early as 1836.[30] Humphrey ap Evans, Margaret Powell's own godson, said: 'many [of the receipts] went back well further than a mere 1857.'[31]

Fred Stedman Jones hailed this statement as: 'a direct quotation from the pen of a first-class witness. [We] couldn't ask for more informed information from a courtroom witness.'[32]

Certainly, there were many more receipts than have survived to the present. Such simple documents would be seen as of no great importance once the cup had been returned and might easily be destroyed. All we can be sure of is that from the time when the *Lleuad yr Oes* articles appeared in 1828 onwards, stories of the cup's 'magical' properties were in circulation.

Here is a sample of the text from a few of these receipts,[33] beginning with the earliest known. This information was printed in an article by Judge David Lewis in 1895:

21st September 1857. Cup lent this day to Ebenezer Vaughan, Gwarcwm, Llwyniorwerth Ucha, for the use of his wife. Left £1. Cup returned 5th October 1857. *Cured.*

3rd January 1858. Cup lent this day to John Edwards. Lluastfawr, Goginan, for the use of his wife. Left a watch. *Cured.* Cup returned 13th February 1858.

26th July 1858. Cup lent this day to James Morgan, Drewen, Dehewyd, for the use of ------------ . Left a sovereign.

November 24th, 1887. The Nant Eos healing cup was lent on the above date to Charles Edwards, for the use of his daughter, Mary Edwards. One pound left. Returned 13th December 1887. *A wonderful cure.*

There is one receipt, dating to 1860, from a William Jones of Llanbadarn, which seems to indicate that the cup was returned two years later. George Eyre Evans was told the following tale by Anna Maria Powell:

Mrs. P. [Anna Maria Powell] told me how that, a very few years ago, a man in being shown round the house, when he came to the

'Relic' scoffed at it, and made fun of it &c. &c. On the following morn when at breakfast, the butler said to Mrs. P. that a man very excited, but most respectful craved audience of her in the hall. When she saw him the man said how that on previous day he had scoffed [at] the Cup and made fun of it &c. that he had passed a terrible night with legions of devils &c. which give him no rest and that with Mrs. Powell's permission, he would now go and make his peace with the relic, by a short prayer over it. Then he did for a few moments alone, when he departed in a perfectly calm and contented frame. Had Mrs. P. not been witness of this herself, or had it only been servants' gossip, she would not have told it to me.[34]

The man in question was the harpist John Roberts, known as *Telynor Cymru*. Although this episode is sometimes dismissed as fable, in fact there is a note in his handwriting kept with the cup, which still exists. It reads as follows: 'The cup was seen and handled by John Roberts, Telynor Cymru, on the morning of the 4th May 1887. Mind completely at ease.'

Ysten Sioned

One of the earliest books known to mention the Nanteos Cup was the Welsh language *Ysten Sioned*, which was published anonymously in 1882. Two years later a second edition appeared which identified the authors as Daniel Silvan Evans (1818–1903) and John Jones ('Ivon', 1820–98). In 1868 Evans translated Welsh medieval texts for William Forbes Skene's *Four Ancient Books of Wales*, the first proper collection in English of early Welsh poetry, and in 1875 Evans became Professor of Welsh at the University College of Wales, Aberystwyth.

Jones was an antiquarian and acknowledged expert on the folklore and history of Aberystwyth. He was also a founder member of the Aberystwyth-based Literary, Scientific and Mechanics Institute. Jones and Evans were close friends for over fifty years. *Ysten Sioned* was a product of weekly meetings held between the two men when Evans was professor at Aberystwyth. The passage on the cup translates as follows:

Very few in our country, especially in the North of Cardiganshire, have not seen the Nanteos Cup or at least will have heard about it. It is a small wooden cup, which will hold nearly a pint, which possesses incredible healing properties, because when all else has failed, using this will provide a definite cure. It is understood that it was made out of the wood of the Cross on which Jesus was crucified...[35]

It is interesting that Silvan Evans and Jones give the volume of the cup as 'nearly a pint'. By our own estimation the true volume was more like half of this.

Women and the Nanteos Cup

It will be noted that the patients mentioned in David Lewis' list (see above) are almost all female. Early documents mentioning the cup, including *Ysten Sioned*, suggest that the cup was used as a remedy for blood-loss,[36] but this source does not suggest that this symptom was something specific to gender. In another early account by Judge David Lewis, he remarks that '[The Cup's] healing virtues in certain cases of female disorder were in great repute.'[37]

Lewis's account is based on the report in *Ysten Sioned*, and he prints a list giving the text of the handwritten notes, part of which is reproduced above. His reference to 'female disorder' might simply be his own inference, based on the gender of the patients named in the list. It might not be the case, therefore, that the cup was expressly intended for this purpose. Other accounts are not gender-specific, for example this description from 1889:

A few years ago, in the upper parts of Cardiganshire, much was heard of 'Cwpan Nant Eos', and considerable search was made for it when anyone had the misfortune to burst a blood vessel. The belief was that by drinking water from this celebrated 'cwpan', the afflicted person would be healed of his rupture.[38]

There might be other reasons why women were the principal borrowers of the cup. What is interesting here is that the most significant aspect of the medieval Grail story is its association with the 'Holy' Blood of Christ. It was, of course, widely believed at the time that women were more superstitious than men. The sixteenth-century tract known as the *Malleus Maleficarum*, which was used in the prosecution of so-called 'witches' during the Middle Ages, specifically comments on the particular vulnerability of females to such beliefs.[39] Such a view is of course tinged with sexist or misogynist conceit rather than fact. However, it still seems, from polls and social studies, that there are a greater proportion of women than men involved with religion, alternative beliefs and superstition.[40]

The reasons for these differences are not biological but sociological, and in the Victorian era the different roles of men and women were much more sharply defined than they are today. In the nineteenth century, for example, it was predominantly women who visited and worshipped at the shrine of the Virgin Mary[41] at Lourdes.

The Placebo Effect

To some it might seem that the healing properties attributed to the Nanteos Cup are the stuff of fairy tales. However, in the field of modern medicine there is a well-known phenomenon in which the human mind is linked with the healing process: the 'Placebo Effect'. The general principle is that the patient's own belief in the power of the healer (or the treatment) can result in a beneficial physiological effect. In the case of the Nanteos Cup, for example, a patient who drinks from the cup may obtain a real, tangible benefit if he or she is convinced that the cup has healing powers; but such theories are fraught with difficulty.

Mary Lewes, a relation of the Powells of Nanteos, described one particular miracle of the Nanteos Cup which seems to fit the notion. In around 1905 a woman from London who had heard about the cup from her parish priest, wrote to Anna Maria Powell. The lady had suffered from a long-term illness that the doctors had failed to cure. She was allowed to visit Nanteos and spend some time alone with the cup in the library. According to Mary Lewes, the lady felt better immediately and later wrote to Mrs Powell saying that her long-term malady had vanished completely; she attributed this recovery to the Nanteos Cup.[42] Lewes commented:

> This absolutely true story is a wonderful instance of the power of faith on the human mind, and, re-acting through the mind, on the body; and listening to the tale, who shall say that the age of miracles – or seeming miracles – is past?[43]

Belief, it would seem, is the key. If he or she is convinced of the cup's curative properties, they will probably benefit. A. G. Prys-Jones, writing in the 1950s, claimed that:

> Amongst the most notable in modern times are the healings effected at Lourdes, healings which have been reported upon by a medical committee open to all doctors. The cures obtained through the medium of the ancient Cup of Nanteos belong to the category of phenomena which modern science, with all its great discoveries and resources, has so far failed to explain: the power of the human mind, through profound faith, to achieve, in the human body, what is apparently impossible.[44]

In fact, the concept behind the Placebo Effect has been known about since ancient times. The Old Testament (Proverbs 17:22) tells us: 'A merry heart doeth good like a medicine: but a broken spirit drieth the bones.'

In the writings of Plato, Zalmoxis converses with Socrates and describes the principle of what became known as the Placebo Effect:

> For all good and evil, whether in the body or in human nature, originates, as he declared, in the soul, and overflows from thence, as if from the head into the eyes. And therefore, if the head and body are to be well, you must begin by curing the soul; that is the first thing. And the cure, my dear youth, has to be effected by the use of certain charms, and these charms are fair words; and by them temperance is implanted in the soul, and where temperance is, there health is speedily imparted, not only to the head but to the body.[45]

In our own time, debates continue about the apparent ability of the mind to heal the body. Experiments carried out in 2003 involving the drug diazepam (better known as Valium) showed that in order for the pill to have any benefit, the patient needed to be told what the medicine was.[46] In the past, scientific explanations have been put forward involving the production of the brain chemical called endorphins. More recently it has been suggested that the type of brain chemicals released which produce the Placebo Effect depend on the circumstances and the expectations of the patient.[47]

Even if the Placebo Effect is a real phenomenon, there surely must be limits as to what it is capable of. In relation to the Nanteos Cup, it should be observed that the claims made in the nineteenth century were relatively modest and might well be within the scope of the Placebo Effect or some other natural explanation; certainly it could explain the case of John Roberts, *Telynor Cymru*, the harpist whose mind was eased by contemplating and praying with the cup.

Women as Healers

We have seen that the early records show that patients of the Nanteos Cup were predominantly female, and that there is a sociological gender link between women and belief in the supernatural. We have also mentioned the number of women healed at Lourdes. Women have, in fact, been closely linked with healing since ancient times. There is evidence for this link from Ancient Egypt, Greece and Rome.

Healer deities such as Ishtar, Isis, Hygieia and Panacea were all goddesses of healing. The priestesses in ancient Egypt during the Dynastic era were all healers. By the third century, the influence of Hippocrates came into play and women were barred from the Greek medical schools. Women were also excluded from learning about the embalming process in Egypt.[48] However, one area of healing where women have always dominated is midwifery, and statistics show that even in the nineteenth and early twentieth centuries women outperformed men at delivering babies, resulting in fewer stillbirths than the professionals.[49]

Healing was also the function of the village wise-woman and this led to accusations of witchcraft. Mary Lewes, whom we shall meet again later – a relation of the Powells of Nanteos – wrote about such superstitious practices, which she asserted were still prevalent in the 1920s:

> ...belief in the powers of 'wise' men and women is now chiefly confined to their abilities as healers, and in this capacity they are still resorted to in the more remote districts of Cardiganshire. The cure – whatever the malady – appears to be always the same and is called 'measuring the wool'. The witch takes two pieces of yarn – scarlet for choice – of exactly the same length. One of these is bound round the wrist or leg of the patient; the other is worn in the same way by the healer. The patient goes home, and

after a few days the witch measures her own piece of yarn. If it has shrunk from the original length, well and good; the yarn continues to grow shorter (so it is said) and the patient recovers. But if on the contrary the yarn grows perceptibly slacker; the patient gets worse and will surely die.[50]

Another, more gruesome, case from 1920s Cardiganshire was reported in the pages of the *British Medical Journal*. On this occasion, a small child was suffering from *enuresis* (wetting the bed). A local wise-woman was consulted and, based on her advice, a mouse was burned alive; its ashes were then ground up and stirred into a bowl of porridge for the boy to eat.[51] We are not told if this cure was effective.

In Britain, women were barred from higher education establishments for most of the nineteenth century and were only finally admitted after decades of campaigning. The first British University to admit women was the University of London[52] in 1878. The first female medical graduates came from the London School of Medicine for Women[53] in 1882. Oxford University only allowed women to study medicine from 1917 and only fully opened up its degree schemes to women[54] in 1920. Cambridge tarried even longer, only allowing women full membership[55] in 1947.

Nineteenth-century Medicine at Aberystwyth
Not far from Nanteos, Aberystwyth in the early nineteenth century was still a relatively small, poverty-stricken town with a population of just over 1,700, characterised by an absence of amenities, poor food and almost completely non-existent healthcare. Medical care for the poor relied on private benevolence and typically came in the form of a donation to allow the pauper to buy drugs or consult a doctor (more often a quack) of his choosing. The fortunes of Aberystwyth and its people were on the verge of change, but that change was slow, and the population of the town was increasing.[56] Advances in medicine tended to happen in big cities and for the most part did not reach rural areas like Cardiganshire until much later.

In 1810, an Aberystwyth doctor by the name of Dr Rice Williams[57] built a bathhouse at the northern end of what would eventually come to be renamed Marine Terrace, on the seafront at Aberystwyth. Rice Williams was every ounce a businessman, and the setting up of the bathhouse was his dream, financed initially by the mortgaging of the

Rhoscellan estate, soon after he had acquired it. The bathhouse was situated where gallows had previously stood, atop a small mound called Penbryndioddef ('the hilltop of punishment').

Rice had lost one of his eyes whilst getting drunk and duelling with a friend, namely the Duke of Newcastle, and as a result of this accident he wore a black band over the empty eye socket. His late eighteenth-century, close-fitting outfits, complete with frills and eye-band, must have given him a striking, swashbuckling appearance! The trend for building bathhouses had already been established elsewhere, such as at Brighton, a few decades earlier, fuelled by the belief that seawater was highly therapeutic. This theory was documented in a book written in 1750 by Dr Richard Russell (1687–1759) called *De Tabe Glandulari*, later translated as *Glandular Diseases, or a Dissertation on the Use of Sea Water in the Affections of the Glands*.

Iron pipes ran far out to sea and the seawater was pumped up to a huge tank. Visitors could take to the waters (hot or cold) in one of a number of bathrooms or showers, or a 'vapour-bath'. Aberystwyth became 'the Brighton of Wales' and enjoyed a huge tourist boom. Bathing machines became popular on the seafront. Aberystwyth was described as a spa town and this was reflected in the street names of the time such as Chalybeate Street, Chalybeate Terrace and Chalybeate Court. The water from one well in Llanbadarn ran red, just as the water from Chalice Well at Glastonbury does; this is due to the iron-rich mineral content of all Chalybeate springs. In order to enhance his reputation still further, Dr Rice Williams spread the word that he was descended from a family of medieval, semi-mythical Welsh herbalists known as the Physicians of Myddfai. Williams may in fact have had some ancestral roots in the Myddfai area, but there can be no doubt whatsoever that this rumour-spreading of his was primarily a marketing ploy.

Nevertheless, herbal medicine was important in nineteenth-century Aberystwyth just as it was elsewhere, in an era before synthetic drugs and free health care. The first synthetic drug was aspirin, which did not appear on the market[58] until 1899, but the benefits of plants containing salicylates (such as willow and myrtle) had been known about more than two millennia before.[59]

It was common practice for people to self-medicate. This was still a time of apothecaries, colourful cures, pills, potions and other treatments, such as 'Dr Radcliffe's Elixir' (for purging), 'Dalby's Genuine Carminative' (to treat flatulence), 'Barclay's Asthmatic Candy', 'Cockle's Compound Anti-Bilious Pills' (to treat vomiting) and 'The Cordial Cephalic Snuff'[60] (for disorders of the head and eyes).

There were quack medicines such as 'Dr Sibly's Reanimating Solar Tincture' which was used for 'debility, consumption, nervous and rheumatic complaints, yellow jaundice, spasms, indigestion, lowness of spirits' and much more.[61] The same medicine had previously been claimed to be able to bring the dead back to life,[62] hence its name.

The use of herbal remedies gained in popularity and it was usual for people to collect herbal remedies from a variety of journals and books. A handwritten manuscript from Capel Seion – just five minutes' drive from Nanteos Mansion – contains cooking recipes from a book attributed to Ellen Powell of Nanteos; the MS also contains herbal recipes, a number of accounts of the Nanteos Cup and other information about the Powells. Here is one such herbal remedy from this manuscript:

To prevent infection.
Take of rue, sage, rosemary, wormwood, lavender, and mint each an ounce. Steep these two or three days in a pint of white wine vinegar. Then pour off the clear and dissolve an ounce of Camphire [henna] in it. When you use it rub the nostrils and upper lip with it.[63]

The Revd Thomas Richards (1754–1837), who was at one time vicar of Llangynfelin in Aberystwyth, also collected such recipes, for example:

For a Consumption.
One Ounce of Gumme Ammoniache.
One Ounce of Barbadoes Tarr.
One Ounce of Elecampane root Powdered.
Mix the whole in 4 Ounces of Treacle and take as much as a Nutmeal, three or four times a day while it lasteth if required.[64]

Among the miscellaneous manuscripts that form part of the Nanteos estate archive is a handwritten Latin text called *Pharmacopaeia*

Chirurgica,[65] while another text deals with herbal remedies for treating livestock.[66]

The importance of herbal medicine continued well into the twentieth century and it is still used today. Even in the twentieth century, many people claimed descent from the Physicians of Myddfai, including some local doctors.[67]

Aberystwyth's first public dispensary was opened on 18 February 1821, 'under the patronage of a charitable public'. It was based in a room owned by a Dr William Bonsall in the Hearts of Oak, in Great Darkgate Street.[68] Dr Bonsall was a son of Sir Thomas Bonsall of Fronfraith, who came to Cardiganshire from Staffordshire and was involved in the lead-mining business.[69] The dispensary's chief patron was William Edward Powell, Esq.,[70] lord of Nanteos manor, Lord Lieutenant and Member of Parliament for the County of Cardigan. In 1825 the Governors included Pryse Pryse Esq.,[71] MP for the Borough of Cardigan and father of Margaret Powell, whose name would become closely associated with the cup later on in the twentieth century. The first dispensary lasted until the end of 1837.

Local antiquarian George Eyre Evans noted: 'During the whole of this period the names of Colonel Powell, M.P. of Nanteos, and Pryse Pryse, Esquire, M.P., of Gogerddan, are found amongst its most active supporters...'[72]

The regulations for patients included the provision that they should provide their own bottles for storing medicine. Another regulation stipulated that 'Strangers visiting Aberystwyth becoming subscribers may recommend the Poor of their own Neighbourhood, who may require Sea-bathing, to the Dispensary.'[73]

Some sources suggest that there may have been two dispensaries in the town, both of which were located in Great Darkgate Street.[74] In the first four years 1,088 patients were admitted to the dispensary.[75]

On 18 January 1838, a meeting was held and a decision was made to replace the dispensary with a more up-to-date institution, and thus was born the Aberystwyth Infirmary and Cardiganshire General Hospital. One of the signatories approving the scheme was Colonel Powell of Nanteos.[76] This was initially opened in a building in Upper-Portland Street, but after the death of Captain Bonsall it was moved to a large building in Little Darkgate Street.[77] In 1886 it moved to a much larger building in North Road and subsequently became known as North Road Hospital. In time, sometime after the opening of Bronglais hospital, it served as a geriatric hospital and only closed its doors in 1998.

We live in a very different world today and it would be hard for many in the UK to imagine an age before the National Health Service. In the early part of the nineteenth century in Aberystwyth, with little medical support and widespread selling of quack medicines, the cup of Nanteos might well have seemed to some to be as good a cure as any. As the century was drawing to a close, the authors of *Ysten Sioned* wrote:

> We do not know whether the present unfaithful generation make use of the Cup; we are afraid that they are putting too much faith in the multitude of doctors amongst us (who, in order to promote their rubbish, shake their heads and condemn old healing beliefs that have been such a blessing for generations) and are neglecting to use the old, simple Nanteos Cup.[78]

Chalice Well, St Brides Well and the Glastonbury Grail

The Nanteos Cup is, unsurprisingly, not the only such wonder-working vessel of which we have knowledge. One that may be said to rival the cup, at least in terms of notoriety, is the Blue Bowl of Glastonbury. In fact, there are no specific accounts of healing miracles performed by the bowl, but the inevitable results of the widespread association of Glastonbury with the Grail story has resulted in a considerable amount of material identifying the Blue Bowl with the Grail.

Chalice Well is a limestone well in Glastonbury, England. It is a chalybeate spring and it supplies a bountiful 25,000 gallons of water a day; even in the fiercest of droughts it never runs dry. It was sometimes referred to as the 'Blood spring' because of the iron contents of the water, which can stain the surrounding stones a brownish red. The well was first mentioned in the thirteenth century[79] and in the mid-eighteenth it enjoyed a brief spell of fame after a man named Matthew Chancellor was instructed by a dream to drink from the well on seven Sundays in succession.

Chancellor stated that the healing power of the well had cured a chronic asthma complaint that he had endured for thirty years.

He opened a health spa in the town, which attracted 10,000 visitors in one year, until a patient died and the spa was closed.[80] There are recorded instances of cures from this period, such as a seven-year-old boy called John Redwood, who was apparently cured of 'the King's Evil' (scrofula) through the healing powers of the well.[81]

In the Middle Ages the well was called *Chalcewelle* or *Chalkwell*, the mutation to Chalice being relatively recent. When the well was excavated by archaeologists, it was discovered that the opening of the well was actually a hole made in the roof of a medieval well house that had become completely immersed in silt with the passage of time. There is also some archaeological evidence that the well was in use in much earlier times.[82] After Glastonbury Abbey had adopted Joseph of Arimathea as its legendary founder, another story arose that he had brought with him the Holy Grail and buried it beneath Chalice Hill, the sacred blood from the Grail thereby leading to the red coloration of the water issuing from Chalice Well. In 1912, Chalice Well House was purchased by the author, poet and playwright Alice Buckton (d. 1944) who authored the Christmas mystery play *Eager Heart*. Buckton also wrote a silent film, *Glastonbury Past and Present*, which features local people from Glastonbury re-enacting events from the history of their town; one of the scenes in the film was the arrival of Joseph of Arimathea.

In 1958, the Chalice Well Trust bought the well and the associated property. The founder of the Trust was the mystic Wellesley Tudor Pole, who under psychic direction and aided by his sister and two of her friends had discovered an ancient blue glass bowl hidden in the depths of St Bride's Well,[83] Glastonbury, in 1906. The bowl was later revealed to have been placed there some years earlier by a Dr Goodchild, again under psychic instruction.

After the bowl was rediscovered from its hiding place in St Bride's Well, it was taken to Bristol and placed in a shrine. The following year, Wellesley Tudor Pole prepared a statement, revealing the discovery of the bowl and his belief that it was the Holy Grail. Numerous scholars, including the esotericist Arthur Edward Waite, who remained doubtful but not wholly dismissive, examined the bowl; others, like Archdeacon Basil Wilberforce, were utterly convinced.

The story is sometimes told how at one point, soon after its discovery, the blue bowl was taken to the London home of the Archdeacon. As a party was taking place on the night it arrived, the bowl was placed on a table in the Archdeacon's library. Next morning it was found to have moved to the other side of the room. It now sat on a book that included the history of Glastonbury.

Whether or not this is to be believed, it is typical of the kind of story that began to gather around this particular relic. Eventually it found a new home in Glastonbury, where it is kept today by the Chalice Well Trust.

Chalice Well itself has been mentioned in fictional works such as Phil Rickman's *The Chalice* and most famously John Cowper Powys' *A Glastonbury Romance*, in which a character called John Geard cures a woman of cancer through the healing power of the well. Powys was open to the idea of psychic phenomena and engaged in some occult practices himself. The magical atmosphere of the Chalice Well and its gardens has not been lost on the New Age community of Glastonbury and the well-known dowser and blacksmith Hamish Miller (1927–2010) proclaimed that powerful earth energy currents ran through the gardens.[84] It was also Miller who sculpted the reproduction of Bligh Bond's *vesica piscis* design, for the underside of the well's circular lid.[85]

In each case, as we have seen, a great deal of faith is required to believe in these miraculous vessels. We can see, following the line of evidence presented here, that the story of the miracles of Nanteos cannot be traced to any date earlier than the nineteenth century, though the probable origins of the cup itself can be traced back further. Subsequently, the stories surrounding the vessel have evolved into something considerably larger.

We are not denying the possibility of actual cures brought about by the cup; these things are a matter for the individual, and can be seen to possess efficacy, at the very least in the examples of the 'cures' recorded at Nanteos. But when did the Nanteos Cup evolve into the Holy Grail? We will now try to answer this question.

W. R. Hall – the Welshman from Somerset

Perhaps the earliest text linking the Nanteos Cup to the Holy Grail appears in a little local guidebook entitled *Aberystwyth: What to See and How to See It*. The earliest copy we could find was the second edition, printed in 1880, in which may be found the following passage:

> **Nanteos.** - Through Trefechan and out by the Penparke road, shown on the plan, to the south turnpike-gate, where the middle road leads to Nanteos, the Nightingale's brook. At the mansion is kept the Tregaron Healing Cup, which bears a resemblance to the mysterious Holy Grail described by Tennyson in his "Idyls [sic] of the King". It is said to have been a chalice made from the wood of the Cross and to have come into the possession of the Nanteos family from the monks of Strata Florida Abbey.[86]

We do not know when the first edition was printed – although it would not have been before 1871 and would more probably have dated to 1879. The second edition of the guide pre-dates Jones and Silvan Evans's *Ysten Sioned* and was printed only two years after the exhibition of the cup in Lampeter by the Cambrian Archaeological Association. As it mentions the 'wood of the Cross' it most likely derives this information from the speech given by Bishop Basil Jones at the Lampeter meeting.

The man who wrote the guidebook was William Robert Hall (1849–1937), a journalist and librarian who originally hailed from Somerset. Hall was born at Combwich on the banks of the River Parrett, one of four sons of educated parents. He grew up at Cannington, near Bridgewater where his father had a shop. Much of his education came from his mother Frances Phippen Mayo, who was a native of Glastonbury. Hall tells us:

> It is through my mother I may perhaps be allowed to claim some remote connection with Wales, for she was born at Glastonbury where Prince Arthur of the Round Table was buried.[87]

Hall's Arthurian interests stemmed from his youth and the teaching he received from his mother, who would of course have been well versed in the traditions of Glastonbury. Hall linked this to his own burgeoning sense of identity, not as an Englishman, but as a Welshman. He attended church at Taunton, then a Congregational chapel, before joining the Plymouth Brethren. By the age of fourteen, Hall was considered an advanced pupil:

Though I had never gone beyond compound multiplication and could not say what a verb was to save my life ... I was considered to be the best pupil in the Church elementary school.[88]

When the time came for young William to take up employment, he went to work with his eldest brother – a printer at Williton – for three years. During this time, he developed a lifelong interest in photography and many of his photographs survive.

Hall returned to Cannington, where his father arranged for him to learn Pitman's shorthand for a month under the tuition of a local policeman in the village. Armed with this meagre knowledge he took up a post as a reporter in Bridgwater, but he was too inexperienced and was quickly sent home. Hall subsequently served an apprenticeship for four years at the *Somerset County Gazette*, before moving to Wales in 1871. He wrote for the *Wrexham Guardian* and *The Salopian*, where he first met Sir John Gibson (1841–1915), founder of the *Cambrian News*. He eventually moved to Aberystwyth, where he wrote for local papers such as the *Aberystwyth Observer*, but is principally linked with the *Cambrian News* – an association that would endure for over sixty years. Towards the end of his life he retired to London and lived with his son, where – at the age of eighty-seven – he wrote his autobiography.[89]

Hall developed strong antiquarian interests and wrote articles for nineteenth-century Welsh journals such as *Bye-Gones* and the *Red Dragon*, based on anecdotes and Celtic folklore he encountered in the course of his journalistic travels through West Wales. A lengthy manuscript entitled 'Cardiganshire Traditions'[90] was one result of these gleanings. In *Bye-Gones* Hall tells us:

I remember hearing a preacher in a sermon in one of the English chapels in Aberystwyth state that he had heard that [George Frideric] Handel was at one time at Llangeitho, where he heard the enthusiastic shouts of 'Gogoniant' by the early Methodists, and in consequence conceived the idea of composing his beautiful and soul-stirring 'Hallelujah chorus' in his 'Messiah'.[91]

He would later mention the story of Handel composing the Hallelujah chorus at Hafod – another West Wales mansion. Hall was a member of the Cardiganshire Antiquarian Society during the period from 1911 until he retired in 1933. He knew and travelled with Sir John Rhys, whose books, including *Celtic Britain*, Hall certainly read. Rhys, a brilliant scholar, was one of the earliest writers to explore the Celtic background to the Arthurian legends. Hall was also influenced by Matthew Arnold's *Celtic Literature*, and Lady Charlotte Guest's translation of the *Mabinogion*. He also knew Professor Edward Anwyl (1866–1914), a scholar of Celtic languages and philology, and Professor Herbert John Fleure (1877–1969), who studied zoology, geology, geography, botany and anthropology.[92] Fleure aided Hall with his understanding of British anthropology.[93]

Hall also read Thomas Stephens' *The Literature of the Kymry*, which makes reference to a medieval poem by the Welsh bard Guto'r Glyn. In this poem, the bard requested the Abbot of Neath in South Wales to loan 'the Grail' to the Abbot of Valle Crucis Abbey in North Wales:

> … He cries for you to send
> The fair Grail to this land,
> The book of the blood, the book of men,
> The place where they fell in Arthur's Court …[94]

The 'Grail' in question seems to refer to a book of medieval Grail lore that had been translated into Welsh rather than a cup or chalice, and while it seems curious that the Grail itself is apparently to be referred to as a book, recent evidence suggests this could be close to the truth. Even so, this poem could well have encouraged Hall to imagine that the Holy Grail came to Wales.

Hall was keen to promote his sense of Welsh identity and always referred to his native Somerset as 'Gwlad yr Haf' (the Land of Summer); this would later become the name of his house in Queen's Road. He sometimes quoted what he described as an old Welsh saying: 'I Wlad yr Haf i fedi rhedyn'; this is actually from part of a verse,[95] the second couplet of which is rather rude! Hall never quoted the second couplet and may have been unaware of its existence:

| Cer i Wlad yr Haf | Go to the Land of Summer |
| i fedi rhedin | to reap ferns |

| Lle ma cwn dion | The place where black dogs |
| Yn cachu menyn | shit butter |

Hall also cited Sir John Rhys in support of his claim for the Welshness of Somerset:

> As Professor Rhys says, 'that there were even so late as the tenth century patches of country here, which were under English rule; but still inhabited by the Welsh, who only ceased to be such by being gradually assimilated to the Saxons around them'.[96]

Hall believed that Cannington – the Somerset village where he grew up – was in former times the centre of a Cymric tribe from whence (according to Hall) it derived its name. In an article he wrote (using the pseudonym of 'Amicus') for the University College of Wales magazine, he refers to Somerset as: 'the summer land ... wherein still linger in feature, language, place names, customs, history and superstitious vestiges of the earlier Celtic inhabitants'.[97]

In the same article, Hall goes on to tell us about Joseph of Arimathea, the Glastonbury Thorn and the wattle church supposedly built by Joseph himself. He also quotes from Tennyson's *Morte d'Arthur*. In another of his *Cambrian News* articles, Hall cites the historian Edward Augustus Freeman to bolster the idea of the Welshness of Glastonbury:

> Glastonbury is a tie between the Briton and the Englishman – between the older Christianity of our island and the newer – the one church of first rank which lived through a storm of English conquest and passed into the hands of our victorious forefathers as a trophy of victory undestroyed and unplundered.[98]

But if the earlier British 'church of first rank' had in some way been preserved 'undestroyed and unplundered', then so too might its doctrines and possibly even relics – or so a Grail-believer might read between the lines. Hall accepted the commonly held belief of the time that many ancient churches were built on 'druidical' stone circles and cited the church at Ysbyty Cynfyn as an example of this. In particular he believed that this was the policy of the 'ancient British Church'.[99]

Hall's guidebook was just one example of his involvement with the promotion of Aberystwyth as a seaside resort. In his application for the post of librarian at Aberystwyth Library in 1918, Hall pointed out his

> ...deep and active interest in Aberystwyth as a health pleasure resort. In former years with others I formed an Improvement Society (of which I was honorary secretary) to make the town better known in the great centres of population in England... For many years I assisted the Town Clerk in supplying information and revising guidebooks sent to him for revision.[100]

As someone who once owned the largest boarding house in Aberystwyth, it would have been in Hall's own interest to promote the town. The Aberystwyth Improvement Society, with W. R. Hall at the helm, operated on many different fronts with the stated aim of promoting Aberystwyth and attracting visitors and income into the town. Hall wrote the Heywood *Guide to Aberystwyth*[101] as well as producing *Aberystwyth: What to See and How to See It*, and worked closely with the Town Hall in the production of their own guide. The appearance of these guides coincides with the time when the Improvement Society was operating. Small wonder, then, that we find references in the *Aberystwyth Guide* saying: 'Nanteos. A short distance, and beautifully situated, contains the Tregaron Healing Cup, which resembles the Holy Grail.'[102]

These words were written by an Englishman from the Land of Summer who wanted to be considered a Welshman. Writing in 1936, Hall noted:

> Once when I was talking to Gwynon Davies of Beuno I told him that I was born in Gwlad yr Haf where the Welsh population had been cut off from the population of Wales as in the case of Strathclyde. I was as good a Cymro as he was. He replied that if I made myself an eminent man, he and others would soon prove that I was a Welshman. That I have been trying to do ever since.[103]

The profile we have painted of Hall, with his Glastonbury and Arthurian influences, combined with his sense of Welsh identity, might well suggest that the Welsh Holy Grail was entirely his own invention. On the other hand, as a gatherer of folklore from the very same area where the cup had its sphere of influence, he might just as easily have been repeating what he had heard from others.

One thing is certain: the Holy Grail legend of the Nanteos Cup was not something that was originated by the Powells of Nanteos; its roots lie well outside the mansion walls. We will encounter Mr Hall again in the next chapter.

4

The Legend Grows

...for this cup is none other than the one from which our Lord drank at the Last Supper

Ethelwyn M. Amery

A Distinguished Antiquary

The history of the Nanteos Cup was about to take a dramatic new direction – one that would establish it in the consciousness of the twentieth and twenty-first centuries as an icon of profound spiritual development and a beacon to be followed by countless seekers.

The story begins, quietly enough, as the nineteenth century ended and the twentieth began. A campaign was already underway to have the National Library of Wales built in Aberystwyth as opposed to Wales's capital city of Cardiff. One of the supporters of this ambitious plan was George Eyre Evans (1857–1939), a noted antiquarian and scholar.

Born in Devon, Evans was the eldest son of Ophelia Catherine Powell and the Revd David Lewis Evans, who was originally from Llanybydder. Evans originally moved to Wales in 1864 but subsequently moved away to pursue his interests. He became a Unitarian minister whilst living in Shropshire and eventually returned to Wales at the turn of the twentieth century, settling in Aberystwyth.

Evans was a founding member of the Carmarthenshire and Cardiganshire Antiquarian Societies and worked for the Royal Commission for Ancient Monuments for a number of years. A highly eccentric, extrovert, intelligent man, a scholar and a prolific writer, he would eventually bequeath swathes of material to the National Library he helped (in a small way) to bring into being. He had a regular column in the *Welsh Gazette* and wrote under the pseudonym of 'Philip Sidney'. He was passionate about the conservation of Cardiganshire's ancient monuments, especially Strata Florida Abbey, knowing full well its great significance to Welsh history and culture.

In early 1901, Evans contacted the Powells of Nanteos with a view to photographing paintings for a book he was writing on the history of Aberystwyth.[1] During one of these meetings at Nanteos on 12 April he thoroughly examined the cup in the company of Anna Maria Powell, who also related its history and mythology to him.[2] This marked the beginning of a serious interest in the cup. It was, at this juncture, mostly significant to him because of its link to Strata Florida, and because he believed that the healing traditions associated with it could possibly be a survival of medieval beliefs – an example of living history.

On examination of the cup at this time, Evans described it as 'a black wood mazer',[3] and related the story of a gold band placed around the cup to protect it from the afflicted borrowers who would try to take a bite out of it.

On Saturday 25 May 1901 (the eve of Whitsun), the 700th anniversary of the opening of Strata Florida was celebrated at the abbey. Evans was present and addressed the crowd. The event was reported by the *Welsh Gazette* who noted how Evans had talked about 'the probable scene of the first celebration of Holy Communion, with the chalice, known far and wide as the Healing Cup of Nanteos'.[4]

The phrase is somewhat ambiguous: does this refer to the first Holy Communion celebrated at Strata Florida Abbey, or does it refer to the First Communion celebrated by Christ and his disciples? It is more likely that he meant the former, but readers of the piece could easily have misconstrued it. Either way, it is clear that Evans thought that the Nanteos Cup was used as a Eucharistic chalice in the abbey.

Evans commented on the occasion himself, declaring: 'Everything seemed to conspire this day [to] make it a thoroughly memorable one. More than ever I feel that I ought to pay more attention to the study of the Abbey.'[5]

To mark the occasion, Evans thought it proper to send a telegram to the Powells of Nanteos. It read as follows:

To Powell Nanteos. On the eve of Whitsun Day 1201 Strata Florida's stately Abbey was opened. Seven hundred years afterwards today['s] party of scholars and friends from Aberystwyth County School assembled in ruins for lectures, send hearty greetings to three generations at ancient house of Nanteos, faithful custodians of Abbey's priceless healing cup. David Samuel, Eyre Evans, lecturers.[6]

Evans had apparently met with the Powells only a few days earlier.[7] His interest in the history of the area, channelled through a series of public lectures on a variety of antiquarian and historical topics, caught the attention of a group that was to benefit from his fount of knowledge. They were known as the British Chautauqua.

The British Chautauqua

The Chautauqua was a Christian organisation that began in America, founded in 1874 by John H. Vincent and Lewis Miller. It was originally formed with the primary aim of training Sunday school teachers and other Christian workers in their vocation. The movement took its name from Lake Chautauqua in New York State, and it was on the shores of this lake that the first assembly was held. These assemblies were organised, educational summer holidays, originally very religious in nature. But over time the scope of these summer schools broadened to include other forms of education, entertainment and culture.

In an age before radio, television and cinema, the Chautauqua assemblies satisfied a particular need and became increasingly popular. This led to independent Chautauquas being formed in other parts of rural America, and the popularity of the movement led to the eventual creation of an equivalent British Chautauqua.

The Revd George Short, president of the Baptist Union, first mooted the idea in 1894. A man named Percy C. Webb took up the challenge. Percy Webb (1862–1942) was a marble and granite merchant from Crouch End in London who was strongly associated with Ferme Park Baptist Church, where he served as a deacon for over thirty years.[8]

With the aid of the Sunday School Union and some like-minded friends, Webb instituted the first British Chautauqua retreat in 1895 at Pwllheli in North Wales, situated on Cardigan Bay. Subsequent British Chautauqua holidays took place at Barmouth (1896 and 1900), Edinburgh (1898), and Saltburne and Folkestone (1899). The first Aberystwyth-based Chautauqua took place in 1897 with subsequent occasions from 1901 to 1906, returning to Pwllheli in 1907. The members were from all over the UK and some came from even further afield.

The movement adopted a biblical quote (2 Peter 1:5) as their slogan: 'Add to your faith virtue, and to your virtue knowledge'. The front cover of their 1901 summer programme tells us:

> The British Chautauqua is a Society to assist Teachers and Christian workers generally. This is its prime object; but it also aims to supply guidance and stimulus to all those who, dissatisfied with the desultory nature of much of the reading of the present day, desire to follow a systematic plan of self-education, to fit them better for service in the Church and in Civic and Social Life.[9]

The British Chautauqua offered their own formal qualifications – an idea first proposed in the year of the initial Aberystwyth meeting:

> The proposal that the British Chautauqua should institute a series of Examinations of gradually increasing importance, and based on a collegiate model, led to the inauguration of a three years' course of study, consisting of a preliminary, an intermediate and a final examination, on the passing of which the student will be invested with the Chautauqua certificate.[10]

One Chautauquan living locally to Aberystwyth was Revd Thomas Williams, and it was through his advice that George Eyre Evans was approached by Percy Webb to be their tour guide, lecturing at all the outdoor locations that the British Chautauquans were to visit. Evans graciously accepted the position.[11] This was a good opportunity to promote Cardiganshire and its history to a wider audience. Evans would subsequently promote the history of Cardiganshire further afield, exhibiting the Nanteos Roll in London.[12]

Reception at Nanteos Mansion

One of the scheduled outdoor excursions for 1901 was to be a coach trip to Cwm Einion (also called 'Artists' Valley') on 17 August. It appears from Evans' copy of the summer programme[13] that this trip was cancelled, for some reason, the coach trip being crossed out and 'Nanteos' written in pencil across it.

A reception was given to about a hundred visitors on the terrace outside Nanteos Mansion. A table was placed on the porch and on the table under a glass case was the Nanteos Cup. Mr and Mrs Powell invited George Eyre Evans to address the audience and describe the history of the cup.

Evans would have been familiar with the history of Strata Florida and had only recently discussed the cup with Anna Maria Powell, so this would have been a simple task for him. He told the crowd that the cup had been handed by the monks to the Stedman family and described how it subsequently came into the hands of the Powells of Nanteos who became its guardians through the ages.

He then dealt with its reputation for healing, producing and reading from the notes written by those who had borrowed the cup and claimed to have been healed by it. He described how a token (such as a gold sovereign or a watch) would be left behind as surety of its safe return. The lady of the manor – Anna Maria Powell – then took up the story. She related from memory incredible anecdotes of the cures which had been effected and how a golden fillet had been fitted to the rim of the cup, to prevent it from being nibbled by pilgrims – adding that the fillet had the effect of inhibiting the cup's curative powers, which only returned when the fillet was removed.

The occasion was reported in the *Welsh Gazette* a few days later, adding one rather intriguing detail. The Revd J. Agar Beet DD, of Richmond Wesleyan College, in responding to the speeches, had added the following:

Dr. Beet also showed how, in the legends of this cup – **said to have been the Holy Grail itself** – in the facts connecting it with the highest act of service in Strata Florida all who saw it to-day, were insensibly drawn very near indeed to the Master himself.[14] [Authors' emphasis]

This was not the first time that the Nanteos Cup had been identified with the Holy Grail in print. W. R. Hall had made the identification – albeit tentatively – in his guidebook more than twenty years earlier.[15] But who, on this occasion, had said the Nanteos Cup was the Grail? Was this a reference to genuine local beliefs? Surely George Eyre Evans would not have meant to refer to the cup as the Grail in any historical sense? We will now try to answer these questions.

With the speeches over, the Chautauquans were invited to roam the house and grounds before eventually returning to their carriages for the return journey to Alexandra Hall in Aberystwyth, where many of them were staying. A week later, Evans, under his pseudonym of 'Philip Sidney', compared the Nanteos Cup to the Grail in the pages of the *Welsh Gazette*:

> Away to your left is Nanteos, the 'Brook of the Nightingale' that country house owned by the family of Powell, which for long played a prominent part on the stage of local affairs, and where today visitors from all quarters of the world are welcomed, who come to see that marvellous 'Cwpan Nanteos', or 'Sacred healing cup', which, resembling the Holy Grail described by Tennyson in his 'Idylls of the King', is said to have been made from the wood of the Cross.[16]

It will be immediately apparent that Evans' wording is almost identical to that used by W. R. Hall in his guidebook, later editions of which were in print at the time. Indeed, the 1901 edition[17] of *Aberystwyth: What to see* used exactly the same wording (in reference to the Grail) as the edition from 1880. Clearly W. R. Hall – or his guidebook – had influenced Evans.

If the tradition was that the cup was made from the True Cross, it follows that it could not also be the cup of the Last Supper. Evans was not making an historical assertion for either case – he used the term 'Grail' in a metaphorical sense, because he thought it was a Eucharistic vessel and because he believed that for the monks of Strata Florida the cup dated to the time of Christ through its link with the True Cross. For Evans, the combination of these two traditions justified his metaphorical use of the term 'Holy Grail'. In his writings he always used inverted commas for this purpose.[18]

The British Chautauquans left Aberystwyth just over a week later, but George Eyre Evans kept in touch with them and bought multiple copies of the *Welsh Gazette* when he received letters from them[19] requesting copies of the newspaper and his reports.

The year 1901 was the first time that this reception and exhibition of the Nanteos Cup had taken place for the Chautauquans, but it was not to be the last. There were 'repeat performances'[20] in 1902 and 1904, which followed a similar formula to the first one; there were also informal excursions at other times.

What had prompted the Chautauquans to visit Nanteos? Doubtless George Eyre Evans had used his connections to make it happen, but the *Welsh Gazette* report seems to imply that the idea came from the Chautauquans themselves.[21] One of their number was Miss Ethelwyn Mary Amery who had been elected to the committee[22] of the group in 1897. We know that this lady had been part of the 1901 visit of the British Chautauquans, but it is questionable whether or not she was present at the original Nanteos Reception. George Eyre Evans requested that the visitors should sign his scrapbook for certain excursions. Ethelwyn Amery signed her name for an excursion to Aberllefenni[23] a few days before, but not for the visits to Strata Florida or Nanteos. However, she was certainly present when the Nanteos Reception was repeated for the Chautauquans in 1902, and her subsequent description of this occasion was to transform the story of the Nanteos Cup forever.

A Scholar of the Grail

Ethelwyn Mary Amery was born in South Hornsey, Middlesex, England, on 19 October[24] 1873, the daughter of chartered accountant Richard Amery (1845–1903) and his wife Catherine Claudius Amery (née Goodwin, 1850–1939). There can be no doubt that she would have attended Ferme Park Baptist church and knew Percy Webb, the founder of the British Chautauquans.

Ethelwyn studied at Bedford College[25] and graduated with a Bachelor of Arts degree from the University of London in 1894. The period coincided with a growing interest in Tennyson's Arthurian writings and it is probable that she studied his poems whilst at University. Amery was an intelligent woman and proud of her academic achievements – she was seen wearing her academic robes at the first Aberystwyth Chautauqua[26] in 1897; a photograph of her[27] from the 1902 Chautauqua again shows her in gown and mortar board, wearing *pince nez* eyeglasses. [**Plate 20**]

During her time visiting Aberystwyth with the British Chautauquans she was living in London at 103 Osborne Road, Forest Gate,[28] later moving to 59 Stile Hall Gardens. According to the 1911 census, she was co-head teacher at a private girls' school and linked to an address in Southport, Lancashire, and she wrote to Evans from this address.[29] The name of the girls' school was 'Wintersdorf'. Amery was co-head of the school with Anne Louise Janau, who studied Mathematics and Physics at Royal Holloway College. Janau also graduated in 1894 – the same year as Amery, having gained a third-class honours degree from the University of London.[30] Amery and Janau lived on the premises of the 'Wintersdorf' school and taught a broad curriculum. The fees in 1913 were 'from 20 guineas per term',[31] suggesting the status of the pupils to be well-to-do.

However, Amery was clearly not satisfied with her life at Wintersdorf and departed England for Canada in 1913, where she became a Canadian citizen, worked as a teacher and joined the Theosophical Society.[32] A census from 1916 shows that she was living in Saskatchewan as a lodger with the family of George and Minnie Hutton; on the census she declared that she was a Baptist and a fluent French speaker.[33] Amery ultimately spent much of her working life in India as an educationalist, writing articles and poems for Theosophical journals – eventually proofreading Madame Blavatsky's huge esoteric volume *The Secret Doctrine*. By 1922 she was Secretary of the Pune branch of the Theosophical Society and principal of a Girls' High school in Dastur Nosherwan.[34] She was later moved to another Theosophical Society Girls' school in Coimbatore, but the school was dropped by the Society because of lack of funds.[35]

Amery produced at least four different versions of the Nanteos Grail story. The earliest of these dates from 1902 and was probably written in the wake of the visit of the Chautauquans to Nanteos Mansion in that year. The British Chautauqua Summer Programme for 1902 had already referred directly to the cup as the Holy Grail:

Saturday, August 16, 2pm. Excursion by Rail to Nanteos, and, by the kind invitation of Mr and Mrs Powell, visit their seat,

where is preserved the Cup of Nanteos, 'the prototype of the
Holy Grail'.[36]]

It is clear from this that the cup was already beginning to be
identified, without qualification, as the one on which the medieval
legends were based.

Ethelwyn Mary Amery would later remove the inverted commas
and present the identification as an actual proposition, within the
context of a modified version of a medieval Grail romance. Her
first effort appeared in the *Ferme Park Magazine* in 1902 under the
title of 'Reminiscences of An Ideal Holiday':

> There was another Cup, a Cup which was handled by the Saviour
> Himself on the memorable Occasion when He drank of the fruit
> of the vine for the last time on earth; that Cup, could we but
> find it, worthy of all reverence and care, and say some THAT
> CUP IS HERE. Tradition tells of its journey to England, and of
> its treasuring in a Church somewhere in the west, and in spite
> of gaps in the story, there is the possibility that this is indeed
> that HOLY GRAIL which was sought for so earnestly by King
> Arthur's Knights.[37]

The first editor of *Ferme Park Magazine* was Percy Webb, and this
is no coincidence since the two of them lived in the same part of
London and both were members of the Ferme Park Baptist church;
Webb was in fact the first editor of the magazine.

It is obvious that Amery had struck up a correspondence with
George Eyre Evans, because he subsequently reproduced extracts
from Amery's article in the *Welsh Gazette* under his 'Philip
Sidney'[38] column for December 1902. In 1903 he did so again
when he produced a sizeable book called *Cardiganshire*.[39] Evans
employed the title 'Through Other Glasses' on both occasions, as
if to emphasise that the perspective was not his own but Amery's.
The 'Church somewhere in the West' in the above quotation may
possibly be a reference to Glastonbury, but it is interesting that she
avoids making this explicit.

Amery's second account of the Nanteos Cup appeared in the
Central Foundation Girls' School Magazine[40] for March 1904.
Called 'A Twentieth Century Quest of the Graal', this account

recalls the visit of the Chautauquans to Nanteos Mansion – however the time, place and people are all disguised. Instead of Aberystwyth we have 'Aber-Nant'. Nanteos becomes 'Nightingale House'; the Powells are replaced by 'the Stedmans'. The events described actually took place in 1902, whereas she says it was 'last year' (which would have been 1903). There is no direct reference to the British Chautauquans. There is no mention of Glastonbury here either, but the Dissolution of the Monasteries is given as the reason for the monks fleeing Strata Florida for Nanteos.

The third account of the cup was to be Amery's best-known work – a small book printed in Aberystwyth called *Sought and Found – A Story of the Holy Graal* (1905). It was George Eyre Evans that Amery contacted to proofread and publish the work, which was only given to the subscribers who had funded it (there were 152 in all). At the beginning there is a dedication 'To Mrs Powell of Nant Eos' – this was a reference to Anna Maria Powell and not Margaret Powell as many later commentators have wrongly assumed.

Chapter One of *Sought and Found* serves as an introduction, in which Amery shows that she was familiar with Grail literature and scholarship. She knew about the French sources that became the foundation of the great Arthurian epic known as *Le Morte d'Arthur* by Sir Thomas Malory (1485). Amery also knew about the academic debate over the authorship of the *Vulgate Cycle* (now known as the *Lancelot-Grail*) and theories concerning the Celtic pagan influences believed by many scholars – then and now – to have influenced aspects of the medieval Christian versions. Amery twice quotes fragments of poetry by Alfred, Lord Tennyson, who had himself mentioned Glastonbury in the context of the Grail tradition:

This, from the blessed land of Aromat –
After the day of darkness, when the dead
Went wandering o'er Moriah – the good saint
Arimathaean Joseph, journeying brought
To Glastonbury, where the winter thorn
Blossoms at Christmas, mindful of our Lord

Tennyson, Idylls of the King

Having given a brief summary of what might be considered the academic view, Amery adds the following:

> Such is briefly the origin which scholars ascribe to the legend, but there are some who think that these old story-tellers were right in their statements, that the cup and the lance are no survivals from Keltic [sic] legend, but are indeed what they are asserted to be, and that some day the Graal will be seen once more in England as it was in olden days.[41]

At this point Amery seems to shrink away from making a blatant assertion that the Grail might be a physical artefact, instead rounding off the chapter by quoting William Caxton's preface to Malory's *Le Morte d'Arthur*:

> ...but for to give faith and belief that all is true that is contained therein, ye be at your liberty; but all is written for our doctrine, and for to beware that we fall not to vice nor sin, but to exercise and follow virtue...[42]

In other words, all is written for the moral betterment of the reader (which of course would be in line with Chautauquan purposes) and the question of historicity is of secondary importance.

The main section of *Sought and Found* (chapters 2 to 5) contains Amery's own version of the Grail legend, drawing upon two medieval romances that form part of the collection then known as the 'Vulgate Cycle' and today as the Lancelot-Grail. These two stories are the *Estoire del Saint Graal* and the *Quest del Saint Graal*. Amery produced a much-reduced summary of these and along the way made some important changes to suit her purposes.

In the *Estoire*, Joseph of Arimathea travels to Scotland and we are told that this is where he died and was buried.[43] In Amery's version, Joseph died and was buried in Scotland, but his body was later removed to Glastonbury.[44]

Another important change concerns the events after the culmination of the quest. In the Lancelot-Grail Cycle *Queste*, the Grail was achieved by the perfect knight, Sir Galahad, who made the ultimate sacrifice, having prayed for his mortal life to end after he had achieved the beatific, sublime vision of the Grail.

Immediately after this event, a mysterious hand took the Grail and the sacred lance up to Heaven and they were seen no more on Earth. Clearly, for Amery's purposes, this ending would not do; she wanted the Grail to remain on the physical plane so that it could be taken to Strata Florida. Rather than omit the well-known version she decided to accommodate both:

> And some say that the Graal ... was received up into heaven, and was seen on earth no more; but others say that it remained for long in the little chapel, and others sought it, and some who were worthy found it and were blessed by the sight of it. And they say also that when at last the road to the chapel was well worn, because many men passed this way, and the noise of war and invading armies came near, the priest bore the cup away to the west, where peace was yet unbroken, and there he found friends with whom he dwelt, and they built another church and established a monastery, and dwelt there many years.[45]

It is possible that Amery had in mind another text, the *Perlesvaus*, also known as *The High History of the Holy Grail*, which dates from the first decade of the thirteenth century. It was first translated by Sebastian Evans in 1838, so Amery could certainly have seen a copy of the book. It describes a seemingly ruinous and deserted Grail castle, visited by two young knights in search of adventure. After a time, they returned, much changed, and when they were asked what they had experienced all they would say was: 'Go where we went and you will find out!'

This was all pointing to the fact that the Grail had returned – or perhaps that it never went away. Again, the small chapel described by Amery may have come from the same source, as Arthur himself experiences a vision of the Grail in *Perlesvaus*.

It is important to note here that there is no mention of Abbot Richard Whiting of Glastonbury spiriting the cup to Strata Florida at the time of the Dissolution of the Monasteries. In Amery's *Sought and Found*, the cup is brought to the vicinity of Strata Florida centuries before the monastery was even built. Moreover, it did not come from Glastonbury but instead was brought to Mid Wales by a priest from the little chapel where, in Amery's story, Galahad had experienced his vision of the Grail. This little chapel is another of Amery's inventions, replacing the city of Sarras in the Lancelot-Grail cycle, where the knights brought the Grail. Although Glastonbury is mentioned once as the location of the original church of the Grail, it is never mentioned again. It is as if there was a determination on Amery's part to downplay its importance.

The main part of Amery's quest ends with a prophecy:

> And some there are who dream that the Graal is still preserved on earth, and is seen by those who seek it diligently, and that some day, when the earth is once more pure and peaceful, the old glory will return to it, and then the reign of Christ will be established for ever.[46]

Here, the Grail has been deprived of its halo, so that all the pilgrim to Nanteos sees is the frail, time-worn relic – although its healing powers were retained.

Having laid the groundwork with this modified version of Galahad's quest, Amery was then able to continue the story of the cup forward to her own time, in the chapter that followed. Chapter Six describes a visit to Nanteos Mansion by 'holidaymakers from Aberystwyth'. These were – of course – the British Chautauquans, many of whom were staying at the Alexandra Hall.

The content of this chapter is very close to the text that Amery had used in the *Central Foundation Girls' School Magazine* mentioned above. The main difference being that the disguised names have been replaced with the real ones. It is not entirely clear why Amery had employed altered names in the earlier account, but for an audience of Chautauquans – most, if not all, of whom would have attended at least one of the Nanteos Receptions – there would have been no sense in maintaining the disguise.

So, whereas the opening text formerly began with 'Not far from the seaside town of Aber-Nant in Mid Wales, stands the Nightingale House, the country seat of the Stedmans',[47] this is replaced in *Sought and Found* with 'Not far from the sea-side town of Aberystwyth, in Mid-Wales, stands the House of Nant Eos, the country seat of the Powells.'[48]

Apart from such simple variations, the two versions are basically identical. The story gives a description of some of the magnificent features of the mansion, before moving on to the cup itself:

Now those who looked at the case wondered what this treasure could be which was thus carefully guarded, and when the cover was withdrawn, the astonishment of many more than equalled their previous curiosity...[49]

There is no mention of George Eyre Evans; instead, Amery makes the Lady of the Manor entirely responsible for relating the story, beginning at the time of the Dissolution:

Many years ago, when Henry VIII was destroying the Monasteries, his servants came into Wales, and, hearing of an ancient Monastery among the hills, where only seven old monks remained to guard their treasure, determined to destroy the Abbey and seize their goods.'[50]

Glastonbury and its last Abbot, Richard Whiting, are again noticeable by their absence. Is it possible that Amery foresaw the possibility of the Church authorities in Glastonbury staking a claim on the cup? Obviously she would not have wanted her book to be a source of embarrassment for the Powells. It is also possible that George Eyre Evans might have expressed to her his doubts about the cup having come from Glastonbury.

Amery, through the voice of the 'Hostess', tells us how the cup was brought to the manor by the fleeing monks and how the last of them entrusted the treasure to the owner of the manor. It is at this moment that Amery introduces a phrase that would be repeated in countless retellings of the story, reverberating down the years:

One by one the old monks died, and when the last one was at the point of death he entrusted the treasure to the owner of the house that had sheltered them, **until the Church should once more claim its own.**[51]

What did this mean? Did the Hostess (Anna Maria Powell) actually speak these words? Amery is the earliest source we know for this phrase. Another similar phrase, 'when Christ shall claim his own', usually refers to the Day of Judgement. The 'Church' might be seen as a way of referring to Christ. In Chapter One of

Sought and Found, Amery had paraphrased Tennyson: 'the holy cup from which our Lord drank at that Last Supper **with his own**.'[52]

Seen in this light, Amery's 'until the Church should once more claim its own' might be seen simply as a variation of the more usual phrase, implying that the Powells were instructed by the monk to keep the cup forever. However, the Hostess (or Amery) then added: 'But the Church has not yet claimed it, and it is that treasure of the monks which you now see.'[53]

Hence the phrase 'its own' in this context must refer to the cup itself and not Christ's chosen; for the same reason the 'Church' must refer to an earthly ecclesiastical authority. Essentially, Amery is claiming that the Powells were expecting at some future time to relinquish the cup to the 'Church', but there is no hard evidence that Anna Maria Powell actually said this.

Not until the final paragraph of the book is the cup's identity as the Grail revealed, although it is not unexpected:

> Not for its healing properties alone was this cup treasured, not because from it the monks had received Communion wine; the cup was older than the Monastery – indeed the Monastery had been built to receive it; it had been handed down from Abbot to Abbot through the ages, and in each age its secret was told to one or two, that they might guard it the more carefully, for this cup is none other than the one from which our Lord drank at the Last Supper.[54]

Amery's role is that of a storyteller, rather like the medieval *conteurs* who originally spread the Grail legends throughout Europe; her academic mortar board has been placed to one side in order that she may weave this tapestry of fact and fancy with its intended purpose of inspiring the reader to great deeds and greater virtue – to be like Galahad, the perfect knight. With this in mind, Amery concludes her work by paraphrasing the Sermon on the Mount: 'The pure in heart shall see God'[55] (cf. Matthew 5:8). In time, the spiritual metaphor provided by Amery's tale would be replaced with a more literal identification of the Nanteos Cup as the vessel used by Christ at the Last Supper – this may or may not have been her intention, but it was what she achieved. Her story appeals to the nationalistic overtones to be found in the Glastonbury legends and so, like William Blake, one is inclined to ponder whether or not these legends are historically true. This leads inevitably to a more materialistic idea of the Grail quest and a more physical concept of the Grail.

Amery's final Grail story was published decades later. The account was called *The Story of the Graal* and appeared in *The Theosophist* in October 1949. Although the essay does not mention the Nanteos Cup directly, the text is drawn from *Sought and Found* with minor grammatical modifications.[56]

Chapters Two and Three have been eliminated completely. The final paragraph of Chapter One is also omitted and some bridging text is introduced to paste over the gap. This includes the phrase:

Of the wanderings of the Graal from Palestine to Britain there are many accounts which can be woven into sequential story, but we will leave that for another occasion, space forbidding its inclusion here.[57]

Presumably, Amery had further essays planned, but these did not materialise in the pages of *The Theosophist*. We may speculate that there may have been more material written but not published. Perhaps it still exists somewhere? The essay concludes at the end of Chapter Five of *Sought and Found*. There is thus no mention of the tourists and their visit to Nant Eos, no wooden healing bowl and no talk of the Church claiming its own.

W. R. Hall and the British Chautauquans
In her writings Amery never revealed who told her that the Nanteos Cup was the Holy Grail. She may have inferred this from George Eyre Evans' speech or from the wording of the 1902 British Chautauqua programme; she may have read the 1901 report from the *Welsh Gazette*. There is yet another possibility – it may have been W. R. Hall himself who revealed it to her.

Hall was, in fact, actively involved in helping with the British Chautauquan visits from the outset in 1897. In the *British Chautauquan* journal we are told: 'Mr. W. R. Hall of Aberystwyth has been untiring and self-sacrificing in the highest degree.'[58]

Hall had provided publicity material which appeared in the journal some months before the visitors arrived. In an anonymously published article we are told:

> In still earlier times it is said, Aberystwyth was a centre of repute among the Druids. Here the ovate was sent to sea in a coracle without rudder, sails or oars. If the winds were favourable, and the frail bark drifted ashore, he was deemed to have been accepted of the gods, and was accordingly initiated into the final mysteries of the order. Whereas if divinely rejected, he was drowned in the trial and was so prevented from disclosing the secrets he had already learned.[59]

This is very probably Hall's handiwork, borrowed in all probability from the writings of the amateur scholar Iolo Morgannwg (the pseudonym of Edward Williams, 1747–1826), whose voluminous writings contained many 'reconstructed' druidic rites such as those mentioned by Hall.

The programme of events for the visitors had to be organised well in advance and publicised. The British Chautauquans, in return, promoted his *Aberystwyth: What to see...* guide, with its reference to the Nanteos Grail.[60]

Hall, in 1897, took the British Chautauquans to the Clettwr Valley and Bedd Taliesin – a low-lying cairn near the village of Talybont, believed to have been the burial site of the semi-mythical bard Taliesin. Hall gave a talk at the site on 'Taliesin and his Times'. The talk was well received although one of the visitors rather irreverently tossed an unwanted sandwich into the cairn cist. According to Hall, Taliesin lived in the days of King Arthur and cited Tennyson's 'Holy Grail' to emphasise that he was regarded as a prophet and the greatest of the Welsh bards: 'Taliesin is our fullest throat of song.'[61]

The British Chautauquans were impressed by the lecture and described it in their journal:

> Mr. Hall conceived from Taliesin's writings that Taliesin was the poet of Unity – uniting the Druids with the Christians of those days and Iberian and Goidel and Brython into an impetuous torrent against the incoming Saxons, whom he described as 'a coiling serpent, proud and merciless'.[62]

W. R. Hall repeated his Taliesin talk for the British Chautauquans in 1902 – the very same year that Amery wrote her first account of the cup.[63]

However it may have happened, it is certain that Hall influenced the key moments during the British Chautauquan visits that lead to the Nanteos Cup, becoming the subject of Amery's storytelling – but this was just the beginning.

The Cup in the Limelight – A Magic Lantern Display

Amery was not the only British Chautauquan to spread the word about the Nanteos Grail. On Monday 27 March 1905, a draper from Harrow by the name of Robert A. Smith put on a presentation about the Holy Grail for the Byron Hill Literary Society. According to one source,[64] the title of the talk was 'The Holy Cup of Nanteos, and How I photographed It'.

Smith had been to Nanteos with the British Chautauquans in 1904 and had taken many photographs of the area and the reception at Nanteos Mansion. Some of these images formed the basis of his presentation at Harrow and included two close-up views of the cup and one of Anna Maria Powell seated at a table outside the mansion, talking to the Chautauquan visitors. There are two that feature George Eyre Evans, Ethelwyn Mary Amery and her mother Catherine, along with Anna Maria Powell and the family of Robert Smith. In these photos, Catherine and Ethelwyn Amery are both dressed in black, most likely indicating that they were still in mourning for Richard, Ethelwyn's father, who had died towards the end of 1903. Amery's writings on the Grail coincided with what must have been, for her, a very difficult and personally stressful time.

Another of Smith's photographs featured the American author W. D. Howells, whom we will meet presently.[65]

A dozen of these photographs were compiled into an album[66] by Smith and sent to George Eyre Evans as a Christmas gift. Evans subsequently featured some of these photos (somewhat cropped) when he published Amery's *Sought and Found*.

In his presentation at Harrow, Smith projected these images using a limelight lantern. He gave a somewhat historically flawed account of the Holy Grail legends, based on ideas circulating at the time. Smith pointed out in an emphatic manner that there was no historical evidence of the Holy Grail at Glastonbury – this at least was correct. We should be grateful to Smith, at least, for preserving in image form these key moments in the evolution of the legend of the cup.

Jonathan Brierley and the Stedman Ancestor

Another visitor to the Chautauquan events at Strata Florida and Nanteos was Jonathan Brierley (1843–1915). Brierley was a Yorkshireman who trained to become a preacher but later became a Fleet Street journalist and author on religious matters. He wrote for a newspaper called *The Christian World* and was very often known by his *nom de plume* of 'J. B. of the Christian World'.[67]

In 1906 Brierley wrote a report in the *Church Times*[68] entitled 'A Welsh Relic – The Nanteos Healing Cup' in which he relayed the story of the mysterious Duke of Arabia, whom we met in Chapter Two. In this version he brings with him a piece of the True Cross, which was subsequently fashioned into a cup. This fabled character, we are told, was given land to the south of Aberystwyth, which included Strata Florida. The cup was given to the monks who kept it until the time of 'the Great Pillage' (Brierley's term for the Dissolution of the Monasteries) whence the cup was returned to the Stedmans.

Brierley informs us that weevils – which infested the cotton wool used to pack the cup – were responsible for the appearance of what he calls a 'rude design' on the inner surface of the vessel. He also recalled that on one occasion when he visited Nanteos, he had raised the question of the type of wood used to manufacture the cup. An experienced woodsman was summoned but was not able to identify it. Brierley then relates how the matter was resolved:

> When, however, a work box and another article of olive wood, happily at hand in the hall, were compared, it seemed plain to all that the wood of the Cup was of similar grain, and although the vessel is black with age where comparatively recent fractures exposed a new surface, the wood shewed the peculiar colour of the olive.[69]

Many subsequent accounts describe the cup as being made of olive wood and this became an accepted part of the tradition, but there exists an anecdotal report from 1985 which suggests that scientists who had examined the cup in 1977 had apparently decided that it was made from wych elm.[70] Brierley then takes the reports of the cup's healing powers and tells us that they were only effective for blood disorders. He recounts how the vessel was sent to a woman suffering from haemorrhaging after giving birth:

> Her life was utterly despaired of by the doctor, and on the woman getting up, and becoming much worse in consequence, the healing cup was hastily sent for as a last resource. In a month the patient had quite recovered.[71]

Brierley's article received a hostile reaction from the famous Arthurian scholar Jessie Weston, who replied to the *Church Times*, claiming that the Holy Grail would not have been made from wood:

> Sir, – In the interesting description of the above relic your correspondent remarks that 'some traditions identify the cup with the Holy Grail;' and goes on to claim for it the honour of being a relic of the True Cross. These two claims are, of course, destructive the one of the other. In its Christian form the Grail is the vessel in which Joseph of Arimathea received the Blood flowing from the wounds of our Lord as he hung on the Cross – ergo, the Grail was not wrought of the wood of that Cross. Nor was the vessel of wood. I am familiar with every extant version of the Grail story, and I know none in which this is the case. The Grail may be of gold, or wrought from a precious stone, it is never of wood. I am not aware that there is any evidence as to the wood of the Cross being olive; the mediaeval tradition, of course, regards it as of the Tree of Life, a branch of which was brought by Adam from Paradise. JESSIE L. WESTON.[72]

Mid Wales Folklore and the Phiol

Not everyone rejected the story framed by Amery, Brierley and the Powells. Around this time Anna Maria Powell showed folklorist Jonathan Ceredig Davies the Nanteos Cup, which was subsequently described in detail by him in his 1911 book *Folklore of West and Mid* Wales.[73] He called it the *Phiol*[74] and referred to an invalid 'wealthy Roman Catholic lady' who had come all the way from London to view the cup – such was her faith in it.

Davies describes again how the cup was believed to have been made from the wood of the True Cross and kept at Strata Florida, but there is no mention of Richard Whiting or the Glastonbury monks. He points out how the cup had been reduced in size by the pilgrims nibbling at its rim and then says, quite plainly:

> It is quite possible that this holy relic was the chalice therein our Lord consecrated the wine and water at the institution of the Eucharist, and in which was said to be preserved some of the blood which fell from the Saviour's wounds as he hung on the cross.[75]

Clearly this contradicts the notion of the cup being fashioned from the wood of the True Cross, but where had this come from? The answer is made known as Davies then simply lifts the whole of Chapter Six from Amery's *Sought and Found*. The reason Davies failed to mention Glastonbury was because Amery did not do so. He was entirely reliant on her book for his statement that the Nanteos Cup might be the Grail.

Davies concludes by mentioning a story about a noble French woman who had asked to have a handkerchief tied around the cup for twenty-four hours and subsequently delivered to her. The cup could deliver its healing in many ways.

The American Writer

The Chautauquans who saw the cup at Nanteos Mansion were frequently joined by guests, possibly the most notable being the American writer William Dean Howells, author of – amongst many other works – *The Kentons, Questionable Shapes, The Son of Royal Langbrith* and *The Landlord at Lion's Head*. Known as the 'Dean of American letters', Howells was noted as a novelist, playwright, critic and editor of the American magazine *Atlantic Monthly*. He was considered one of the most influential American writers of his day. In 1904 he was awarded the degree of D. Litt. *Honoris Causa* by the University of Oxford and having journeyed to Oxford to receive his honour, decided to spend a few days in Aberystwyth with his wife. He was requested by the British Chautauquans to join them on their excursions and accepted their invitation.

On Wednesday 10 August 1904, the Chautauquans went to
Nanteos. The party was led by George Eyre Evans. The British
Chautauqua Summer Programme for that year recorded the
occasion as follows:

Wednesday, August 10. 1.30pm. – Excursion, Coach drive
to Nanteos. Visit the Gardens and grounds by invitation of
Mr and Mrs Powell. 'The Healing Cup of Nanteos', or, 'Holy
Grail,' will be shown.[76]

There were 134 British Chautauquans[77] at the reception; a number
of them signed their names in Evans' scrapbook as a memento of the
occasion. Amongst the signatures are those of Ethelwyn M. Amery
and her mother, Catherine, both giving Stoke Newington as their
address.[78] William Dean Howells, who was also present at the
event, struck up an accord with Evans and later that evening visited
him at his home. Evans recorded the day's events in his notes:

On the following afternoon [10 August 1904] I had the pleasure
of taking Mr [William Dean] Howells to Nanteos with a party
of the British Chautauqua, to whom I lectured on the 'Cup of
Nanteos' or the 'Grail'. The same evening, he called upon me, &
spent some time in my library & eagerly asking questions &
himself imparting information on many topics. It was a time of
much refreshing and value to me. He told me that all he writes is
taken by Harper Brothers who deal with it as seems to them fit.
Accompanied by Mrs Howells, he proceeded from Aberystwyth
to Chester en route to Edinburgh.[79]

Before his departure, Howells signed Evans' visitors' book,
adding 'D. Litt, Oxon, honoris causa, New York'.[80] The British
Chautauquans were pleased to have a notable guest in their midst
and a photograph of Howells appeared in the Summer Programme
for the following year.[81] The *Welsh Gazette* proudly declared that
William Dean Howells was 'of Welsh Ancestry'.[82] Neither was
Howells to forget the occasion, as he documented it in his book
Seven English Cities, published five years later.[83]

The format of the Nanteos Reception had become more elaborate
by 1904. The Lady of the Manor brought out the cup and placed

it on a table. After the Chautauquan guests had arrived and congregated on the lawn outside the mansion, an open-air religious service was held. A soloist, Madame Lizzie Owen, singing a sacred hymn followed this. According to W. D. Howells, 'she sang divinely',[84] although he could not remember whether she sang in English or Welsh. This performance was followed by the speeches, the first of which was made by the unnamed 'Unitarian minister' referred to by W. D. Howells in his *Seven English Cities*; the minister was of course George Eyre Evans. Howells tells us:

> He [George Eyre Evans] told us how the Holy Grail had been deposited with the monks of Strata Florida ... but I forgot who made them this trust, unless it was King Arthur's knights, and I am not sure whether the fact is matter of legend or history.[85]

Once again there is no specific information as to how the cup was deposited in Strata Florida and the report in the *Welsh Gazette* is similarly unrevealing.[86] The Lord of the Manor was absent on this occasion and so the Lady of the House, seated with her grandson on her lap, told the story of how the fame of the cup had spread throughout the whole area. Howells tells us that it was customary for the sick to nibble a piece of wood from the cup and then swallow it, as if the cup itself were part of the medication.

The Last Generation
Towards the end of 1911, William Beauclerk Powell and his wife Anna Maria both passed away. They died within days of each other and were buried in the family vault at Llanbadarn church on the same day. Nanteos was inherited by William's son, Edward Athelstan Lewis Powell (1870–1930), who moved in with his wife Margaret and their only child, William Edward George Pryse Wynne Powell, known as Billy.

Edward was born in Denbigh, educated at Rugby school and Oxford and returned to Nanteos after graduation to administer the estate. He subsequently joined the Leicestershire Militia and later re-joined the 3rd Battalion in August 1914. He served with this battalion until May 1915 and then with same unit in Northern Command Humber Defences near Hull, Yorkshire, until February 1916. He then joined the 2nd Leicestershire Regiment in

Mesopotamia, as part of the relief effort for General Townshend at Kut. Edward was present at the first and subsequent battles at Sunniyat on 6–19 April 1916.[87]

We know that Billy was destined for a military career from a young age. His father was a retired captain and a portrait at Nanteos shows him in military uniform. Perhaps it was expected that Billy would follow in his father's footsteps and in the early years of the twentieth century Billy attended a military preparatory school at Aldershot called Winton House.[88]

Billy joined Sandhurst in September 1917 and subsequently entered the regiment of the Welsh Guards, gaining a commission as a second lieutenant. The regiment had been formed just over two years earlier in February 1915 and had been immediately honoured. They were chosen to mount guard at Buckingham Palace on 1 March – St David's Day – just three days after their formation.

Major C. H. Dudley Ward was promoted to be acting commander of the 3rd Battalion of the 1st Welsh Guards during the last stage of the First World War – the period when the heir to Nanteos was a subaltern in his battalion. After his demobilisation from the army on 1 August 1919, Ward began to write his *History of the Welsh Guards*. His first book was well received, and he went on to produce several more histories of Welsh regiments including *The 53rd (Welsh) Yeomanry* and the *Regimental Records of the Royal Welsh Fusiliers*. In his *History of the Welsh Guards* he writes:

> We feel we have not done justice to the valour of those who formed and fought in the Battalion of Welsh Guards. Amongst the fallen are officers, from Randolph, Mawbrey and Smith, who were the first, to Powell who was the last, whose names are merely mentioned. There are hundreds of private soldiers who are not mentioned at all... Every soldier who fought and fell has his reward in the memory of his friends; but an adequate monument worthy of his sacrifice can only be erected by the future action of his countrymen – men whom he never saw.[89]

The action in which Billy Powell lost his life reflects the courage and loyalty of all these men and the shameful gossip that is apparently still occasionally recounted in his home town[90] that he was shot in the back 'by men he never saw' – i.e. his own men – needs to be silenced once and for all. This is provided for us by the description by Dudley Ward of the manner in which this man died among his brave and loyal Welsh compatriots.

Ward relates that 'the engagement near the village of Bavai was entirely L. F. Ellis and No.3 Company's fight,'[91] describing Ellis as 'a little man who indulged at times in quick, fretful outbursts of temper'.[92] Ellis had formed up his company on the east of the village and advanced through the extremely fine, misty rain, leading his men through the hedges until they made contact with the enemy at the railway. When he found that his leading platoon had checked, he went forward to see what was happening. With enemy machine guns firing out of the mist he realised that nothing was coming from the railway some 50 yards in front of him. His halted men told him that the railway cutting was held by the enemy, which caused him to lose his temper. 'Nonsense, there is no one there,'[93] he fumed, and ran across the intervening 50 yards and jumped into the cutting – to find himself in the middle of around fifty Germans with nothing but his walking stick, which he flourished over his head.

A loud report from the bank immediately behind him felled a facing German, announcing that Lance Corporal Gordon and Sergeant Jones had followed him and were firing from the top of the bank. The startled Germans took flight, but Jones accounted for five and Gordon for six before the enemy all disappeared into the mist to entrench themselves on the rising ground on the opposite bank behind them. This example of 'Squiff' Ellis, who led his company into battle fearlessly, by dashing forward alone and waving them on with a walking stick, received the highest praise from Ward, who describes him as a 'wonderful little man ... who really ran the whole battle in the front line'.[94] Ellis had fired his men by his own example, and they advanced up the slope in a series of short rushes.

The gunfire was continuous at this point, but there were surprisingly few casualties. Ellis was now leading a Lewis gun team and he took over the gun himself when the No. 1 was shot through the neck. Ward specifically tells us[95] that Powell was killed trying to rush a light machine gun, and *at his heels* Private Hammond also fell. The enemy were either killed or they ran, Prehert Farm was reached and Bavai held. Ward has this entry in his diary for 8 November:

> There was a brigade funeral at 11.30 a.m. for men killed at Amfroipret – including six of ours. At 2.30 p.m. we had another funeral at Buvignies. Poor young Powell was amongst the first killed and Private Hammond, the H.Q. orderly, a first-rate fellow. When Mog had finished I announced to the battalion over the graves of the dead that the result of their gallant efforts and the supreme sacrifice of their comrades was at hand; that German Plenipotentiaries had come through the French line under a flag of truce to ask for terms.[96]

On 11 November news reached the battalion that an armistice had been signed and took effect 'at 11.00 hours today'. The order posted outside the battalion HQ read:

> Hostilities will cease on the whole front as from November 11th at 11 o'clock (French time). The Allied troops will not, until a further order, go beyond the line reached on that date and at that hour. (Signed) Marshal Foch.[97]

At Nanteos Captain E. A. Powell and his wife Margaret were preparing to celebrate their heir and only child's return from the war when they heard that he had fallen in what was a meaningless sacrifice, two days after the poet Wilfred Owen's death. Owen's famous poem 'Dulce et Decorum Est', which speaks of the horror and futility of war, perfectly expresses the needless death of Second Lieutenant William Powell, advancing against the stuttering machine guns that were to be silenced at last tragically within hours of his death; a meaningless attack led by a nineteen-year-old youth with nothing but a revolver in his hand.

In 1897 the artist George Frederick Watts had presented a painting of Sir Galahad to Eton College – Billy's old school – and it now hangs in the chapel there. The revival of interest in the Arthurian legends in Victorian times, imbued as they are with knightly ideals of heroism, chivalry and self-sacrifice, is reflected in the poetry of Tennyson and other works of literature of the time:

> So all day long the noise of battle roll'd
> Among the mountains by the winter sea;
> Until King Arthur's table, man by man,
> Had fallen in Lyonnesse about their Lord…
> *Morte d'Arthur*, Alfred, Lord Tennyson

This was an expression of the *zeitgeist* which ultimately inspired a generation of young men like Billy, many of whom would make the ultimate sacrifice on the field of battle during the First World War just as Arthur's knights had done in the ancient stories.

It was none other than Billy who was, in 1904, the small child who sat on his grandmother's knee as she regaled the British Chautauquans with the story of the Nanteos Grail and the seven monks who brought it to their home.

Billy was buried in France at the Maubeuge Cemetery. In 1922, tenants and employees of the Nanteos estate built a memorial to Billy Powell in Penparcau, Aberystwyth. It consists of a 12-foot-high Celtic cross of grey granite, made by Messrs Whittiple of Exeter.[98] In May of that year, the memorial was formerly unveiled in a ceremony at which Captain E. A. L. Powell and Margaret Powell were both present.[99]

Mary L. Lewes

Not long after the British Chautauquans visited Aberystwyth, word of the Nanteos Cup was spreading in esoteric circles and an article appeared in *The Occult Review*[100] for 1910. Mary Louisa Lewes of Ty Glyn Aeron, a member of another ancient and powerful Ceredigion family, wrote this article. Mary Lewes was a distant cousin of Captain John Hext Lewes of Llanllŷr, a man named in Margaret Powell's will and who would be involved in a legal battle to gain control of the Nanteos estate[101] in the 1950s. An aunt of Mary Lewes, Louisa Jane, was married to Sir Pryse Pryse of Gogerddan, who was father to Margaret Powell. Mary Lewes wrote frequent articles on Welsh folklore, fortune-telling and the supernatural, and her books included *Stranger than Fiction*[102] and *The Queer Side of Things*.[103] Her sister, Evelyn, was on the

Executive Committee of the Cardiganshire Antiquarian Society in 1910. In the *Occult Review* article, Lewes relates how a Roman Catholic lady came from London and was cured by the cup, adding that there was 'nothing really extraordinary' about the healing. Lewes explanation for the healing effect was drawn from psychological ideas:

> A Roman Catholic, her mind was trained to receive with faith suggestions from her spiritual director, and it is this very attitude of unquestioning openness to suggestion, which sets working that wonderful set of faculties, called by Dr. Schofield 'the unconscious mind', and by the late Mr. Frederick Myers 'the subliminal self'. As Mr. Percy Dearmer remarks in his book *Body and Soul*, the authenticity of relics is a side-issue; faith in them is the main point, and the factor that makes for healing.[104]

Her article mentions both the True Cross and Holy Grail traditions but describes the latter as 'a picturesque, but I fear, too far-fetched idea'.[105] Some years later, when writing her book *The Queer Side of Things*, her tone seems to have softened somewhat and the True Cross tale is labelled a 'much less regarded tradition'.[106]

A. E. Waite and Arthur Machen

Shortly before Lewes' article appeared in *Occult Review*, the mystic and occultist Arthur Edward Waite (1857–1942) had made reference to the cup in his 1909 work, *Hidden Church of the Holy Grail*:

> There are historical memorials of mystic and holy cups, possessing great virtues and preserved in old Welsh families. Among these is the Holy Cup of Tregaron, which was made of the wood of the True Cross and its healing virtues were manifested so recently as the year 1901.[107]

Born the son of a sea captain in Brooklyn, New York, Waite was intensely religious as a child; his Roman Catholic faith suffered after the death of his sister, but he subsequently developed a deep interest in spiritualism, Theosophy and the occult. Waite was the translator of a work on magic – *Dogme et Rituel de la Haute*

Magie – written by a nineteenth-century French occultist, Alphonse Louis Constant (1810–75), who adopted the pen-name of Eliphas Levi. Waite subsequently became a prime mover in esoteric circles and was a founding member of the Hermetic Order of the Golden Dawn, given over to the study and practice of ritual magic. Among its members were the infamous 'Black Magician' Aleister Crowley, the poet W. B. Yeats, and the eccentric esotericist Samuel Liddell MacGregor Mathers. Waite is probably best remembered today as the creator of the *Rider-Waite Tarot*, one of the most important developments in the history of cartomancy.

Another famous writer who mentioned the cup at this time was the novelist and essayist Arthur Machen (1863–1947), who, in his novel *The Great Return*, refers to it directly as 'the Healing Cup of Nanteos, or Tregaron Healing Cup'.[108] The cup is also mentioned in an essay entitled 'The Secret of the Sangraal' published in his book *The Shining Pyramid*.[109]

Machen and Waite were introduced to each other via Machen's first wife, Amy Hogg. The two of them became close friends for life, finding commonality in their belief in a spiritual reality underlying the mundane world; in spite of this there were differences between them. In one of his most well-known books, *The Hidden Church of the Holy Grail*, Waite mentions that the hypothesis he developed in *Book VII – The Holy Grail in light of the Celtic Church* was based on material given to him by Machen.[110]

However, in a private letter to a Mr Wood, dating from 11 December 1916, Machen expressed strong reservations about *The Hidden Church*:

> I do not believe that there is a word to be said for its main thesis. Indeed, I do not believe that Waite knows what his main thesis is: he talks of the 'Secret Church' but he has confessed to me that there was no Church, no organised body though there was a 'higher Christian consciousness'.[111]

Machen himself was certainly fascinated by the story of the Grail. On 12 February 1906, he wrote to his friend Paul England:

> I have been amusing myself lately by going to the B[ritish] M[useum] where I make researches into the origin of the Holy

Grail Legend to gratify a curiosity excited by Waite's ingenious but (I think) mistaken theory on the subject. He is inclined to believe the Legend the cryptic manifesto of the 'Interior Church'; he would love to connect it with Cabalism, the Templars, the Albigenses. Now I am always telling him that nothing ever good comes out of heresy, but he won't believe me... On the general question of the Grail, I am happy to say that I do not think it will be possible to come to any cut or dried conclusion. [Alfred] Nutt and the folklorists have done their worst with it in the worst spirit, but it has eluded them.[112]

He continued his researches for a further six months and filled a large notebook with quotations from numerous texts. He had already collaborated (to what degree is uncertain) with Waite in 1903–4 on a verse drama with the resounding title *The Hidden Sacrament of the Holy Grail*, but in 1907, just one year after he had been occupying himself in the British Museum reading room, he began work on *The Secret Glory*, a strangely fragmented and patchy novel about a character named Ambrose Meyrick, very much an alter-ego for Machen himself.

Between mystic revelations and satire of the public school system, the book is an uneasy mix, shot through with moments of great beauty. Machen makes it clear that for him the Celtic Church and Celtic Christianity were widely separated from orthodoxy and held secrets that were lost to Rome. The Grail was central to this. In *The Secret Glory*, he has Meyrick meditate on the mystical revelation of the Grail:

The Celtic church was the Company of the Great Errantry [i.e. the Grail seekers] of the Great Mystery, and, though all the history of it seems but a dim and shadowy splendour, its burning rose-red lamp yet glows for a few, and from my earliest childhood I was indoctrinated into the great Rite of Cor-arbennic [Machen's version of Corbenic, the Castle of the Grail]. When I was still very young, I had been humoured with the sight of a wonderful Relic of the Saints – never shall I forget that experience of the holy magic of sanctity.[113]

In *The Secret Glory*, the Relic of the Saints is not the Nanteos Cup but the Cup of St Teilo, kept in secret in an old whitewashed farmhouse by its last surviving guardian. It is tempting to believe that this was in part a reference to relics which Machen himself had seen as a boy, and that one of them was the Nanteos Cup, but this is not certain.

Machen continued to develop his ideas concerning the Grail, finally publishing them as a series of essays written for the *Academy*, the journal edited by Oscar Wilde's notorious friend Lord Alfred Douglas. In these, Machen made it clear that he saw the Grail as a liturgy which had survived, via the Celtic Church, and been enshrined in the romances of the Grail. The actual vessel was, as he had stated in his novels, the relic of a Celtic saint.

Just how much this was inspired by the legend of Nanteos is difficult to say. Certainly, the spirit of the story is everywhere present in Machen's writings. In what is possibly his most famous book, *The Great Return* (1915), the 'spirit' of the Grail is brought to West Wales along with a return of 'the Celtic Mass' in a local parish church. A dying girl is restored to health overnight and peace and goodwill comes to the village. Again, the details are reminiscent of the reports of the Nanteos Cup's healing properties and essentially, all of this reflects Machen's ideas of an ecstatic Celtic observance, while celebrating the native saints of Wales.

Perhaps his most concise statement was in a review of Waite's *Hidden Church of the Holy Grail* written for *T. P.'s Weekly* in 1909:

> Personally, I am of the opinion that the story is of Celtic origin, and that the Knights of the Graal are Welsh saints in armour. A relic of peculiar sanctity – a portable altar, perhaps – used by St. David, and famed for its miraculous properties, became confused at a very early period with the Magic Cauldrons of Pagan tradition; the ruin of the Celtic Church and the Celtic state found its symbolism in the desolate 'enchantment' of Britain; the loss or concealment of the relic became the vanishing of the Graal; the flight and death of Cadwaladr the Blessed one translated into the Passing of Galahad.[114]

This is so at variance with the Grail's history, which Machen and Waite had studied at such length; it shows how very partisan towards the Celtic and particularly the Welsh traditions Machen was. His views are certainly in keeping with the vision evinced by

Anna Maria Powell and Ethelwyn Amery, and it is tempting to believe that the latter had read Machen's essays before she wrote her full-length story of the Grail in 1905.

Waite's own interest in the relic did not end with the publication of *Secret History*. In a letter he wrote on 23 July 1938 to a Mr Miller, he remarked:

> As regards Skene's translation of 'Four Ancient books on Wales' [sic], it must be explained that I have been far away from Celtic Subjects since my volume on 'The Holy Grail' appeared in 1933 - The Sacred Cup of Tregaron has brought me back thereto, and I am very glad to have the references which you send, I need to be reminded of many things in these days, as my recent work has been anxious and I am very tired. (John Matthews archive)

The story of the Nanteos Cup continues to grow. W. R. Hall's guide, *Aberystwyth: What to See and How to See It*, had mentioned the cup as early as the 1880s, but by the 1920s it was spreading to other guides, including the official *Aberystwyth Guide*. It is not surprising to learn that W. R. Hall was involved with the revision of this guide:[115] 'Nanteos. A short distance, which contains the Tregaron Healing Cup which resembles the Holy Grail.'[116]

By the 1930s the wording had changed:

> ...the picturesque Nanteos Valley with the mansion of the Powell family, where is preserved the precious mediaeval relic called the Cup of Healing, the surviving portion of a wooden bowl, a large part of which has been taken by believers in its magical properties.[117]

By 1938 there was no mention of the cup in the *Aberystwyth Guide*. It was also absent from the 1912 edition. However, the story had not been forgotten.

During the summer of 1932, two warships cast anchor at Aberystwyth. These were the aircraft carrier HMS *Furious* and the destroyer HMS *Vimy*. The presence of these impressive naval vessels at a small Welsh seaside town must have caused a stir, but the Royal Navy put aside military manoeuvres in order to take part in the local carnival week.

Putting on a Show

Aberystwyth's Carnival Week was organised by a committee which mainly consisted of local town councillors and tradesmen. The event consisted of a variety of celebrations, competitions and parades. One major event was a pageant, which took place within a stone circle in the ruins of Aberystwyth Castle. The stone circle was modern – erected for the National Eisteddfod of 1916. The pageant itself was, for the main part, a celebration of Aberystwyth and Welsh culture and consisted of a number of plays on such well-known themes as 'The Flooding of Cantre'r Gwaelod' and 'The Arrival of Owain Glyndwr'. Reporters, photographers and movie cameramen were there to record the occasion. Cheek-by-jowl with these traditional Welsh plays was one called 'Cwpan Ystrad Fflur' or 'The Healing Cup of Strata Florida' and this story seems to have been accepted as a genuine and venerable tradition – as much part of the Welsh cultural fabric as any tale from the *Mabinogion*.

Two years previously, on 30 July 1930, the Cardiganshire Antiquarian Society held a meeting at the Strata Florida Abbey.[118] One of the speakers at this occasion was Samuel Morris Powell (1878–1949), who was at one time headmaster of Tregaron County School and known as an historian and bard.[119] His paper was entitled 'Pilgrim Routes to Strata Florida'[120] and – as inferred by its title – covered the subject of pilgrimage to Strata Florida Abbey during the Middle Ages. As far as Powell was concerned, there was a particular reason why 'sick folk' would have made the journey to Strata Florida, namely, to come and seek the curative powers of the *Cwpan* or healing cup held at the abbey.

One person we know was present at this meeting was the newly appointed vicar of St Mary's Church, Strata Florida – the Revd Hugh Lunt (1872–1941). Hailing from Pwllheli, North Wales, Lunt attained a First Class Licence in Divinity from St David's College, Lampeter,[121] and was ordained in 1900. Lunt became curate of Llangwnadl, Llanberis and Llanllyfni churches and later ministered at Ystradyfodwg in the Rhondda before becoming vicar of Strata Florida in 1930. He was a man of many talents – composer, musician, playwright and a notable member of the Gorsedd of the Bards. He adopted the *nom de plume* of 'Gwynodl' for the purposes of his bardic writings, derived from Llangwnadl – the church of which he was once a curate.

It was possibly the 'Pilgrim Routes' lecture by Samuel Powell that was the inspiration for the play penned by Revd Lunt. Here was a subject with a suitably pious tone, deeply rooted (it was assumed) in the local tradition with the added mystique provided by the captivating tale of the cup. Moreover, writing such a play would allow Lunt to combine his many talents and cast himself in a role to which he was already well accustomed, that of a priest.

The organisers had invited local villages in the Aberystwyth area to take part in a pageant competition with fifteen pounds and fifteen shillings as the first prize. Hugh Lunt, aided by the villagers of Pontrhydfendigaid, plus one other group from Machynlleth, may well have been the only entrants.

The play was based around the very simple idea of sick pilgrims coming to Strata Florida to be healed by the waters of the cup. The script is sadly missing but there are some observations we can make about the play, based on the newspaper reports of the time. We know from a review[122] of a later performance for 'Aberystwyth Week' in 1934 that the play was partly or wholly in Welsh. Three photographs held at the National Library of Wales[123] depict the 1934 performance and these have lines from the script etched onto them, entirely in Welsh (for example, 'Yf o'r cwpan hwn' – 'drink from this cup'). An earlier report[124] from 1932 indicates that Lunt had ignored the 'Chalice of the Last Supper' account in favour of the 'True Cross' version of the tale. This may have been simply because he was aware of the practicalities involved, such as the necessity of setting the play at a single location. Alternatively, Lunt may have had a preference for the 'True Cross' account. Either way, it is likely that Lunt had done his own research into the cup and he maintained his antiquarian interests even after his time at Strata Florida.[125]

Lunt cast himself in the central role of the abbot of Strata Florida (calling himself 'Abbot Gwynodl'[126]) and is quite recognisable in the photographs[127] as his habit is distinctly lighter than those of his fellow 'monks' whose dark habits look more like those of Benedictines; 'tonsured' wigs completed their costumes.

The natural amphitheatre provided by the castle ruins, complemented by a cloudless sky with the sun setting on a becalmed sea, would have enhanced the sense of wonder. The stone circle at Aberystwyth Castle represented the area outside the monastery. Lunt was obviously aware that Cistercian rules forbade the admission of women, so the healing would take place outside the abbey walls. The North Tower of Aberystwyth Castle substituted for the west gate at Strata Florida.

The play begins with the arrival of the afflicted pilgrims, who had travelled many miles from the banks of the River Dovey to the north. In the background, the monks could be heard chanting. The pilgrims speak to the 'gate-keeper' Bleddyn, who instructs them in prayer. The monks then emerge from the abbey, carrying the cup and a pitcher of water. Abbot Gwynodl, played by Lunt, would then bless the cup and minister to the sick, allowing each of them to drink from the cup in turn. The abbot would then tell the pilgrims that they had been healed, although according to another report[128] the sick 'manifest miraculous healing, the blind receiving sight, the withered arm is made whole, the cripple walks'. The pilgrims then depart, praising not the cup but Almighty God.[129] The monks also depart, returning to the confines of the abbey through the gate.[130]

Reviewers were effusive with praise for the play and its performance. They seem to have been particularly impressed with the solemnity and dignity of the occasion – something about it struck a chord. Most of the players were from Pontrhydfendigaid (the village closest to Strata Florida) and nearby Tregaron. There were multiple performances of the play during the weeks it was shown in 1932 and 1934 and it was viewed by thousands of visitors.[131] At the very least, the performance would have left them with the impression that something extraordinary was kept at Nanteos. Doubtless some would have assumed that here was a celebration of a very ancient tradition.

In the summer of 1935 Lunt became vicar of Capel Bangor and there were to be no repeat performances of his play. He passed away in 1941. The script of his 'Cwpan Ystrad Fflur' may be missing but another of his plays has survived and is preserved at the National Library of Wales. The play is in Welsh and is entitled *Cwmcynfelin*.[132] In the play, a lazy, inept priest called Nathan Vaughan condemns belief in the cup as 'nonsense' and 'Popery'. In spite of this, for Lunt, the Nanteos Cup represented a genuine Christian tradition worthy of protection and public celebration.

There is a sad postscript to the story of Lunt's pageant-play. Just over a year after Lunt's passing, his younger daughter Selina, who played 'Esther, the blind girl' in the play, died[133] after a long illness at the tragically young age of nineteen.

Wagner and Nanteos

The list of famous visitors to Aberystwyth is a lengthy one. The poet laureate Alfred, Lord Tennyson visited the town[134] and is believed to have stayed in the Belle Vue on the seafront.[135] In 1896 Edward VII came to Aberystwyth and was made chancellor of the university.[136] Another gentleman of note who has long been thought a visitor was the renowned German composer Richard Wagner, whose portrait hung in the hall of Nanteos Manor. It is assumed that the presence of this portrait was in commemoration of a visit and that he journeyed all the way to West Wales to see the Powells' famous cup; this idea reinforces the notion that the cup must be an artefact of great importance.

When the *Welsh Gazette* was promoting the Aberystwyth Week pageant in the summer of 1934, Margaret Powell was simultaneously getting publicity for Nanteos in the pages of the *Western Mail*, which printed a two-part article on the mansion entitled 'The Treasure House in a Cardigan Glen'.[137] The report was based on an interview with Margaret Powell by the writer Tom MacDonald, who commented: 'A beautiful world it is to-day and beautiful it must have been for Wagner. For here [Nanteos] he wrote something of his opera *Parsifal*.'[138]

Parsifal was Richard Wagner's final opera, based on the story of the Holy Grail. It might therefore be only natural to assume that his presumed visit to Nanteos had something to do with the 'Holy Grail' kept there by the Powells. In 1965, a local newspaper reported on what was said to be the very first performance of a scene from *Parsifal* in Aberystwyth. The reporter could not resist making a reference to the cup:

As a point of interest, tradition has it that the Holy Grail is at Nanteos, near Aberystwyth, having been moved from Strata Florida at the time of the dissolution of the monasteries. Our performance may be thought, therefore, to be in a most appropriate setting.[139]

Margaret Powell was not specific about when Wagner's supposed visit to Nanteos took place, however, many websites[140] and books[141] have stated in a matter-of-fact way that it took place in 1855 and the visit was at the request of George Powell.[142] It has been further suggested that seeing the cup and hearing its legendary history so inspired Wagner that he wrote his opera *Parsifal* as a result.

However, this is simply not true. Much of Wagner's life is well documented, not least by the man himself in his autobiographical *Mein Leben*[143] (*My Life*[144]), or in the immensely detailed diaries written by Wagner's wife, Cosima. There is not a single word in any of these documents to suggest that Wagner ever came to Wales to view the Nanteos Cup. Moreover, the story handed down to us by Margaret Powell is essentially impossible.

Wagner is known to have visited Britain on three occasions,[145] in the years 1839, 1855 and 1877. The first two years can be ruled out for very good reasons. Firstly, the only known link between Wagner and Nanteos was through his friendship with George Powell, an ardent fan of Wagner's music. We know from a letter to the poet Algernon Swinburne (dated 11 September 1876) that George Powell once dined with Wagner. However, George was born in 1842, so even in 1855 he would only have been a teenager and in 1839 he was not even born.

The libretto for Wagner's *Parsifal* was partly based on Wolfram von Eschenbach's *Parzival*. Wagner had read this work as early as 1845. In his own words: 'I lost myself in Wolfram's strange, yet irresistibly charming poem. Soon, however, a longing seized me to give expression to the inspiration generated by this poem.'[146]

So, the principal source of the inspiration came not from the Nanteos Cup (which would be a naive suggestion, to put it mildly) but from the medieval romance of Wolfram von Eschenbach. In fact, Wagner only started thinking about the opera *Parsifal* in 1857, supposedly on 'Good Friday', although this was not literally true:[147]

> Since the sojourn in Marienbad [in 1845] ... I had never occupied myself again with that poem; now [1857] its noble possibilities struck me with overwhelming force, and out of my thoughts about Good Friday I rapidly conceived a whole drama, of which I made a rough sketch with a few dashes of the pen, dividing the whole into three acts.[148]

This was two years after many popular sources say Wagner came to Nanteos. He cannot possibly have composed part of *Parsifal* there in 1855 or any time earlier.

Wagner's last visit to Britain (in 1877) was to give a series of concerts in the Royal Albert Hall in London. Would he have broken his busy schedule to make the journey from London to Aberystwyth to visit George Powell at Nanteos? Every single day of the period in question (1 May–4 June) is accounted for in the diaries of Cosima Wagner,[149] with the sole exception of one day – 2 May. To travel from London to Aberystwyth and back in a single day – a distance of at least 500 miles – would be a long journey, even today. In 1877 on steam-powered locomotives it would barely have been feasible, if at all.

In fact, the diaries of Cosima Wagner tell us exactly when Wagner began the musical composition of *Parsifal*, namely on 2 August 1877 – two months *after* his third and final journey to Britain had come to an end. Cosima wrote: 'But he has arranged his studio for Parsifal, and today I heard a few of the first notes!'[150]

These first few notes were the very beginning, and there is no evidence of anything before this. The Wagner/Nanteos story is clearly a myth, although more recently, mutations of the original have since emerged,[151] which aim to skirt around the difficulties we have raised. Ultimately, perhaps, the story will never die, but this is typical of the way the Nanteos Cup has become, for each succeeding generation, a symbol of such importance that it has acquired its own set of 'heroes'. This echoes the way in which the Grail story, originally unconnected to the Arthurian legends, drew the British king and his knights into its orbit from the twelfth century onwards. In the next chapter we shall see how this has continued to the present day, widening its sphere of influence beyond anything either the Powell family or Ethelwyn Amery could have imagined.

5

The Struggle for the Cup

I have always heard in the family that it was made out of a
piece of the Cross, but the oldest printed account I have seen
said it was the cup Joseph of Arimathea caught our Saviour's
blood in when He was pierced.
                    Reported words of Margaret Powell[1]

The Sole Survivor

As the twentieth century gathered momentum, the story of the
Nanteos Cup took a new direction, incidentally extending its
influence outward beyond the confines of Wales. It also became
the centre of a struggle for possession that was to continue for
several years.

The member of the Powell family we most strongly associate
with the cup today is the late Margaret Powell (1861–1951). It
was her reinterpretation of the legend that has become the root
of most of the subsequent retellings, although more elaborations
and nuances were yet to come. It cannot be emphasised enough,
however, that she played no active role in the receptions given
to the British Chautauquans in the early years of the twentieth
century; the 'Mrs Powell' referred to by Ethelwyn Mary Amery
was Anna Maria Powell, not Margaret. The census of 1911 shows
William Beauclerk Powell and his wife still in charge at Nanteos
and makes no mention of Margaret or her husband Edward.

Margaret Powell was daughter of Sir Pryse Pryse of Gogerddan,
a large estate near Aberystwyth. She showed a keen interest in
the Nanteos Cup and was close friends with Lord Ystwyth of

Tan-y-Bwlch, Matthew Vaughan Davies (1840–1935). It is known that when her husband was away or intoxicated, she would use a bedsheet as a flag and raise it up the flagpole as a signal to Lord Ystwyth that it was safe to visit Nanteos.[2] She was deaf, a problem that got worse throughout her life and by the 1930s she was using an ear trumpet.

The death of her only child, Billy, during the First World War must have been emotionally painful and would have left a deep void in her life. Her brother had died shortly before Billy and her husband Edward died of pneumonia in 1930, leaving Margaret grieving alone, with no family at Nanteos. Her Christian faith, under such wretched circumstances, must have been a source of solace and the cup would have become linked with this. There can be no doubt that Margaret Powell went out of her way to help people and her kindness is attested to by those she helped.[3]

Thus, the use of the cup in the service of the sick and the proclamation of its story became increasingly important in her life and perhaps helped ease the pain of the loss of Edward and especially Billy. Perhaps in her eyes Billy was Galahad, the perfect knight and the Grail awaited his return to Nanteos – but it was never to be.[4]

In 1934 Margaret Powell commented that the cup was better known in America than it was in Wales. She claimed that hundreds of Americans came to Nanteos every year wishing to see the cup and that she would often pour water into it that was subsequently bottled so they could take it away.[5]

When a visitor came to see the relic, Margaret Powell would greet them in the Morning Room. In the meantime, the housekeeper, Maggie Williams, would retrieve the cup from the cupboard, fill it with water and make it ready for display. Margaret Powell would then invite the visitors into the library to drink from it. After this was done, she would take the guests into the dining room and slam the door. This was the signal for the housekeeper to take the cup away and put a replica, made by Richard Rees Jones of Rhoserchan, in its place.[6] This strange ritual was performed to ensure that the real cup was not left unattended, lest it be stolen by thieves.

Despite any such fears, Margaret Powell made the cup available for exhibition away from Nanteos, thereby increasing its fame and the sense that it was part of the Welsh tradition. One such occasion was in 1916 when it was loaned out to Penparke National School.[7]

Another occasion was in January 1930 when it was loaned to the National Library of Wales. Margaret's maid, Maggie Williams, suitably attired for the occasion, took the relic by pony-trap to the home of librarian Sir John Ballinger, in whose care it was placed until its return. The cup was also exhibited in 1936 at Aberystwyth Town Hall; the man who made this possible was the antiquarian George Eyre Evans we met in Chapter Four.[8]

A Mysterious Account

Occasions when the cup was displayed in public would have required a written account to be displayed along with it. It is likely that this was the purpose of the anonymously penned 'Blue Manuscript',[9] a handwritten account of the story of the Nanteos vessel. It bears no signature and is undated. At some point early in the twentieth century it was deposited at the National Library of Wales (NLW MS 3297B) but the depositor and date that it was deposited remain a mystery.[10] The blue manuscript is not part of the Nanteos estate collection, which was only given to the National Library in 1957, yet it certainly emanated from Nanteos.

The document has the Welsh title of 'Cwpan Nanteos' though the remainder of the text is in English. It consists of three sheets of pale blue paper, with a slight sheen on the reverse side of each page. After comparing the handwriting against other Nanteos documents, we concluded that the handwriting was that of Margaret Powell's husband Edward,[11] although the content is most likely Margaret's composition (as we hope to demonstrate). This may not have been a deliberate attempt at concealment, as she was known to occasionally dictate letters rather than write them herself.[12]

The paper of the blue manuscript is slightly stiff, and it would crease awkwardly when folded. It has been folded on two separate occasions – once fairly neatly in half and once rather clumsily into thirds.

The blue manuscript provides us with a new version of the Nanteos story. It may well have been the 'master' from which the later versions were copied, but as the manuscript is undated, we can't be completely sure. What is certain is that this new story comes to us through Margaret Powell.

Margaret Powell was anything but reticent about getting publicity for her cup; nor was she afraid of linking it to the Grail. A statement written by her – mentioning her by name – was published in full in a 1930s edition of *Aberystwyth: What to See and How to See It* and in it she refers to the cup as 'The Healing Cup, that tradition says is the 'Holy Grail.'[13]

The quote at the head of this chapter, drawn from Tom MacDonald's 1934 interview with Margaret Powell, contains text that is identical to the statement reproduced in the guide, so she was promoting the cup as the Grail at least as early as the 1930s, if not before.

According to Amery's *Sought and Found* a priest had brought the cup to Mid Wales generations before Strata Florida was even built. In the new account, it was the last abbot of Glastonbury, Richard Whiting, who spirited the cup to Wales during the time of the Dissolution of the Monasteries, prior to his own bloody, brutal demise on Glastonbury Tor, where he was hanged, drawn and quartered. The blue manuscript gives no details of how the cup travelled to Strata Florida. It is in this new account that we first encounter another phrase that has been repeated ever since, whenever the story has been retold:

> This cup was kept at Glastonbury until the Abbey was threatened with destruction in the reign of Henry VIII, when Richard Whiting, last Abbot of Glastonbury, sent it **over the 'impassable mountains'** to their Brethren at Strata Florida (Ystrad Fleure)[14] [Authors' emphasis]

The use of the phrase 'over the "impassable mountains"' indicates that Margaret Powell influenced this version of the story, for reasons we will shortly explain. In the new account the monks have to flee twice: first, from Glastonbury to their 'brethren' at Strata Florida, then from Strata Florida to Nanteos. They fled Glastonbury in fear of their lives to keep the cup from the clutches of King Henry VIII.

They took flight from Strata Florida some years later when it was destroyed by fire, to seek refuge at the manor with an unnamed Powell ancestor.

There are, of course, some obvious historical problems with the new account. Glastonbury had no relationship with Strata Florida at any point in its history and Strata Florida was dissolved in the same year as Glastonbury – months before, in fact. There had been fires at Strata Florida, but these were well before the dissolution. Margaret Powell was aware of this fact having made a written enquiry to a man named W. H. Davies[15] in 1937.

The ending of the new account is essentially the same as Amery's – the old monks perished and the last of them, lying on his deathbed, handed the cup to the unnamed lord of the manor, revealing its hidden mysteries at the same time. However, there is no mention in the blue manuscript of Amery's phrase 'until the Church should once more claim its own'.[16]

Possibly the earliest book to contain a version of this new account was *A Hunting Diary* by Newton Wynne Apperley.[17] Apperley (1846–1925) was proud of his achievements, which included hunting otters with hounds in Nanteos Pool.[18] He was equally proud of the fact that his father had slaughtered 300 tigers in India.[19] Printed posthumously in 1926, his book has an introduction written by E. W. Cuming containing a descriptive account of the cup and its story.

In Cuming's introduction, the reference to the 'impassable mountains' is ascribed to certain 'old historians' who are never named. As well as the seven old monks who go to the manor, the book refers to some young monks who 'went into the country to earn their living'. Cuming offers an explanation as to why the monks had chosen to come to Wales, namely that 'there were then no monasteries left in England.' This is very similar to the statement made by Margaret Powell in *Aberystwyth: What to See...* published years later.

Cuming also informs us that the Trustees of Cardiff Museum had offered the Powells £9,000 for the cup, but the offer had been turned down. This tale is most likely more Nanteos mythologizing, especially given the fee stated, which was a very large sum of money at the time. The National Museum of Wales had already received superior-quality items for no money at all. At the ceremony of the laying of the foundation stone of the museum in 1912, King George V made a speech in which he commented:

> I am glad to have been able to commit to the charge of the Museum the Dolgelley chalice and paten. I hope the treasures which are to be stored here will be continually enriched, and that

many others will emulate the generosity and public spirit of the donor of the Caergwrle Cup.[20]

The Dolgellau Chalice and paten were magnificent silver-gilt medieval ornaments discovered near Dolgellau in 1890. At some point prior to being declared Treasure Trove they had been sold[21] for £3,000 – one third of the supposed asking price for the Powells' broken wooden bowl. Sir Foster Cunliffe, Bart., of Acton Park, near Wrexham, had donated the Bronze Age Caergwrle Cup[22] in 1912.

The Lionel Lewis Letters

In 1938, Nanteos was to receive another famous visitor, one who would enhance the cup's reputation as the Grail still further. Revd Lionel Smithett Lewis was educated at Oundle and Queens' College Cambridge.[23] He was appointed vicar of St John the Baptist Church, Glastonbury, in 1921. He was a passionate believer and staunch defender of the Glastonbury traditions and authored two books that aimed to bolster the legends of its connection to the Grail by referring to known history. Lewis was later responsible for reinstituting the tradition of sending a sprig of the Holy Thorn to the British Monarch at Christmastime[24] and in 1923 instituted a series of annual Glastonbury pilgrimages.[25]

His two most well-known books are *St Joseph of Arimathea at Glastonbury* and *Glastonbury – Her Saints*. Lewis was a great philanthropist and an antivivisectionist, but the quality of the scholarship in his publications is poor and would be best described as pseudo-history. His books draw upon earlier questionable works such as R. W. Morgan's *Saint Paul in Britain* and J. W. Taylor's *The Coming of the Saints* and are also influenced by the writings of Archbishop James Ussher of Armagh, famed in his day as dating the precise moment of the creation of the world from Biblical evidence as 'the entrance of the night preceding the twenty third day of Octob [sic] in the year of the Julian Calendar 710'.[26]

There still exist a number of letters from Lionel Lewis to Margaret Powell of Nanteos. These are held at the National Library of Wales, Aberystwyth, and date to between 1938 and 1940. We know that this colourful correspondence is incomplete and that the two of them had communicated years before[27] and Lewis wrote again at a later date, but these letters have not been preserved.[28]

The first three letters deal with arrangements for a visit to Nanteos Mansion to see the cup. This visit would later be referred to as the 'little pilgrimage' and the pilgrims included Revd Lionel Lewis, Sir Charles Marston and Revd Russell Warrilow.[29]

The 'little pilgrimage'[30] to Nanteos took place on 22 September 1938. During that visit, Margaret Powell told her guests her version of the 'Holy Grail' story. She also related another tale, which was to become the subject of much of the subsequent correspondence. According to Margaret Powell, she had – some thirty years before – seen a very ancient history book which contained the tale of the Nanteos Cup. She could not remember the title of the work or its author but recalled certain details. It contained a dedication to a Prince Charles, consisted of eight volumes[31] and used the phrase 'over the impassable mountains' to describe the journey of the cup from Glastonbury into Wales.[32] This is how we know that the blue manuscript was influenced by Margaret Powell – it was she who was witness to the account in the 'ancient history book' which contained the 'impassable mountains' phrase. Since the blue manuscript is in the hand of her husband Edward, it is possible that he was also witness to the same ancient history.

Lewis wanted to validate the legend of the Nanteos relic, and it was obviously important to recover this book (or a copy of it), if indeed it existed. If Mrs Powell's recollections of it were accurate it would contain the oldest reference to the Nanteos Holy Grail legend, pre-dating Amery's writings by possibly hundreds of years.

The man who allegedly owned this mysterious book was John Maunsell Bacon (1866–1948), the one-time headmaster of a military preparatory school at Cargate, Aldershot. Lewis referred to this school as 'Mr. John M. Baron's'[33] (a typographical error for John M *Bacon*) but it was otherwise known as Winton House.[34] This military school was at one time attended by Margaret Powell's son, Billy, and according to the version of events related to Lewis by Mrs Powell, she had been shown this book with its reference to the Nanteos Cup story by Billy's headmaster, John Bacon.

During his stay at Nanteos in 1938, Lionel Lewis had visited the National Library of Wales to find out everything he could about the cup. He was aided in his search by the Chief Librarian at the insistence of Sir George Fossett-Roberts, who had attended dinner at Nanteos with Lewis and his fellow pilgrims the evening before. When Lewis arrived at the library he was greeted by a slew of books and documents, especially retrieved in advance for his perusal. He did not find a copy of John Bacon's mysterious book, but he did find an anonymous, handwritten account of the Nanteos Holy Grail legend that used the phrase 'over the impassable mountains'. In his next letter[35] to Mrs Powell he identified it by its reference code – MS 3297B. This of course was the 'blue manuscript' itself.

Lionel Lewis wanted Mrs Powell to examine the blue manuscript because he thought that it might have been her handwriting or that she might at least be able to identify the hand. It is clear that by the time Lewis had written his own report[36] he was still none the wiser. In his report, Lewis speculated on whether this handwritten account was copied from the 'missing' chronicle supposedly in the possession of John Bacon.

Sometime after the pilgrimage party had departed for home, Lewis started to make enquiries about the mystery book which (it was believed) contained the reference to the cup. A friend of Lionel Lewis, a Mrs Arthur Stallard of Bath (real name Constance Louisa Stallard, 1870–1959), had previously corresponded with John Bacon[37] in 1932. She was able to track down the former headmaster, who was by this time a collector and vendor of antiques and books in London with a particular interest in glass ornaments.[38]

Mrs Stallard bought a book from Bacon, which had a dedication to Prince Charles, as it was believed that the sought-after book contained such a dedication. Bacon was reluctant to sell it and stated that Mrs Stallard had invoked the name of Mrs Powell as emotional leverage, a claim described by Lewis as 'bunkum'. Whatever the truth of the matter, Bacon sold the book to Mrs Stallard for just two pounds.

The book purchased by Mrs Stallard was a copy of *The Annales or Generall* [sic] *Chronicle of England*[39] by John Stow (1525–1605), an English historian and antiquarian best known for his 1598 *Survey of London*. Mrs Stallard gave the book to Lewis and it was soon discovered that it did not contain the required passage about the cup and the 'impassable mountains' – Mrs Stallard had bought the wrong book.

Lewis struck up a correspondence with Bacon, who hinted that he might have a book that fitted the description of the mystery tome: 'I may mention that I have a book pub. 1738 in 8 volumes, the only one in my possession, and it has been in my possession many years.'[40]

To the dismay of Lewis, Bacon refused to name the work in question and was unwilling to do any further dealings until he got his copy of Stow's *Chronicle* back. It is clear that these two men did not see eye to eye. Lewis found Bacon evasive and difficult to negotiate with ('I have had to pin him out like a dead butterfly')[41] whilst Bacon found Lewis 'very difficult to deal with'.[42] Bacon was using his refusal to name the 1738 book as leverage to have his Stow's *Chronicle* returned; this infuriated Lewis: 'He has never told me the title of the 8-volume book which he dangles before my eyes.'[43]

Towards the end of October, Mrs Powell offered to go and see Bacon herself. Lewis was not keen on the idea and advised against it adding the following postscript: 'P.S. You can't touch Bacon without getting greasy.'[44]

There is a hint in a letter from Boots Lending Library,[45] reminding her of the immanent renewal of her subscription, that Mrs Powell was about to embark on a journey in November 1938. Whether this meeting between Bacon and Mrs Powell happened or not, no more information regarding the Nanteos Cup was forthcoming. This is evidently the case because by January of the following year Lewis had decided to change tack and search for the mystery book elsewhere. He was keen to have photographs of the cup because he was convinced that it had a pattern on it, which he thought was a stylized form of Hebrew writing.[46] It seems that his request for photographs was accepted.

By mid-January 1939, Lewis had sent his completed report[47] to Mrs Powell. This recounts the Nanteos Cup/Holy Grail legend and what was learned by the 'little pilgrimage' on their visit to see the cup. This included the story of the still missing book with its reference to the dedication to Prince Charles and the mention of the phrase 'over the impassable mountains'. The report describes the physical appearance of the cup and concludes optimistically that: 'All members of the little Pilgrimage party were deeply impressed by it, and think its history true.'[48]

However, Lewis was aware that there were one or two problems with the story as presented in the blue manuscript: 'The destruction of Strata Florida by fire was long before the dissolution. Unless there was a later fire also, this is probably an error.'[49]

Lewis then enumerates and describes all of the sources he had come across during his visit to the National Library at Aberystwyth. The list includes the blue manuscript, which is referred to as 'Cwpwn Nanteos' (*sic* – the word is actually 'Cwpan' but the handwriting arguably gives the appearance of 'Cwpwn') and Leland's *Itinerary in Wales*, which includes the Latin phrase *invia saxa* (impassable rocks) in geographical relation to Strata Florida.[50]

Mrs Stallard of Bath had also told Lewis about a 'tradition' concerning the tower at Ozleworth Church, Wotton-under-Edge, Gloucestershire. This story had been communicated by the Rector of Ozleworth, John Richard Rimes (1873-1962).[51] According to Rimes' story, the Holy Grail was once stored in a recess in the church tower. Lewis cleverly wove this tradition into the story of the Nanteos Cup, suggesting that this tower was an overnight resting place for the Glastonbury monks, who were en route to Strata Florida with their precious cargo. Lewis also found an interesting reference in *Monasticon* – a large work by the Tudor historian Sir William Dugdale. This contained the following: 'The Bennet College Manuscript quoted by Tanner speaks of seven Monks at Stratfleur.'[52] (Stratfleur is derived from the Welsh name for Strata Florida.)

Lewis also cited another work called *Mitred Abbies* by Browne Willis and this seemed to give the names of the seven monks: 'To Lewis LanSadurne alias Lleus, David Richard Smythe, Morgan Johnes 3 l. each. Thomas Derham 4 l. John Yorke 3 l. 19 s. 8 d. Richard Mayot 2 l. 13 s. 4 d. and to David Morgan 2 l.'[53]

The names of the monks are all of a much later date than the suggested date of the cup's movement; however, the fact that these earlier historical books gave the requisite number of monks seemed to affirm (for Lewis at least) the story recounted by Mrs Powell. Lewis was probably unaware that there was a precious, three-volume copy of Dugdale's *Monasticon* in the Nanteos library; it was listed in an inventory[54] dating to 1861 and was auctioned[55] in 1957 where it sold[56] for £22.

Also cited in his report are Amery's *Sought and Found* and two sources by Stephen Williams,[57] both of which suggest that the cup may have been a mazer cup; obviously Lewis would either have not accepted this suggestion or otherwise misunderstood what this implied for the dating of the vessel. As we have seen, this identification is extremely likely to be accurate.

Lewis read his completed report on the Nanteos Cup to the Clergy of the Glastonbury Jurisdiction. According to Lewis 'it was received not only with great interest but very favorably' and he sent copies to the National Library of Wales, the British Museum and the British Library.[58] He was still intent on finding the missing mystery book but by January 1939 he had given up on 'the unsavory Bacon'[59] and was resolved to go to the British Museum Library in search of it. By this time the quest for the book was becoming an obsession – in one letter he says 'the book must be found'[60] and repeats the phrase later; in the same letter he refers to himself as 'a hound keen on the scent'.[61] In spite of his dogged persistence, Lewis's researches at the British Museum Library drew a blank.

Some months prior to Lewis's 'little pilgrimage', Margaret Powell had herself written to the British Museum concerning the identity of the book. She received a reply from F. G. Rendall who was unable to identify the book from her description but hazarded a guess at a work by Cardinal James Ussher – '*Antiquitates ecclesiarum britannicam* [sic]'.[62] The fact that she was making enquiries suggests that Margaret Powell genuinely believed the book existed.

By February 1939 Lewis's cousin, Revd Ernest Sankey, had discovered the reference to the 'Holy Cup of Tregaron' in A. E. Waite's *Hidden Church of the Holy Graal*.[63] Lewis guessed correctly that Waite was referring to the Nanteos Cup, but no more fresh information was forthcoming – Lewis's search had been in vain.

There is then a *hiatus* in the extant correspondence of just over a year. The next letter that we have is dated Feb 9 1940. There was no mention of any quest for a missing book; instead, Lewis was questing for the cup itself. His letter began innocently enough with the usual pleasantries about the weather and Mrs Powell's health. Lewis then quoted Amery's *Sought and Found* passage about the cup staying with the Powells 'until the church should once more claim its own'. He assumed (wrongly) that Margaret Powell herself spoke these words. He then described a specifically fashioned cupboard to be made for the North Transept of Glastonbury St John's Church and then, finally, revealed its purpose – to house the Nanteos Cup!

> If you could trust us with your priceless treasure which originally hailed from here, & is everlastingly interwoven with the names of Glastonbury, & St. Joseph, we would have a special little cupboard in the wall made... If this plan pleased you, you could know that the Glastonbury-Nanteos Treasure was safe for all time, yet accessible for all; that the Trust had been fulfilled, & once again St. Joseph's Cup was in Glastonbury.[64]

We do not have Margaret Powell's response to this, but we can garner the tone of its content from Lewis's response. She had obviously raised concerns about the safety of the cup and the risk of damage to it. Lewis had a touché to this: 'Just one point. Your kind generosity in lending the cup has been so abused that only about one third of it remains!'[65]

Mrs Powell had obviously raised the issue of free access to the cup to which Lewis had countered that this could be guaranteed by a Trust deed. We do not have her response to this suggestion, and it is here that the extant correspondence ends.

Why did Margaret Powell not accede to Lionel Lewis's request? Perhaps a clue might be revealed in a comment from one of Lewis's earlier letters:

> But I have been full of so many plans in case of war... If the enemy devise to wide-spread frightfulness, a town of 5000 inhabitants with 2 beautiful church towers, one of which (mine) looks like a Cathedral might tempt some returning bomber.[66]

Thankfully this dreadful scenario did not take place, although potentially it could have done. Perhaps a large church with a tall spire, not too far from a major city might have been a bigger target than a mansion in far-off rural Mid Wales? At any rate, Lewis's own comments cannot have helped his cause. The city of Bath (just over 20 miles from Glastonbury) was indeed a target for the Luftwaffe only two years later. There might be other possible explanations, the simplest being that perhaps she didn't want to let the precious relic go; after all, she never spoke the phrase 'until the church should once more claim its own' to the British Chautauquans.

Another possibility is that she may have been aware of the openly played-out battles between Lewis and Dean Armitage Robinson (1858–1933) whose critical scholarship of the Glastonbury legends put him in direct opposition to Lewis. Lewis was not above making personal attacks on his opponents in his writings and his language could be quite scathing.[67] The idea of a British 'National Church' with Glastonbury as the 'Mother Church' as emphasised by Lewis in his books[68] stands in marked contrast to the Roman Catholicism of the Cistercian monks who had provided the Powells with the cup. Why hand over a Catholic relic to a Protestant church? Moreover, should a relic whose traditions and history are so firmly rooted in West Wales have been handed over to Glastonbury in Somerset? According to a letter written by a Mr Frederick Blight[69] to the *Western Mail*, 'Mrs. Powell was not averse to the idea but said she could not make up her mind then.'[70]

This diplomatic strategy might have been adopted to overcome the possible offence that a definite refusal might have caused. The matter did not completely rest in 1940. Ten years later, Lewis brought the matter before the Glastonbury Parish Council who sent Mrs Powell a request to have the cup 'returned'. This failed and Lewis wrote to Sir George Fossett-Roberts, hoping that he might act on his behalf. His letter ends: 'In these days of uncertainty, it would be good to know that the Cup had returned to its ancient home.'[71]

Clearly, he thought that the story was worth believing in, even to the end of his life. The fact that there is not a shred of real evidence connecting the cup with Glastonbury did not deter the Revd Lewis. For him the Nanteos relic was the Grail and the Grail belonged in Glastonbury, sometimes known as 'This Holiest earth'.

Charles Marston and Revd T. R. Warrilow

Before moving on, we ought to say something more about Sir Charles Marston and Revd Warrilow, both of whom attended the 'little pilgrimage' to Nanteos in 1938. Sir Charles Marston (1867–1946) was the son of John Marston (1836–1918), a successful businessman who founded the Sunbeam company who manufactured bicycles, motorcycles and motor cars. Sir Charles continued the successful management of the family business interests but his true passion was archaeology, in particular biblical archaeology. Although he was not for the most part involved with the actual excavation work, he funded archaeological digs in the Middle East, wrote books and gave lectures. His goal from the very outset was to prove that the Bible, in particular the Old Testament, was historically true. This is borne out by the titles of his best-known works: *The Bible Comes Alive* and *The Bible is True*.

Sir Charles is known to have had an association with Frederick Bligh Bond, the archaeologist of Glastonbury Abbey. In 1938, not long before the 'little pilgrimage' to Nanteos, Marston had been involved in a plan to restart archaeological excavations at Glastonbury Abbey involving two friends from America, Mr and Mrs George Van Dusen, but permission was denied.[72]

Three years before these events, Marston had visited ongoing excavations at Lachish (an ancient city located in present-day Jordan) to view pottery sherds that had an ancient form of writing on them. Marston referred to this as 'Sinai Hebrew script',[73] a kind of cuneiform script used to represent Hebrew letters. It was suggested that Moses himself originated the alphabet or at least was responsible for popularising it.[74] Marston was fascinated by one particular piece which had what he claimed was a religious inscription. This was a reddish pottery bowl with Canaanite letters written in white lime using a brush, now known as 'Lachish Bowl No. 1'. This raises the possibility that the suggestion of Hebrew writing on the Nanteos Cup, put forward by Lionel Lewis,[75] might have been linked with Sir Charles Marston's interest in the early writings he thought he had identified on the Lachish bowl and other similar items. The Hebrew connection to the origin of the Grail myth may have been in his mind also.

The Revd Thomas Russell Warrilow (1879–1967) was a friend of Sir Charles Marston. He was vicar of St Andrew's in Grimsby and later moved to Frome. He does not seem to have had any especially deep interest in biblical archaeology, although he seems to have gone abroad to Port Said in 1933 with Sir Charles Marston and his wife Ruth aboard a vessel called the *Strathaird*,[76] presumably to visit one or more of the archaeology excavations sponsored by Sir Charles. There is no correspondence from him to Margaret Powell in the Nanteos estate archive and he does not appear to have added anything to the conversation with regard to the cup.

Barbara Waylen

Lionel Lewis had failed in his quest to discover the 'mystery book' that would have verified the link with Glastonbury and raised the status of Mrs Powell's account to one that had genuinely ancient roots. However, even with the Second World War in full swing, someone else would take up the challenge.

Barbara Waylen (née Williams, b. 1906) was an author of books on spirituality and faith-based subjects who in 1952 was nominated for the Nobel Peace Prize for her work, *Creators of the Modern Spirit*.[77]

She had visited Nanteos as a child[78] and during her visit was told the story of the Nanteos Cup by Margaret Powell. In 1941 she married a Greek and Hebrew scholar called Hector Waylen, whose family was from Devizes in Wiltshire. Hector's father was James Waylen, who wrote well-known books on the history of Devizes.

Barbara Waylen turned her attention to writing and in 1943 wrote to Margaret Powell asking for information on the Nanteos Cup with the expressed intention of publishing on it.[79] Mrs Powell responded positively, informing her about two ancient books including '*The History of England* (circa 1600) dedicated to Prince Charlie'.[80] Waylen's correspondence says nothing about the work being in eight volumes and it pushes the date of publication back more than a century; however, the mystery book now had a definite title.

Waylen was aware that there is no mention of the Nanteos tradition in well-known Arthurian sources such as *Le Morte d'Arthur* or the Welsh *Mabinogion*, but in spite of this declared herself to be convinced of the authenticity of the relic. Armed with the details given to her by Mrs Powell, Waylen expressed her intention to search for the mystery book in the National Library of Wales and the Bodleian Library in Oxford. At every stage, Waylen asked Mrs Powell's permission to go ahead, so we can be sure that when Waylen's account appeared in print, it was with Margaret Powell's full approval.

Waylen's retelling appeared seven years later in her book *Evidence of Divine Purpose*.[81] The story is attributed to an unnamed 'sixteenth-century historian'[82] and follows a similar pattern to the blue manuscript, with some modifications. Waylen was less specific about which treasures were taken from Glastonbury to Wales. She related how the seven monks fled Strata Florida and rather teasingly added: 'An account which has recently come to light confirms this event.'[83]

But which account? Waylen does not say. Could she have come across John Bacon's mystery book in the Bodleian? Or perhaps some third party had found it? Might this simply refer to the discovery of the blue manuscript by Lionel Lewis? No citation is given, and the book lacks a bibliography, so unfortunately we are left in the dark.

We are told that the cup stayed in Monmouth, concealed in a secret cupboard when the monks were travelling to Nanteos. This seems to be a variation on the Ozleworth episode cooked up by Lionel Lewis (see above), with Monmouth substituted for Ozleworth. Monmouth is certainly not en route for anyone travelling from Strata Florida to Nanteos! We are also told that the cup was the inspiration for Malory's *Morte d'Arthur*, which is unlikely as most of Malory's sources are well known and it is extremely doubtful that he ever visited Strata Florida. Since Malory's book was published in 1485, the suggestion was probably added to imply a more ancient origin for the relic.

The Postcards

As its fame grew, postcards of the Nanteos Cup began to appear for sale in local shops. At least three probably date from the first half of the twentieth century. One early card shows the cup without any background and has some text on the front which reads 'Cwpan Nanteos. The Healing Cup. Originally in Strata Florida Abbey. & believed to be made from the wood of the Holy Cross.'

Galloway of Aberystwyth printed this early postcard. Sidney Victor Galloway (1873–1951) was a bookseller who set up his business in New Street, Aberystwyth, in 1904 but subsequently moved to Pier Street. He was President of the local Chamber of Trade, which in 1932 organized the pageant on the grounds of Aberystwyth Castle,[84] including of course the Revd Hugh Lunt's play about the Nanteos Cup (Chapter 4). It is theoretically possible that the inclusion of Lunt's play was what prompted the publication of the postcard by Sidney Galloway.

The card was reproduced in Barbara Waylen's *Evidence of Divine Purpose*,[85] but the part of the text referring to the 'Holy Cross' fable has been deliberately censored – the new myth was beginning to supersede the old.

The best-known postcard was taken for Mrs Powell by Pickford's photography, a firm based in Pier Street, Aberystwyth. This card shows the cup resting against the wooden box in which it was normally kept. On the side of the box is a small blob of wax bearing the impression of the seal of the Powells. We can only conjecture as to the date that the photograph was taken, but Revd Lionel Lewis had specifically asked for photographs of the cup to be made[86] in 1939.

A third postcard probably dates to the time that a new family, the Mirylees, occupied Nanteos, and is also the most intriguing. It shows the Nanteos Cup resting on an ornately bound book. Scattered around are a handful of handwritten notes attesting to the curative properties of the cup; the date '15th October 1857' can be discerned on one of the notes, which rests on one corner of the book, partially obscuring the spine. The whole display is on a table in one corner of the room near to a window, which is mostly out of shot, but the light from the window illuminates the scene.

The identification of the book should concern us, especially as it bears the title *The History of England*. Could this be the mystery book sought after by Lionel Lewis and Barbara Waylen? The answer is 'very probably not', but how do we even know which book it is? No author appears on the spine, neither is any volume number visible. Underneath the title is the subtitle, which under high magnification we discovered to be 'Henry VIII to Elizabeth'. We include here a computer-enhanced image of the spine which shows this quite clearly. [Plate 6]

Also on the spine of the book are heraldic symbols. Towards the top of the spine is a royal crown reminiscent of that borne by the early Stuarts, but it might instead be the coronation crown of Queen Alexandra[87] (consort of Edward VII) or even the Imperial State Crown of Queen Victoria. Towards the bottom of the spine, partially obscured, is another heraldic device known as a 'naval crown'.[88]

A similar shot to this postcard appears in E. Raymond Capt's[89] film *The Traditions of Glastonbury*, made in around 1963. It seems that Elizabeth Mirylees informed Ysatis De Saint-Simone,[90] a much more recent Grail seeker, that the book in the photograph traced the history of the cup back to the time of Joseph of Arimathea.[91]

Countless books have been printed entitled *The History of England* and many of them have been reprinted and rebound in many different ways. An inventory of the books in the Nanteos Library[92] dating to 1861 shows that they had multiple works entitled *The History of England*. The authors mentioned include Gleig, Goldsmith, Echard, Hume, Smollett and Gunthrie, but there are a couple of references to works with the same title for which the author's name is not given.[93]

In 1739 John Oldmixon produced a *History of England* which again covers Henry VIII to Elizabeth,[94] but his work is not explicitly listed in the Nanteos inventory. It would be ironic if the cup – this famous relic from a Catholic monastery – were linked with the writings of a man whose sentiments were vehemently antipapist. Another candidate is volume six of the second edition of Tobias Smollett's *A Complete History of England from the Descent of Julius Caesar to the Treaty of Aix La Chapelle*,[95] printed in 1759. This work is partly based on the *History* written by David Hume (1711–76).

According to the inventory, Nanteos had an extremely rare version of this, which was printed in seven volumes, with a four-volume continuation. Additionally, in the Morning Room at Nanteos was kept a sixteen-volume work consisting of ten volumes by David Hume and six volumes by Smollett. This may match an octavo-sized imprint published by J. Wallis in Paternoster Row, London, in 1803, and there may be other imprints of Hume which also fit the bill.

The book was chosen for the photograph partly because of its impressive appearance and partly because of the text on the spine. It implies – visually but tacitly – that the history of the cup was written down by ancient historians and as such it is meant to act as testimony to the veracity of the legend and the sanctity of the cup. The book is a silent witness, but most likely a false one, because upon examination, none of the works in the inventory (by known authors) say anything about Abbot Whiting secreting Glastonbury's treasures into Wales. The book might just have been borrowed from another library or it may have been one of the anonymous volumes named in the 1861 inventory; either way, no more can be said about it.

The fate of the book used in the photograph is unknown. In 1958, Elizabeth Mirylees donated around sixty valuable books from Nanteos to the National Library of Wales; however, the book was still in Nanteos when E. Raymond Capt filmed it in the 1960s.[96] According to a Nanteos booklet produced in the mid-1960s, several hundred volumes were loaned to the National Library of Wales.[97]

If such a book ever existed, it is highly unlikely that none of the many researchers into the history of the Grail would have come across it. Yet such a volume would be hugely important, not only in helping establish the history of the Nanteos Cup, but also of what we might call 'The Joseph Grail'. We ourselves searched extensively but were unable to locate the book used in the photograph.

Margaret Powell's Missing History of Nanteos

There is a possibility that Margaret Powell was writing her own history of Nanteos. The only evidence for this comes from a letter from a P. I. Turner;[98] from this we deduce that he was in the process of producing a typed version from Margaret's own handwritten notes, perhaps for sending to a publisher. The letter dates from the period when she was corresponding with Lionel Lewis and had it been printed it would have portrayed the Powells in a very positive light. Mr Turner comments:

> It is very pleasing to see, from these notes, that the Powells, in general, were much respected in the county, and good to the poor, and were not the dissipated monsters that some people would like to make out all landowners were.[99]

It would have doubtless revealed to the world the Nanteos Cup, and had Lewis been able to discover John Bacon's mysterious history book, it would have mentioned that as well. However, by the time Barbara Waylen came onto the stage, the history project must have been abandoned. The whereabouts of Margaret's manuscript and the typewritten pages from Turner are unknown.

In the early hours of 12 March 1951, Margaret Powell died, and her funeral took place at Llanbadarn church[100] on Thursday the 15th. Many people mourned her passing. An anonymous contributor in the *Welsh Gazette* wrote:

A great Welsh lady has passed away in her 91st year, and no one who had the honour to know her can forget the impact of a real personality... Young people loved her and she made the old feel young. Her eyes were so blue and her welcome something to warm the heart. Zest for life and the capacity to radiate happiness were hers to the end.[101]

By the day of the funeral, three people – Myfanwy L. R. Loxdale, P. L. Saunders-Pryse and Elinor Briggs – had come forward and identified themselves as the heirs to the Nanteos estate and had instructed Margaret Powell's solicitor to run the estate on their behalf.[102]

There were those, however, who seemed more concerned with the future of the Nanteos Cup, which had been placed in an Aberystwyth bank vault whilst the legal arguments over who should inherit the Nanteos estate were being played out.[103]

Gwladys Tobit Huws and Maxwell Fraser

Shortly after Mrs Powell's death, an article appeared in the *Welsh Gazette*, written by one G. Tobit Huws. The author was almost certainly Gwladys Elen Tobit Huws (née Evans, 1879–1972), daughter of the schoolmaster, journalist and author Henry Tobit Evans (1844–1908) who had written a book on the Rebecca riots called *Rebecca and her Daughters*.[104] The book was edited by Gwladys and published in 1910, two years after her father's passing. In her later years, Gwladys Tobit Huws moved to Llandaff, Cardiff, but was previously linked with Sarnau and Neuadd Llanarth, both of which are in Ceredigion. She occasionally wrote under the pseudonym of 'Non'.[105]

Huws' article, entitled '*Cwpan* Nanteos',[106] relates a faith-based, romantic account of the relic. We are told that the cup was 'carved in whorls' – in accord with the widespread belief (promulgated by

Lionel Lewis) that the cup had a mysterious pattern etched on it which needed to be deciphered. Unusually, Lindisfarne Abbey is suggested as Joseph of Arimathea's initial destination instead of Glastonbury, although 'there is nothing tangible to prove this theory correct.' Then, as well as Lindisfarne, the author also suggests as Joseph's destination 'Glastonbury Abbey in Gloucestershire' [sic]. She also claimed that Strata Florida was the 'sister abbey' of Glastonbury, which of course it was not.

When we examined a manuscript written by Gwladys' father, Henry Tobit Evans,[107] we found some loose papers within, one of which stated that the monastery of Llanbadarn Fawr had been 'claimed by the Abbey of Gloucester'. This claim is indeed historical – the monastery of Llanbadarn Fawr was given to the Benedictine abbey of St Peter's, Gloucester, thanks to the Norman lord Gilbert Fitz Richard.[108] However, this state of affairs did not last for very long and had no bearing whatsoever on the history of Strata Florida, which was always a Cistercian house and completely unrelated to any Benedictine abbeys in England. However, it is possible that this snippet of history concerning Llanbadarn Fawr's brief annexation by Gloucester Abbey reveals how the slip-up may have been made.

Gwladys Tobit Huws then informs us that the Holy Thorn grows not only at Glastonbury but also at Strata Florida. The importance of this abbey as a destination for pilgrims is emphasised. As per the account in the blue manuscript, King Henry's men destroyed the abbey by fire.

A newspaper cutting of Huws' article was sent to the author Dorothy May Fraser, who wrote under the pseudonym of Maxwell Fraser. She married the poet Edgar Phillips who was known by the pseudonym Trefin and who was Archdruid of Wales between 1960 and 1962. Maxwell Fraser's correspondent (a 'Mr Aubrey') had obviously filed the newspaper cutting away, as Fraser's response is dated 25 August 1952 – more than a year after Huws' article appeared in the *Welsh Gazette*. In her response to 'Mr. Aubrey', Maxwell Fraser noted the 'glaring errors' in Tobit Huws' article: 'Fancy putting Glastonbury in Gloucestershire!! It's a wonder the Somerset folk have not stoned him!'[109]

Fraser had briefly mentioned the Nanteos Cup in one of her books[110] and this may have prompted the correspondence from Mr Aubrey, but there is no strong evidence that the cup was of especial interest to her. That said, in 1962, her husband, the Archdruid Edgar Phillips, received a booklet from Isabel Hill Elder, a leading light of the British Israelite movement; this was her recently published *The Cup of the Last Supper*.[111] In her book, Elder relates the familiar story of the Nanteos Cup. She also sent 'Trefin' a covering letter in which she revealed that she had been to Nanteos and drunk from the cup. She concluded: 'That it is the genuine Holy Grail one cannot have any doubt.'[112]

The British Israelite Connection

The British Israelites are a fundamentalist Christian movement who believe that the British (and Americans of British stock) are descended from the 'lost' Ten Tribes of Judah – a hypothesis that is generally rejected by mainstream historians. Isabel Hill Elder wrote a number of books and pamphlets that expound on the British Israelite take on history and which aimed to prove their claims. Her best-known work was *Celt, Druid and Culdee*, which developed her views on the druids and the early development of the British Church, prior to the influence of Rome. Poorly researched, it is more a matter of fantasy rather than fact.

Another booklet of hers was *The Story of Glastonbury*, which made direct reference to the Powells and the Nanteos Cup. In this account the Glastonbury monks stayed a full three years at Strata Florida before it was sacked by the King's men (which would have been historically impossible). She speculates that the westward journey of the monks towards Aberystwyth implied an intention to escape by sea. We also learn: 'There seems no reason to doubt that the Cup is of olive wood and made, in all probability, from wood cut from the olive grove in Joseph of Arimathea's Gethsemane Garden.'[113]

Just how the author is supposed to know about Joseph's garden, or what grew there, or how it could have been turned into a cup, is unclear, but the account concerning the cup is almost identical to that given in *The Story of Glastonbury*. Elder was emphatic in her insistence that 'In the tradition as handed down from one generation to another, the number never varies, seven monks including their chief, the Prior.'[114]

This is not borne out by the facts and is only one of many errors in her work.

Another of Elder's works, *George of Lydda*, deals with the patron saint of England. In this work, Elder draws on the medieval *High History of the Holy Grail* (*Perlesvaus*) and *The Grand St. Graal* (*The Queste del Saint Graal*) to assert that King Arthur and most of the knights of the Round Table were of Hebrew lineage.[115]

Elder's friend, Florence Annie de Ste. Croix (1872–1946), was another enthusiastic believer in the Nanteos Holy Grail story. In a letter to Margaret Powell, she claimed that the Antioch Chalice and the Nanteos Cup were both used at the Last Supper of Christ. She also contrived some novel speculations regarding the origin of the Nanteos Cup:

> Do you know I feel sure our Lord carved this Cup Himself when He was in our land here at Glastonbury – hence the miraculous healings which were affected with it when taken to sick folk. Was it not here first, then allowed to be taken to Jerusalem by Him by permission of The Ancient Patriarchal Church held then by The Druids – on condition that Joseph of Arimathea who was the Uncle of Our Lord's mother should bring it back to Glastonbury?[116]

This information apparently came from an ancient Celtic manuscript in the possession of Isabel Hill Elder, but the manuscript is unidentifiable and probably did not exist. The connection of the Nanteos Cup with the Antioch Chalice is interesting, since there are several clues that associate the latter with the Grail – but again, the evidence is absent.

Perhaps it need only be added that the view of the druids adopted by the British Israelites was a romantic one popular in the nineteenth century, which drew on the writings of authors such as William Stukeley and Edward Williams, better known as Iolo Morganwg – a forger of Welsh manuscripts. Elder also believed that some members of the Israelite tribe of Levi visited Britain and that the Levitical faith thus became the source for the religion of the British druids.[117] Thus, for the British Israelites there was continuity between the ancient Hebrew faith, British druidism and their own ethnocentric brand of Christianity.

Florence de Ste. Croix believed that the Nanteos Cup, being one of the two chalices of the Last Supper, was the property of the

Israelite folk of Britain and in her letter, she warned Mrs Powell that someday the cup would be 'needed':

> Therefore, I feel certain that the Precious Cup you hold in your keeping & guardianship ... is truly National, is ours, by right of Heritage as being Israel Folk... When Britons are unveiled [as God's chosen] then that Cup will be needed & will be 'seen' as our National Treasure when we were made One Nation again.[118]

Her belief was that a revelation was imminent – one which would 'reveal Britons as The Israel of God, His Chosen Race from Abraham, Isaac & Jacob-Israel',[119] but something terrible had to happen first:

> The tragedy is the Lie that the 'Jews' are The Chosen People is about to be destroyed & the Rightful Heirs are about to be revealed! The Signs of the Times & all that is happening Today reveal this to those who are 'Watching'![120]

Bear in mind that the letter dates from 1942, when the Nazis were systematically exterminating the Jews in what today is known as the Holocaust. The only true revelation to emerge from those times was the full extent of man's capacity for inhumanity towards his own kind.

A third character from the British Israelites we have already met, namely E. Raymond Capt, whose films showed some footage of the relic.[121] Eugene Raymond Capt (1914–2008) was a building contractor from California and the author of several books and films on British Israelite-related topics. Reading George Jowett's book *The Drama of the Lost Disciples* stimulated Capt's interest in the Glastonbury traditions. This book was first published in 1961, so Capt's first film, *The Traditions of Glastonbury*, must post-date this time.

Some of the footage of Capt's film shows the Nanteos Cup at the mansion; however, this footage also appeared in another film, *Light of the West* by Chrest/Gateway Film Productions in 1977. The footage may have been borrowed from Capt's film or it may have been stock footage.

Capt's book *The Traditions of Glastonbury* was first published in 1983. Much of his account[122] of the Nanteos Cup draws from that of Isabel Hill Elder, and repeats her assertion (almost verbatim) that the monks intended to escape by sea when they reached Aberystwyth.[123] Capt did not utilize Elder's account in its entirety and he failed to mention the number of the monks who, according to the legend, came from Glastonbury. As with Elder's account, Capt asserts that it was the function of the glass bowl (rather than the golden fillet) to prevent the sick from biting the cup. Capt goes into some detail concerning the receipts and letters connected with the cup and cites the remarkable case of Father Wharton, which we will discuss in the next chapter.

Regardless of what one makes of the dogmas of the British Israelites, it must be admitted that the interest shown in the Nanteos Cup by some key figures within this movement helped to spread the fame of the cup and elaborate the stories even more.

The Glastonbury Crusade

In the wake of the passing of Mrs Powell, a number of people wanted the Nanteos Cup to be 'returned' to Glastonbury, mainly Glastonian supporters of the Revd Lionel Lewis. However, not all Lewis's supporters were Glastonbury-based and one such was Frederick M. S. Blight (1875–1963) who lived near Lampeter in Mid Wales.

Frederick Maurice Spurway Blight[124] was born in Lewes, Sussex. He attended Manchester Grammar School and the London School of Journalism. He moved to Wales in 1894 and worked as a Post Office executive in Cardiff for some forty years before moving to Cardiganshire. He worked as an accountant for a while before retiring and devoting his time to his many artistic talents.

He was a skilled draughtsman who copied the works of famous artists and illustrators including Aubrey Beardsley and Toulouse Lautrec. His skill was such that experts were concerned that his work might fall into the wrong hands and be passed off as originals. Blight was an honest man, however, and towards the end of his life donated his unsold works to the National Library of Wales.[125] He was something of a controversialist who enjoyed writing letters to the press.

On one occasion he had written on the subject of incorporating the Welsh dragon into the royal coat of arms.[126] Blight had previously written to the *Sunday* Times,[127] joining an ongoing discussion on the topic of mazer bowls. In this letter, he had related the story of the Nanteos Cup and divulged the relatively recent news of Margaret Powell's death to an international audience:

> Mrs Powell of Nanteos, recently deceased, left no direct heirs and now there is considerable argument whether what is left of the bowl should be treated as a museum piece or be stored in some sacred edifice.[128]

He naturally found himself on the receiving end of some correspondence, not least from Revd Lionel Lewis himself, who of course wanted to obtain the relic for his church in Glastonbury. Blight seems to have been aware that some 'considerable argument' was going on, but how he knew this is unclear. The mention of the 'sacred edifice' might suggest that Blight could have corresponded with Lewis before or otherwise knew of his plan to store the cup in an aumbry.

At first, Blight was not a believer in the Joseph of Arimathea legend and had doubts as to the Nanteos Cup being the Holy Grail but was convinced that the cup was a holy relic from Glastonbury and felt very strongly, therefore, that it ought to be 'returned' there.

In order to sway things his way, Blight wrote to the influential Dr Thomas Jones who had served on the council of the University of Wales, the council of the University College of Wales, Aberystwyth, the council of the National Library of Wales and the council of the National Museum of Wales. Jones was also formerly Chairman of the Royal Commission on Ancient Monuments for Wales from 1944 to 1948. Such a well-connected individual surely would have been able to sway the argument for Glastonbury, if only he could be brought on side – or so Blight must have thought. In his first letter to Dr Jones, Frederick Blight expressed his aversion to the idea that the Nanteos Cup should be placed in a museum, an idea proposed by members of the Cardiganshire Antiquarian Society.[129]

In his first letter to the *Welsh Gazette*, Blight declared the Nanteos Cup to be the property of Glastonbury Abbey. Rather surprisingly perhaps, he publicly cast doubt on the Joseph of Arimathea legend and the authenticity of the relic as the Holy Grail, citing the work of Dean Armitage Robinson as his authority.[130] Instead he argued that since it was a holy vessel which Glastonbury Parish Church Council had laid claim to, it should therefore be handed over to them.[131] Blight's public denial of the Glastonbury legends upset the Revd Lionel Lewis who responded by sending him free copies of his own books in an attempt to refute Robinson's arguments and bring Blight on side.

In Blight's first letter to Dr Thomas Jones, he confessed that he may have upset Lewis through his reference to Robinson and thereafter he wholly accepted Lewis's account of how the cup came to Nanteos. Blight declared himself to be against the idea of the cup becoming a museum piece and added: 'I even think it was quite wrong of the Powell family to keep the Cup for some 400 years.'[132]

Blight then asked Dr Jones to reveal the identity of the executor of Mrs Powell's will; it seems likely that Dr Jones obliged. He also appealed directly to Dr Jones for help in his cause: 'I should be so very glad if you could lend your influence for the return of the cup to Glastonbury.'[133]

Shortly after this, Blight contacted Mrs Powell's executor, Mr John Noel Davies Jenkins, who responded that the cup would become the property of whoever inherited Nanteos. This did nothing to deter Frederick Blight's letter-writing campaign. In his second letter to Dr Thomas Jones, Blight expounded on a rumour that Mrs Powell had bequeathed the cup in her will:

Yesterday I had a letter from the Rev. Lionel Lewis; he says he had heard from a Sister of Clewer (I believe that is a Protestant 'nunnery' near Windsor), who heard from a R. Catholic priest, who had heard from a Jesuit priest (sounds rather 'house-that-Jack-built') that Mrs Powell had bequeathed the Cup to the Welsh National Museum![134]

This rumour was, of course, utterly false. Blight wrote again to the *Welsh Gazette*, rebutting the rumour and quoting a statement from the executor saying that the relic would go to the new owners of Nanteos. He then cited the passage from Amery ('until the Church should once more claim its own') almost as if it were legally binding on the Powells. To make it doubly clear that this was what he was hinting at, he referred to Revd Lionel Lewis as 'the church as by Law established'.[135]

According to Blight's version of events, Lewis, Sir Charles Marston and company had arrived at Nanteos in 1938 and had requested the cup's 'return' to Glastonbury that very evening – the church 'as by Law established' had staked a claim. However, Lewis was only a parish priest and could not be said to be acting under the direction of any higher ecclesiastical authority at that time. In any case it would have been somewhat brazen of Lewis to make such a demand of Mrs Powell on a first meeting.

A closer examination of the correspondence between Mrs Powell and Lewis reveals that in fact he did not openly make any request for the 'return' of the cup until[136] 1940, although the question must surely have been on his mind. There is a suggestion from later correspondence[137] that Lewis may have written to Mrs Powell *c.* 1949, but this letter is missing. By Lewis's own admission, she did not reply.

According to Blight,[138] Lionel Lewis had secured the support not only of the Glastonbury Parish Church Council but also the Bishop of Bath and Wells, Harold William Bradfield. Lewis also appealed to Geoffrey Fisher, the Archbishop of Canterbury, in aid of his cause.[139] In the 1960s another vicar of Glastonbury, the Revd Hugh Knapman,[140] appealed for the relic to be returned.[141] None of these attempts were successful.

In stark contrast to his earlier public rejection of the Glastonbury legends, Blight wrote that:

> Reputable historians consider that the first Christian settlement in Britain was founded at Glastonbury by Joseph of Arimathea and his reputed tomb is now in Glastonbury Parish Church.[142]

This reversal of opinion may have been brought about through his correspondence with Lionel Lewis and reading Lewis's 'refutation' of Dean Armitage Robinson.[143] Nevertheless, he still considered the identification of the Nanteos Cup as the Holy Grail to be 'problematical'.[144] Needless to say, he did not list any of the 'reputable historians'.

In spite of the slightly legalistic tone of his argument, Blight was aware that his attempts to sway the legal process might fail, so he also made a plea to the future inheritor of Nanteos, whose identity was not decided at that time. Finally came the most baffling argument of all: 'The remaining fragment, riveted and enclosed within a glass bowl, has no artistic value to recommend it as a museum-piece; its value is purely sentimental.'[145]

In the previous paragraph of the same letter, Blight had heralded the Nanteos Cup as 'the greatest treasure of Glastonbury Abbey',[146] only to reduce it to a sentimental folly a few sentences later. Perhaps he thought that playing down the value and importance of the cup would persuade the future owners of Nanteos to part with it.

In May 1952, Blight resumed his attack, writing to the *Welsh Gazette*. The question of whether or not the relic was legally an heirloom had not been completely resolved. Blight, in all seriousness, wrote that the Nanteos Cup was 'never, strictly speaking, a possession of the Powell family',[147] citing Amery's familiar passage, 'until the Church should once more claim its own', as proof of this. Blight – repeating his curious gambit – wrote that the cup was in such a poor condition that it had 'no value whatever as a museum piece'[148] and by implication should therefore be given to the Church of St John in Glastonbury.

For a short while, *c.* 1953, Blight returned to Sussex. He wrote to the *Western Mail* in 1953 from his address in Plaistow,[149] claiming that Mrs Powell had told Revd Lionel Lewis that she could not make up her mind about parting with the relic. The fact that the earlier correspondence between Mrs Powell and Lionel Lewis broke off almost as soon as he requested the cup, allied with the fact that she did not even reply to Lionel Lewis's final request, surely reveals how she truly felt.

Blight decided that he much preferred Wales to his native Sussex, dubbing it a 'Land of Snobs and Yahoos'[150] and so he departed England for Wales once more. He requested that when he died, his mortal remains be buried at Strata Florida and this request was granted.[151] Given his sympathies towards Wales and the legends surrounding Strata Florida and its famous cup, perhaps this is no surprise.

Legal Battles

Following Margaret Powell's death, with the Nanteos Cup concealed in an Aberystwyth bank vault,[152] a legal battle ensued to decide who would inherit the estate. The dispute would last some years and was only resolved in the High Court in late 1955. The principal competitors were Captain John Hext Lewes (1903–92) and Elizabeth Mirylees (1920–86), both related to Margaret Powell.

Margaret Powell had bequeathed the Nanteos estate to Elizabeth Mirylees, but there were strings attached. According to the stipulations in her will, Mrs Mirylees would be required to pay death duties (amounting to £16,000) and was required to raise this money without re-mortgaging the estate or by selling any part of it. If Mrs Mirylees was unable to fulfil all of the requirements of the will, then the estate should go instead to Captain Hext Lewes.

Captain Lewes contended that he was able to raise the funds required to pay the death duties, but the judge (Justice Upjohn) ruled that the stipulations were either too vague or unfair and the whole of the estate should go to Elizabeth Mirylees and the restrictions set aside.[153] Thus Elizabeth Mirylees (known as 'Betty') became the new owner of Nanteos Mansion and guardian of the Nanteos Cup.

In the early years of her guardianship of the relic, Betty Mirylees contemplated a course of action that might well have spelled disaster for believers by potentially jeopardizing the legitimacy of the cup – she wanted to have it scientifically dated. Once again, the cup – or the narrative power of the cup – was under threat by those who were closest to it.

6

Exile and Return

For 200 years the Cup has been here, and the story of its healing power has become known all over the world. The present owner herself has received requests for water from every continent.

From the booklet *Nanteos Historic Monument*, *c.* 1965

With the court battle finally won, Betty Mirylees and her family finally moved into their new home. The grand old mansion of Nanteos, once a place of pomp and aristocratic grandeur, had become run-down through more than a century of neglect and unpaid bills. Betty had won her five-year-long high court case to become the new lady of the manor, but the real battles still lay ahead: how to fix the mansion? How to make it pay? She also had a young family of five children[1] to bring up, the youngest less than a year old. Then there was the other problem, waiting silently in a bank vault – what about the Grail?

In the wake of Margaret Powell's death there was much speculation as to what might happen to the cup and where it truly belonged. In spite of the attempt by Revd Lionel Lewis and others to 'return' the cup to Glastonbury or some other religious institution, it became clear at a fairly early stage that the new owners of Nanteos would also become the new owners of the cup – it would be up to them to decide its fate.

The 'Light Ray' Test
Betty knew about the stories surrounding the cup and its supposed identity as the Holy Grail – there can be no doubt that she regarded

it as sacred. Even so, she seems to have been racked with doubt and had an urge to discover whether or not the stories were really true. Betty had evidently read a popular science account on the early radiocarbon test performed on the Dead Sea Scrolls. We may never know which account she had read but it seems that Betty (or the author of the report) had misunderstood the method of radiocarbon dating.

In 1957, radiocarbon dating was still in its infancy. The only testing of this kind done in relation to the Dead Sea Scrolls was the dating of a piece of linen from one of the caves at Qumran, where the scrolls had been discovered. The work was carried out by the pioneer of radiocarbon dating, Willard Libby, at the University of Chicago; this revealed the piece of linen to be 1,917 years old, give or take around 200 years.[2]

Radiocarbon dating is an invasive method which requires a sample of the material to be dated to be taken from the source. Dating the cup by this method would have meant removing a small amount of wood, thereby causing some damage. However, it seems likely that Betty did not fully understand this because when she announced in the *Cambrian News* that the cup was to be scientifically dated, she referred to it as a 'light ray treatment'.[3]

Accounts describing radiocarbon dating frequently refer to the fact that the radioactive isotope Carbon-14 is generated by cosmic rays bombarding the upper atmosphere. Perhaps because of this, Betty seems to have misunderstood radiocarbon dating as a non-invasive method that would not have harmed the cup.

According to the *Cambrian News* article, her intention was to take the cup to London, to 'the same laboratory that carried out the Dead Sea Scrolls tests' – in other words the British Museum, which had taken an interest in radiocarbon dating almost since its invention.[4] However, as explained above, Libby had done the work at the University of Chicago.

The first list of samples tested at the British Museum was published in 1959 and this list does not mention the Nanteos Cup.[5] If Betty had radiocarbon-dated the cup, this could have jeopardised its reputation as the legendary Holy Grail, and even if it had been dated to the time of Christ, this alone would not have identified it beyond doubt as the one true Grail. The following week she was photographed in the Belle Vue hotel on Aberystwyth's seafront, dining with her husband, the Major, alongside tenants from the Nanteos estate.[6] There is no mention of the cup in the photo caption and the reason for the occasion is not given.

It was not so long afterwards that Betty was organising an auction event that took place in a marquee in the grounds of Nanteos. Many items were up for sale including prints, engravings, porcelain, plate, furniture and books from the Nanteos library. Among the latter were the rare three-volume copy of William Dugdale's *Monasticon*[7] and the *Works* of Henry Spelman.[8] With so much on her plate, taking the cup to London can't have been a high priority. We searched extensively for a follow-up report but were unable to find any. If the so-called 'light ray' test did happen Elizabeth Mirylees never made the outcome known and since there are no records, we can conclude that it never happened. This would seem to be confirmed by Father James Wharton (see below) who wrote in 1959: "Major and Mrs. Mirylees have decided not to send the Cup to the British Museum for testing as to its age.[9]

Betty soon became a firm believer that the Nanteos Cup could heal and stated publicly her belief that it was the Holy Grail.[10] She turned against the idea of subjecting it to scientific dating. She came to recognize the link between the cup's ability to heal and the power of faith,[11] reasoning that negative statements from a recognized authority might undermine the ability of the believer to believe – this in turn might take away the cup's ability to heal (or perhaps the patient's own power to heal himself). According to Fred Stedman Jones, as mentioned in the Introduction: 'Her pragmatic view was that it heals, and nothing would be gained "by finding out that it was made in Birmingham", as she put it to me.'[12]

The Remarkable Case of Father Wharton

There is one specific case that may well have been responsible for changing Elizabeth Mirylees' mind about radiocarbon dating the cup. Indeed, the cure was so complete and so spontaneous that it defies all scientific explanation.

Less than two weeks after the announcement about the 'light ray' test, a gentleman in his mid-sixties arrived at Nanteos.[13] His name was Father James Henry Shields Wharton BA (1891–1966), former priest at St Joseph's Church in Upton-on-Severn, Worcestershire; he

This page, overleaf: 1–4. Images of the Nanteos Cup as it is today. (By permission of Llyfrgell Genedlaethol Cymru / The National Library of Wales)

THE NANTEOS CUP.

Above: 5. Photo from the early 1960s showing
the Cup resting on top of a mysterious *History of
England*. (By permission of Llyfrgell Genedlaethol
Cymru / The National Library of Wales)

Right: 6. Enlargement of the image showing the
spine of the elusive book against which the cup is
shown. (By permission of Llyfrgell Genedlaethol
Cymru / The National Library of Wales)

Above, left: 7a, 7b. Photos showing the shape of the inner boss of the Cup, with enlargement showing further detail in the wood. (Photos Ian Pegler, with thanks to the National Library of Wales)

Below: 8. Nineteenth-century engraving showing Nanteos House and grounds. (Public domain)

Stannard & Dixon, lith 7, Poland St.

1854

NANTEOS,— C? CARDIGAN.
THE SEAT OF W.E. POWELL, ESQ. M.P.

Above: 9. Nanteos Mansion today. (Photo by Ian Pegler, 2006)

Right: 10. Modern sculpture in the grounds of Nanteos House showing the Cup. (Photo by Ian Pegler)

11. The Great Arch, part of the ruins of Strata Florida Abbey. (Photo by Ian Pegler)

12. Nineteenth-century print of Strata Florida Abbey. (Public domain)

13. Photo of the *Cwpan Ystrad Fflur* pageant-play from 1934 by the Reverend Hugh Lunt. (By permission of Llyfrgell Genedlaethol Cymru / The National Library of Wales)

14. Mynachlog Fawr farmhouse, once home to the Stedman family, now owned by the Strata Florida Trust. (Photo by Ian Pegler)

Above left: 15. The occultist Arthur Edward Waite (1857–1942). (Public domain)

Above right: 16. The author Arthur Machen (1863–1947). (Public domain)

Above left: 17. The composer Richard Wagner (1813–1883). (Public domain)

Above right: 18. Worthington George Smith (1835–1917) was one of the first people to examine the cup. (Public domain)

Right: 19. The oldest known illustration of the Nanteos Cup, produced by Worthington George Smith *c.* 1900. (Photo by Ian Pegler)

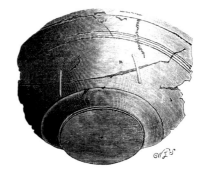

Left: 20. Miss Ethelwyn Mary Amery in academic robes, 1902. (By permission of Llyfrgell Genedlaethol Cymru / The National Library of Wales)

Below: 21. Margaret Powell in the 1940s with unknown gentlemen. (By permission of Llyfrgell Genedlaethol Cymru / The National Library of Wales)

had been chauffeured in a car over a hundred miles to come and see the cup. He could not drive himself and as he was helped from the car it was obvious that this sickly priest was crippled with arthritis and had problems bending his knees. He was allowed to drink from the cup and then asked to be alone with it for a short while. Betty overcame her initial hesitancy and granted his wish.

A few minutes passed and suddenly Father Wharton was healed – his arthritic condition had vanished completely, he was moving about quite freely and without pain, overjoyed at what he deemed a miraculous recovery. He literally ran towards Betty shouting 'Look! Look!' This incredible transformation was witnessed by, amongst other people, Revd Wharton's housekeeper, Phyllis Woodward,[14] and a young Fiona Mirylees.[15]

Word got out about the cure, resulting in a flood of correspondence requesting water from the cup. Father Wharton was so moved by the experience that he wrote three sermons on the cup and these have been preserved to this day.[16] The venerable priest lived another nine years with no recurrence of his old illness. Probate records reveal the name of his last abode[17] – it was called 'Avalon'.

This apparent miracle, so hard to comprehend, had occurred at precisely the critical moment for Betty Mirylees. It was enough, surely, to dissuade her from travelling to London and to give her pause for thought. In her possession was a vessel with the power to change people's lives for the better – that was what mattered. Now she knew what to do with the cup and dating it was unnecessary.

Opening Nanteos to the Public
Curing Father Wharton of his arthritis was one of the earliest feats of the cup after it was restored to the mansion from the cloying darkness of the bank vault. More strange occurrences were to come of course but there were other, more pressing needs on the mind of the new lady of the manor. Nanteos Mansion was in a run-down condition and the roof was in an appalling state. To ease the financial burden, the Mirylees decided to apply for a special heritage grant. The application to the Historic Buildings Council for Wales was successful and the amount awarded was substantial[18] – £10,400 (over £180,000 itoday).

There were, of course, strings attached. One of the conditions was that once the alterations had been made, the mansion should be opened up to the general public for one day a week from May to September each year.[19] For the first time in its history, people would be free to wander the halls and rooms of this stately home. The cup would have been an obvious selling point to attract more visitors and as early as 7 February 1961 the cup was featured on a Television Wales and West programme with the Welsh title of *Amser Te* ('Teatime').[20] The man who presented the talk on the cup was Gildas Tibbott, a member of the Cardiganshire Antiquarian Society and Deputy Librarian at the National Library of Wales.[21]

Most newspaper reports seem to suggest that the first occasion of the house being opened was on Easter Monday, 3 April 1961, when more than 300 visitors came to look at the mansion.[22] An admission fee was charged, eventually a guidebook was printed, and more postcards of the cup and the mansion were made and sold. One report suggests that Betty had intended to go ahead sooner and had insured the Nanteos Cup for £10,000. So worried was she about the safety of the cup that when the general public were allowed into the mansion, the cup would be kept in a padlocked box and constantly guarded by a member of the family.[23]

Later that year, a Welsh Language programme, *Dirgelwch Nanteos* ('The Mystery of Nanteos'), was shown by the BBC in Wales; it was presented by the academic Dr Glyn O. Phillips and produced by Selwyn Roderick.[24] The cup inspired novelists such as Elizabeth Yunge-Bateman who, in 1961, wrote and self-published a children's novel, *The Flowering Thorn*, in which five young people seek the Grail in modern-day Wales.

Nanteos opened to the general public the following year and there was more publicity for the cup. An article in *Country Quest* by Cynric Mytton Davies records[25] that a sufferer of paralysis was cured in January 1960.

Sometime in 1959 before the doors to Nanteos were opened to the public, there was another remarkable occurrence. Betty's youngest child, Jean, had a life-threatening accident when a ladder toppled and fell, crashing down onto her, cracking her skull. The mortally wounded infant (she would have been around two years old at the time) was rushed to hospital. The doctors did their best to save her, but she was haemorrhaging heavily and was not expected to live. Elizabeth Mirylees, out of desperation, took the

Nanteos Cup from its box and started praying. Within the space of ten minutes she received a phone call from the hospital – Jean's haemorrhaging had suddenly stopped, and the child was now expected to survive. The child did indeed survive and grew up none the worse for her ordeal.[26] Events of this kind were now to occur with increasing frequency.

A Distinguished Voice

We have already encountered the Christian movement known as the British Israelites, a group who believe that the British are descended from the 'lost' tribes of Israel. Certain of their number, such as Florence de Ste. Croix and Isabel Hill Elder, had been to Nanteos some years before, but when the mansion was advertised as a tourist destination in the 1960s, more took an interest. One was E. Raymond Capt, whose films and book *The Traditions of Glastonbury* we mentioned previously.

An even more famous enthusiast was Cyril Frederick 'Bob' Danvers-Walker (1906–90), who is best remembered as 'the voice of British Pathé News' for more than three decades. Bob also presented the BBC radio show *Housewife's Choice* and served as an announcer on another popular show, *Take Your Pick*.

Bob had close links with the custodian of Glastonbury Abbey, who presented him with a thirteenth-century capstone in recognition of his services to the place. Bob in turn named his cottage 'Abbey Thorn Cottage', but had great difficulty in his attempts to grow the Glastonbury Thorn at home.[27] He also told a story of being almost caught by the Nazis in January 1940 while reporting from France on the Dunkirk operation. The place where he was so close to being captured was Fecamp – which possesses its own Grail-related story, in which a hollowed-out log of wood washed ashore containing a phial of Christ's blood, which is still kept in the Benedictine Abbey of the Holy Trinity at the site, and is said to liquefy at Easter. Perhaps this fuelled his undoubted fascination with the Grail.

Bob's stentorian tones will be familiar to anyone who has watched old British Pathé newsreels, some of which were used as propaganda during the Second World War in order to boost the morale of the British people and inspire them with a patriotic will to fight the Nazis. One newsreel from 1940 was entitled 'Our Island Fortress' and subtitled 'There's a Land, a Dear Land' – the kind of sentiments one would expect from a British Israelite and patriotic Englishman. It also gained him the doubtful honour of being placed on Adolf Hitler's 'kill list' in the event of a successful invasion of Britain.

When Nanteos was about to reopen in the summer of 1963, Bob Danvers-Walker publicised the fact in a magazine called *Coming Events in Britain*.[28] Bob's own interest in the Nanteos Cup dated to the 1950s; he went on to produce a number of slide-show lectures for Covenant Publishing, a firm based in Glastonbury, Somerset, who are strongly linked with the British Israelite movement. Danvers-Walker travelled widely, presenting the lectures himself – more than 230 times in the UK over a decade – and duplicates of the lectures were distributed abroad. One of these lectures was called 'They Came to a Land', which focused on the coming of Joseph of Arimathea to Britain. Several of the slides concerned the story of the Nanteos Cup, about which Bob was very open-minded. His view of the Glastonbury Legends as presented in his slides was uncritical – a fund of Glastonbury lore most likely based on the work of earlier British Israelites and the report by Lionel Smithett Lewis.

Bob Danvers-Walker was given permission to photograph the Nanteos Cup in 1977, when it was exhibited at the National Library.[29] He seemed to be convinced that the cup had been 'botanically analyzed' at Kew Gardens and that this test had proven that the cup was from the Levant[30] – we have no evidence to suggest that this examination ever took place.

Bob received correspondence from an unnamed priest who had written to him describing how the cup had cured his 'semi-crippled condition' – almost certainly Father Wharton. Danvers-Walker's connection to the Nanteos Cup did not end there, as we shall see.

Departure from Nanteos

With costs of running the mansion on the rise and the clamour surrounding the Nanteos Cup on the increase, the Mirylees family decided to move out of Wales to a new home in Herefordshire – and they took the cup with them. Betty Mirylees claimed that one of the reasons for moving away was because of the incessant correspondence and the work generated by the requests for water from the cup. It reached the point that she was sending out hundreds of bottles of water per week, at her own expense.[31]

She was also subjected to a fair amount of unwanted attention from cranks demanding that she hand over the cup to them whilst others barged their way into Nanteos (still a private residence) demanding to see it.

With the decision of the Mirylees to move out of Nanteos, the estate was broken up and sold off to the tenant farmers and the mansion itself was eventually sold to a scrap dealer named Geoffrey Bliss. Many people wondered what would happen to the cup and there was correspondence to this effect in *Country Life* magazine.[32]

In spite of her stated desire to get away from it all, Betty continued to make water from the cup available and even courted attention for it, as witnessed in an interview with her which appeared in *Woman* magazine[33] in 1969 and a television appearance in the BBC programme *What's Happening to Camelot?* made the same year. The article in *Woman* resulted in a deluge of more than 3,000 letters.[34] Elizabeth Mirylees would get Christmas cards with messages saying, 'Remember me – I was blind and now I can see.' In spite of the many reports suggesting that the cup was kept in a Herefordshire bank vault, the article[35] indicates that it was kept in a drawer in Major Mirylees' bureau.

Did the Cup Leave Britain?

The cup apparently did not always remain in Herefordshire. Letters from Bob Danvers-Walker to Fred Stedman-Jones suggest that it was loaned to the 'Sangreal Foundation', founded upon the work of the British Occultist W. G. Gray (1913–92). In 1974, a Texas oil millionaire named Carr Collins is said to have paid to have the cup transferred to the US, where it was to be tested. This seems, on the face of it, an unlikely event, given the rigid refusal of the Powell and Mirylees families to allow the cup to be taken away – never mind subjected to tests. Yet, the story persists, and one of the authors of this book, John Matthews, bears testimony to the fact that Carr Collins certainly knew Fiona and Clementina Mirylees, since both were present at one of several extravagant parties thrown by Collins in the 1980s, to which the cream of British esotericists were invited. John attended more than one of these events and remembers meeting the Mirylees sisters in 1983.

Both were formally dressed – even to the white lace gloves much beloved of ladies at the time – and both looked very out of place amongst characters like Israel Regardie (former secretary to Aleister Crowley), esotericist Gareth Knight, and others. John decided to strike up a conversation, and began with a very direct question: were they really the guardians of the Nanteos Cup? It was Fiona who responded, with a very guarded look and an abrupt nod. She then turned away and stared out of the window. John decided to press the matter a little further and asked her directly if she believed that the cup was indeed the Holy Grail. Without turning around, and almost in a whisper, she replied: 'Oh, yes. It is the Grail – or so they say.'

The obvious dichotomy of these two statements begs further interrogation, but Fiona Mirylees refused to be drawn further.

We spoke to several people who both knew Carr Collins well and assisted him in planning his extravagant parties. None of them recall any arrangement to send the cup abroad, or to have it tested. In 1977, a lady named Nora Brook, then in her eighties and apparently a personal friend of Betty Mirylees, wrote to John Matthews having read his work on the Grail, offering him a set of papers concerning Nanteos, which had been passed to her by 'a friend' following the death of 'Mrs. Mirylees'. These consisted of 'A memorandum of the Reverend Lionel Smithett Lewis, M. A. Vicar of Glastonbury, touching the Nanteos cup and a visit to Nanteos, Co. Cardigan, 1n 1938, together with related papers'.

Mrs Brook sent John a few scattered press cuttings and some correspondence with the Bishop of St David's and later the librarian of the National Library of Wales concerning the cup. Interestingly, in her letter to John, she mentions hearing that the cup had been sent away to America, which she found 'horrifying'. She had clearly expressed her concerns to the librarian, David Jenkins, who in his reply mentioned the 'exhibition of manuscripts, books and paintings &c. to be arranged by the staff of the library' for the period of mid-July to mid-August 1978. He then continued:

> I wrote to major Mirylees shortly before Christmas and he has very kindly agreed to let us include the Nanteos Cup In the exhibition... You will therefore gather that the Cup has been returned from U.S.A. or, at least will be returned before next summer. (John Matthews archive)

This suggests that it was known that the cup had indeed been sent abroad, though no further evidence for this has so far come to light.

A passage in W. G. Grays' unpublished memoir relates the story as he saw it (including some interesting variants to the story told by the Powells and Ethelwyn Amery):

Carr [Collins] had once got on the track of another item once reputed to be the historical Holy Grail but was factually the remains of an ancient olive wood bowl, with reputed healing properties and known as the Nanteos Cup which gets occasional unwanted publicity. Its story was that after the dissolution of the English Monasteries, a few ex-monks from Strata Florida Abbey were seeking fresh homes in Welsh valleys, and a farming family were so kind to them that they said they would leave their Most precious relic with that family to guard until the Abbey should be restored again. It was just a small and quite plain bowl turned from olive wood, originally some five or six inches across and maybe three inches deep. It was supposed to be filled with water and left to stand overnight. The sick person should drink it next morning and await cure. It remained in the same family for several centuries and acquired a great reputation for healing both humans and animals among the local farming communities. Over the centuries it had been chipped and broken so often that less than half of it remained. This fragment could still be placed in an ordinary glass bowl, which was filled with water, and apparently its healing properties were still operative.

The chances are that this could indeed have been an early Celtic Mass-Cup of no special intrinsic value except as a relic. Chalices of precious metals were not obligatory in the Christian Church until about the sixth century, and the consecrated wine was often offered in small bowls of pottery, glass, or base metal. Wooden drinking bowls were not uncommon in old times and known as masers in this country. Strata Florida in Cardiganshire had been a Cistercian house, and that Order was well known for their plain and non-precious style of sacred utensils. Be that as it may. Carr had located the present holder of the famous fragment, and we went to see it together.

It was held by a pleasant widow-woman with two grown up unmarried daughters, and they lived at the edge of a village where they bred pedigree dogs. The lady herself was almost crippled with arthritis and the Cup had availed her nothing. She actually kept it in a plain wooden box under her bed, together with a glass bowl and a fairly large collection of letters attesting to cures. At her invitation I held the relic in my hands for a while as she told its story and how her family came to inherit it. She had refused enormous amounts of money for what I held, and I would not have supposed her to be a wealthy woman at all.

I asked her if she herself knew of any instances of unusual healing, and she told me that one of her daughters had fallen from horseback, cut her head badly, and was in hospital where there was apparently great difficulty with checking the loss of blood. 'I went home and got the Cup,' she said, 'and just sat there, holding it and hoping. I didn't pray because I don't know how to pray, but I just kept thinking of my daughter. Presently the phone rang, and it was the hospital to tell me the bleeding had stopped all by itself.' Apparently, a previous possessor in the past century had tried to preserve the remains of the Cup by having a silver rim fitted, which promptly prevented any cures, though these recommenced when the rim was removed. I gather Carr made his bid for it also, which was turned down like those of his predecessors. It is nice to know there are some items beyond the power of the Almighty Dollar to reach.

We note the variants, including the accident to Betty Mirylees' daughter, which is here transferred from her being hit by a ladder to falling from her horse – a story that has a slightly more romantic ring to it. W. G. Gray wrote most of his autobiography from memory however, so it may simply be that his recollection was faulty. The references to the Carr Collins' interest are fairly clear. Carr had asked and was refused; though it appears from Gray's statement that he may have tried to *buy* the cup. However, amongst the papers collected by our late collaborator Fred Stedman-Jones, we find another – very different – account, involving the redoubtable Bob Danvers-Walker who, as we have seen, showed a considerable amount of interest in the cup from the 1950s up to his death in 1980.

According to Fred, Danvers Walker wrote and told him about the apparent loan of the cup to the Sangreal Foundation in 1974. Then, in 2001, Fiona told him that 'they would not send it back [so] that Jean and her boyfriend went over to fetch it and were told that it had been loaned elsewhere or some such tale.' She also told Fred that they had taken out the rivets and stuck it together – she and her mother had doubts that it was the real cup when Bob Danvers-Walker recovered it for them from the USA.

These are startling statements, and ones that cannot be ignored, despite the fact that no evidence for any such events seems to have survived. Fred notes that Bob had invited him to visit and promised to show him correspondence relating to this. Unfortunately, he died before this could happen. Fred also quotes some of the letters he received from Bob Danvers-Walker, in which the latter states: 'The Cup was taken on loan for an exhibition in 1974 by the Sangreal Foundation in Dallas, Texas. I refrain from commenting further on this matter.'

This is a curious statement. Why would he not wish to comment? Later on, Danvers-Walker remarks:

> A Carbon dating of a mere fragment of the Cup was proposed but Betty Mirylees demurred on the grounds that though it would assure its age it would not prove its historic origin since bowls were commonplace articles in the first century A. D.

This of course implies that no tests were carried out, as all the evidence we have been able to assemble also demonstrates. So just how was Bob Danvers-Walker involved in bringing the cup back from the USA? Apart from anything else, it implies very clearly that the cup *did* go out of the country and was passed from hand to hand until he recovered it. Could this possibly have happened, and what does it add to the story of the relic?

A possibility might be that when Danvers-Walker and Fiona Mirylees mention the loan of the cup to the Sangreal Foundation, the assumption is that because the foundation was based in Texas, the cup must have been taken there. However, it is possible that the cup was indeed leant to Carr Collins, who kept it for a time in Britain. Until the papers of Bob Danvers-Walker are properly explored we cannot know the truth, but so far, an extended search has failed to discover them.

In the last weeks of completing this manuscript, two letters came to light from the archive of Dr Helmut Nickel, late curator of Arms and Armor department at the New York Metropolitan Museum.

These were copies sent to Dr Nickel, whose interest in Arthurian and Grail traditions was widely known, from a colleague at the Cloisters Museum, also in New York. The first was addressed to Carr Collins:

The Cloisters
Fort Tryon Park,
New York,
N. Y. 10040

November 24, 1975

Mr. Carr P. Collins Jr.
4801 St. John's Drive
Dallas, Texas 75205

Dear Mr. Collins:
This is a response, rather belatedly, to your letter to the Curator of The Cloisters regarding the "Nanteos Cup."

If it is still in your possession and you plan to visit New York in the near future Dr. Helmut Nickel, Curator of Arms and Armor at The Metropolitan Museum of Art, and Mr. J. L. Schrader, Curator-in-Charge here at The Cloisters, would both be very much interested in seeing the object.

Thanking you for bringing this object to our attention, I am,

Yours sincerely
(signed)
Aphrodite Hagiegeorgiou
Administrative Assistant
(John Matthews archive)

To this Collins replied, in a letter dated 16 December 1975, responding to Ms Hagiegeorgiou. In this Collins states:

Thank you for your note about the 'Nanteos Cup' and hope that I will get to bring it up with me in the early Spring. The Nanteos Cup belongs to Mrs Mirylees in Herefordshire, England, and she was kind enough to lend it to me to show and share over here...
(John Matthews archive)

The implications are that Carr Collins had indeed taken possession of the cup and had sought a means of dating it from the best experts he could find. The dating of the letter seems to confirm this. However, neither the archives of Dr Nickel nor Mr Schrader reveal any evidence that any such tests were ever carried out, and the exact meaning of the letters remains unclear as to whether Collins actually had the cup in his possession.

For the moment, the mystery remains.

The Aberystwyth 700 Exhibition

In 1977 the cup made another public appearance when Aberystwyth celebrated the 700th anniversary of its Town Charter. The celebratory events continued throughout the summer until the end of the year. One of the events was the Aberystwyth 700 exhibition, which took place at the National Library of Wales. This event ran from 22 June to 9 August,[36] but there was an official opening event on Tuesday 21 June. One of the exhibits was the Nanteos Cup, which proved to be a star attraction throughout the summer.

Speaking at this opening event was Professor E. G. Bowen (1900–83). In his opening address[37] given in the Gregynog Gallery,[38] Bowen stressed the historical links between the Aberystwyth area and Strata Florida and used this to lend a rationale for the exhibition of the Nanteos Cup, which had been loaned to the National Library by the Mirylees family. Bowen then referred to the cup directly – he called it a 'turned wooden mazer or drinking bowl probably of the fifteenth or sixteenth century'.[39]

This attempt at dating was, of course, educated guesswork. However, Bowen had no problem with the tradition that the Nanteos Cup had come from Strata Florida. For Bowen the strength of its reputation for healing (which was thought to cover an extended time period) was enough to suggest a real historical context. He must have subsequently amended his paper as he refers to the enormous popularity of the cup during the course of its exhibition at the National Library. The local newspaper had run a headline that read 'Holy Grail on display at National Library', without inverted commas and stated in a matter-of-fact way that the cup had been brought to Britain by Joseph of Arimathea.[40] Professor Bowen's address – by way of contrast – made no mention of the Holy Grail story.

The Antiquarians Visit Nanteos

On 19 August, ten days after the Aberystwyth 700 exhibition had officially ended, a group from the Cardiganshire Antiquarians visited Nanteos Mansion. This field trip was part of their Annual General Meeting,[41] which ran from 13 to 20 August. The group were given a tour of the mansion by the antiquarian Douglas Hague and an audio recording was made of the occasion, which has survived.[42]

Douglas Bland Hague (1917–90) was a Birmingham-born antiquary. He had worked as a surveyor and briefly as an architect before being employed as an investigator at the Royal Commission on Ancient and Historical Monuments for Wales, which is based in Aberystwyth; he held this position for over three decades.[43] Although he worked in archaeology, he was not, strictly speaking, a qualified scientist. On the audio tape he describes himself rather self-effacingly as a 'minor civil servant' and while this may – strictly speaking – have been true, it does not do justice to his many talents. He was a pioneer in industrial archaeology, worked on archaeological digs, had a keen interest in lighthouses and was passionate about the preservation of nineteenth-century structures. He was at one time appointed to the Welsh Group of the Council for British Archaeology and was also involved with the Royal Archaeological Institute and the Victorian Society and became Vice-President of the Association for Industrial Archaeology in 1987.[44]

The audiotape of Hague's guided tour of Nanteos Mansion is interesting in terms of what is included and what is omitted. Having given a fairly long, rambling talk on the architectural features of the various rooms, Hague finally turned his attention to the Nanteos Cup. He reveals that he had seen the cup in the 1950s and had measured it and drawn a diagram of it that he had subsequently lost, having sent it off somewhere and had not had it returned. Hague also says that he 'knew exactly' what the Nanteos Cup was, bearing in mind that this was said *a week before* the 'examination by experts' took place.

He then recounts how Geoffrey Bliss had a replica of the Nanteos Cup made that was on display at the mansion and how the original was at that time in the National Library of Wales (although formally the Aberystwyth 700 exhibition had ended).

The audiotape monologue then jumps to Hague speaking about a completely different topic and no more is said about the cup.

The recording was made a matter of days before Hague was due to examine the Nanteos Cup, yet – sadly – there is no mention of the forthcoming examination on the tape.

When we made a formal enquiry at the Screen and Sound Archive, we were informed that the tape contained no splices or edits whatsoever, and the CD-R copy provided to us reproduced the entire content of the audiotape. However, the possibility was admitted that at some point prior to its being deposited at the archive, the content of the tape may have undergone some editing and it was likely that part of the recording had been omitted. In summary, we will never know what else Douglas Hague may or may not have said about his plan to examine the cup. We can be certain that one of the motives for borrowing the vessel was that he wanted to redraw the diagram that he originally produced (and subsequently lost) in the early 1950s and also that he wanted to identify the species of the wood.

Correspondence from Douglas Hague to Fred Stedman-Jones[45] seems to suggest that Elizabeth Mirylees was fully aware of Hague's desire to identify the wood and this was no spur-of-the-moment plan. Seven years prior to the examination, Hague had sent a photograph of the Nanteos Cup to a laboratory called Forest Products Research in the hope that they might identify the wood of the cup. It is obvious from the response that Hague had described the cup as a 'Mazer bowl', but the laboratory expert was unable to identify the wood except to say that it was a ring-porous hardwood.[46] Contrary to information on the World Wide Web and elsewhere, Hague was not a specialist in wood identification; neither was he a 'Commissioner' – his job title was 'Investigator' until the day he retired.[47]

Examination by Experts

Hague's examination of the Nanteos Cup most likely took place at the headquarters of the Royal Commission; at the time this was at Edleston House[48] in Queen's Road, Aberystwyth. This rather charming Victorian structure, complete with veranda, was built for a Dr Bonsall in 1898 as a private nursing home. Apparently, it was designed along the lines of a Spanish villa,[49] although Hague thought the place was more in the style of an American Colonial building.[50]

The only primary source we have found that documents what happened when the cup was examined by Hague and his experts is a three-page, manually typed report (NLW ex 720) held at the National Library of Wales. The Royal Commission for Ancient and Historical Monuments Wales holds a copy[51] of this report along with Hague's diagrams of the cup.[52] A date on the diagrams tells us when the measurements were taken: 26 August 1977 – five weeks before the university 'freshers' were due to arrive.[53] However, there is a second date on Hague's diagrams which tells us when they were delivered: 17 March 1985. Looking at the date on the report itself we find it to be 16 March 1985, and Hague deposited it at the National Library in the same month. This comes as a surprise; why had Hague waited nearly eight years to write up a three-page report?

The bulk of Hague's papers held by the National Library was donated posthumously and primarily concerns his passionate interest in lighthouses. This makes his report on the Nanteos Cup rather exceptional – one of only two documents deposited by Hague during his lifetime, the other being a handwritten Arthurian work called *In Arthur's Land – an Account of the Traditions and Antiquities Relating to Arthur and His Knights in South Wales and Monmouthshire* by Ada Mary Merry,[54] also styled *An Appendix to the Idyll's of the King and Lady C Guest's Mabinogion*. This work is an attempt to analyse the Arthur of history by examining various manuscript sources, but it is flawed and frequently cites the work of Iolo Morganwg, particularly the *Iolo Manuscripts*. Iolo has been called a forger by some experts; while this is perhaps an extreme accusation, his work has made it very difficult for modern researchers to separate fact from exaggeration. At the very least, the donation of this work to the National Library by Hague would indicate that he had an interest in Arthurian history.

Hague's Nanteos Cup report – like the audio tape – is notable not only for what it reveals, but also for what it conceals. The Hague document does not attempt to date the cup, apart from a brief statement by Hague that it is a 'late medieval mazer bowl'.[55] Hague mentions that he had difficulty in identifying the species of the timber himself because the patina had been damaged; this was the reason why Hague put together a team of experts to examine the cup – it had nothing to do with a desire to date the wood by some scientific means.

The experts were from the 'University' (a reference to the University College of Wales, Aberystwyth) and the Forestry Commission (which had its offices in Aberystwyth) but Hague does not name any of the individuals concerned. We know from correspondence with Fred Stedman-Jones that one of the university scientists was an amateur woodturner who frequently made bowls from ash, elm and wych elm.[56] According to the Hague document, the bowl was subjected to 'careful examination over two days',[57] during which the experts visually compared the bowl with modern bowls made of those three woods.[58] On the basis of this, they concluded that the bowl was made from wych-elm (*Ulmus glabra*). In short, Hague's account of what actually happened during the 'scientific' examination amounts to less than one sentence. Moreover, there is nothing whatsoever in Hague's report that describes an attempt to date the wood of the cup scientifically.

In order to obtain a better appreciation of what might have happened during this examination we searched for information on wood identification. We found pamphlets aimed at customers visiting furniture shops, books aimed at woodworkers and books with a more rigorous approach. From the latter[59] we learned that reliable wood identification depends upon being able to optically examine a clear view of the end grain at high magnification. The expert then must draw on his own knowledge and experience to identify the species of wood, perhaps aided by written information in the form of flowcharts or similar. Moreover, it is important to be able to view a clean cross section of the growth rings with as little disturbance to the cellular structure as possible. Microscopic examination is preferable because of the greater level of detail that this allows; otherwise a small, hand-held magnifying lens may be used. Either procedure would require the timber to be cut with a sharp blade. For microscopic examination, a tiny sliver of wood needs to be sliced off and placed under the microscope; sometimes a machine called a microtome is used for this purpose.

To prepare the wood for the microtome, various methods are used such as boiling the sample in water or softening the wood with hydrofluoric acid.[60] Even in the simpler case of examination with a hand-held magnifier, the wood still needs to be very carefully and cleanly sliced with a sharp blade in order to get a clear view of the end grain. Since Elizabeth Mirylees had expressly forbidden any procedures that would mark or damage the cup,[61] none of the above methods could have been employed without incurring her wrath.

We must conclude, therefore, that the circumstances of the optical examination were not ideal – the scientists were restricted by the terms and conditions under which the cup was loaned. Not only were the scientists unable to get a clean view of the end grain at high magnification, they were very restricted in terms of the wood samples available to compare it against. Moreover, if the surfaces of the cup were as badly damaged as Hague stated in his report,[62] they would have been further hindered in their attempts to view the end grain clearly. Success in optically identifying a timber species in this way also relies greatly upon the skill and experience of the experts doing the examination – we have no idea of the level of experience of the experts concerned.

There is no hint from the Hague document that any attempt was made to compare the Nanteos Cup against a sample of olive wood; this might at the very least have been a good idea, even if only to be able to say that the possibility had been eliminated.

Scientific Dating: The Shroud of Turin Versus the Nanteos Cup
By way of 'compare and contrast' we will briefly explore the dating of another famous holy relic and invite the reader to draw his or her own conclusions.

The Shroud of Turin is believed by some to be the burial cloth that wrapped the body of Jesus when he was laid in the tomb provided by Joseph of Arimathea following the Crucifixion. The shroud bears a folded front-and-back image, purportedly of the tortured and crucified Christ, which miraculously imprinted itself on the cloth at the moment of His Resurrection.

Back in the 1980s the decision was taken by the Holy See to allow the Turin Shroud to be scientifically dated. On 21 April 1988 at the Sacristy of Turin Cathedral, samples of the shroud were taken and sent to laboratories in Arizona, Oxford and Zurich. Samples of cloth from three other sources were also sent to each of the laboratories to act as controls. The samples were purged of contaminants and subjected to a process known as 'accelerator mass spectrometry'. The end result was a radiocarbon date for the shroud which placed it firmly in the medieval period. The whole process was properly documented, the paper was subjected to peer review, and the results were published in the science journal *Nature*.[63]

When we set out to investigate claims regarding the dating of the Nanteos Cup, the document produced by Douglas Hague (NLW ex 720) was the obvious starting point. It is quite obvious that this document was never considered a scientific report of any kind; neither does it name any of the scientists who examined the cup. In addition, NLW ex 720 gives no clue as to whether or not a report might have been published elsewhere. We conducted a thorough search but were unable to find any scientific report on the examination of 1977. By way of contrast, the report in *Nature* cited above was found by a simple electronic search in a very short space of time.

Although the science report on the dating of the shroud was later criticised, we can at least say that the science was documented. We know that the results were independently replicated, we know what controls were put in place and the methods used as well as who conducted the experiments. The paper was published in a reputable science journal and at least bears the stamp of identifiable scientific authority and accountability.

Can the same be said of the 1977 examination of the Nanteos Cup? Clearly not, but through a process of repetition combined with exaggeration and careless rephrasing – Chinese whispers we might say – many Internet commentators and authors of derivative histories have overplayed the 'scientific' nature of what took place in 1977. The effect has been to treat Hague's document as if it were the last word in scientific reporting, very often without having examined it at all.

The delay of nearly eight years between the examination of the cup and the writing up of the report may be explained fairly simply. Hague never initially intended to write a report but seems to have done so in response to correspondence that appeared in *Country Life* magazine in March 1985. A letter was published by a Mrs Lloyd Matthews to which Hague responded and which was published in the April edition.[64]

The Hollywood Film-star and the Waters of Plenty

Yet another interesting character now enters the story of the Nanteos Cup. Antoine Jean-Baptiste Marie Roger de Saint-Exupery (1900–44) was the author of *The Little Prince*, a children's novel which is now one of the best-selling books of all time, having been translated into over 230 languages.[65] The phenomenal success of the book was such that it spawned a number of adaptations and spin-offs. One of these was a book entitled *The Return of the Little Prince* written by Ysatis De Saint-Simone (b. 1945), a niece of Antoine de Saint-Exupery's wife Consuelo (1901–79).

Ysatis De Saint-Simone had a successful career as an actress on stage and screen, including some film and television roles. Her on-screen name was Malila Saint Duval and it was as such that she appeared in the 1970 film *Airport*, which featured Burt Lancaster, Dean Martin and George Kennedy. Ysatis also appeared in episodes of *Dragnet 1967*, *Bonanza* as well as the 1977 western *The Great Gundown*[66] and a 1973 Wide World of Mystery adaptation of *Frankenstein*.[67]

A profound near-death experience following an accident transformed her life, and she started taking an interest in oriental spiritual training. She also took an interest in the Holy Grail and in 1985 found herself led to the Mirylees' Herefordshire residence. In April 2006, a month before the release of Ron Howard's movie adaptation of Dan Brown's bestseller *The Da Vinci Code*, Ysatis issued a press release[68] to the world. This statement was a protest over the *Da Vinci Code* movie, and she urged people to boycott the film. However, Ysatis also took the opportunity to reveal the 'most likely' Holy Grail to the world – the Nanteos Cup.

It seems that during her visit to the Mirylees residence she had witnessed a physically impossible – in other words miraculous – event. Elizabeth Mirylees placed the Nanteos Cup inside the glass bowl and poured water over it; she then poured the water into several bottles for Ysatis and her friends to take away. According to the account by Ysatis[69] this all happened without Betty having refilled the bowl once – as if the cup was conjuring endless amounts of water out of nowhere. If the account by Ysatis is accurate, then here we have a phenomenon beyond all rational comprehension. Ysatis also reproduced a letter by Fiona Mirylees (although her name was removed) which clearly suggests that Fiona was a witness to this strange occurrence. We can confirm from private correspondence[70] that Fiona mentioned the extraordinary event to Fred Stedman-Jones in 2001, thus entering it firmly into the growing corpus of legends surrounding the cup.

A Brief Word about Dowsing

We are about to introduce two more extraordinary characters into the story, both of whom practised the mysterious art of dowsing, or water-divining. In order to make the following sections comprehensible, we must first explain something of this ancient craft.

Dowsing is a form of divination used for locating water, minerals and many other things, tangible and intangible. It typically involves the use of a hand-held device such as a rod or pendulum. During the later Middle Ages, dowsing was used for mining for ore in the Erzgebirge in Central Europe. The first written European reference to the art dates to 1546, in a book called *De Re Metallica* by a German physician called Georgius Agricola.

Although many people associate dowsing with water-divining, historically it was associated with the hunt for minerals and today it is used for a much wider variety of purposes. The earliest known articles linking ancient sacred sites to dowsed underground water date to the 1930s; French dowsers Louis Merle and Charles Diot made the connection in 1933 and 1935 respectively. A British dowser called Captain Boothby also tentatively made the connection and later so did the one-time Keeper of the Department of British and Medieval Antiquities at the British Museum, Reginald Allender Smith.[71]

A talk given by Smith in 1939 influenced Guy Underwood, a barrister who spent much of his spare time investigating stone circles, standing stones, cathedrals and other ancient sites with his dowsing rod. He was a skilled artist and draughtsman, capable of surveying ancient sites and drawing accurate diagrams, showing how the 'water-lines' he detected by dowsing flowed through them. Although he wrote many of his papers in the 1950s, it wasn't until five years after his death that he became better known, thanks to the posthumous publication in 1969 of *The Pattern of the Past*.[72] His book has since become one of the best-known twentieth-century works on the subject of what has since been termed 'Earth Energy dowsing'.

Dowsers 'feel' and 'see' lines of energy within the earth, using senses that are nowadays usually neglected or passed over as fantasy. The 'lines' that Underwood found with his rod were almost always in groups of three. Each of the individual lines that made up a triple-band was of negligible width, so he termed these 'hair lines'. Groupings of triple-bands constituted the main patterns that he found. For example, a 'water-line' was a single triple-band, a 'track-line' was made of two triple-bands, whilst an 'aquastat' (sic) was two pairs of triple-bands with a larger gap in the middle. Underwood found that many sacred places are built over what are known as 'blind springs'. A blind spring occurs when underground water, rising vertically under pressure, hits an impermeable layer of rock. The water then escapes outwards through whatever fissures are available. The dowser should sense this as individual streams spreading out in different directions, emerging from a single point. In addition to this, the blind spring has its own characteristic 'energy signature', which is usually perceived as being in the form of a spiral, centred on the blind spring. This spiralling energy Underwood classifies in a number of different ways and it is a very prevalent feature in the sites he listed as examples.

The spiral is a two-dimensional representation of the vortex which is commonly observable in Nature (whirlpools, eddies, etc.) and more recent dowsers such as Billy Gawn have suggested that some dowsed spirals may actually be vortices.[73] The spiral was widely used as a pattern in Celtic and pre-Celtic art. The magnificent West entrance to Strata Florida includes several spiralling forms on the arch mouldings.

The discovery of this link between blind springs and ancient sites is attributed to Reginald Allender Smith,[74] but Underwood added his belief that the altars and spires of churches, abbeys and cathedrals were also deliberately positioned over blind springs.[75]

Michael Poynder

Around the same time that Ysatis De Saint-Simone paid a visit to the cup at its new home on the Welsh border, another New Age author also came to call. Born in London of Anglo-Irish parents, Michael Poynder lived for much of his life near Carrowkeel Mountain in County Sligo.[76] He attended Wellington College and the Royal Military Academy, Sandhurst, before being commissioned into the 7th Queen's Own Hussars. He had a fascination for gemstones, which he studied for over thirty years, and opened shops in London selling silver and jewellery. He wrote *The Price Guide to Jewellery* for the Antique Collector's Club of Great Britain.[77]

Poynder had a middle-class Christian upbringing, his parents being of traditional Protestant stock. His father had ancestry from the Clapham Sect,[78] Church of England moral and social activists in the early 1800s. He eventually moved away from his conventional Christian roots after he discovered that many of the Christian 'truths' he had held to in his youth had no biblical source and were the result of Pagan concepts having been assimilated into Christianity. One turning point (which he described as 'a pretty shattering event in my life')[79] was the discovery that the traditional date of Christmas –25 December – is not mentioned in the Bible and has more to do with the Winter Solstice celebrations of Pagan tradition and the birthday of the Roman god Mithras.

Rather than throw out Christianity completely, Poynder began to investigate it and relate it to other faiths and cultures, specifically those that pre-dated its foundation. He took on board New Age concepts, practised meditation and dowsing and took an interest in the Indian guru Sri Sathya Sai (also known as Sai Baba). He also became a landscape painter, poet and a spiritual healer.

One of Poynder's books, *The Lost Magic of Christianity*, is of particular interest because it devotes space to Strata Florida Abbey and the Nanteos Cup. It was written sometime after his mid-1980s visit and contains a photograph and sketch of the cup, both of which he produced himself.

The book presents us with a blend of New Age ideas including Sacred Geometry, chakras, earth energies, dowsing, landscape figures and 'Earth Stars'. We are given alternative historical accounts, but the references and bibliography are less than comprehensive, so it is not always possible to say where these accounts come from. Poynder's version of Celtic Christianity he conceived of as having been compatible with Druidism[80] and as such would not have been recognized by someone like Revd Lionel Lewis. Poynder also believed – with Holger Kersten[81] – that Jesus survived the Crucifixion. However, whereas Jesus and Thomas Didymus (we are told) disappeared into India, his closest followers came instead to Britain.[82]

His account of the tale of the Nanteos Cup is based on the familiar 'Holy Grail' version but with some notable deviations. For many Christians the appeal of the Nanteos Cup on a symbolic level is in its simplicity. It has none of the ostentatious pomp of most of the other Grail claimants and is emblematic of the humility of the man they call Saviour – this explains its appeal to Poynder.

The account[83] begins with the Last Supper and we are told that Christ and his followers used vessels made from olive wood. The cup is blessed by Jesus and used to catch his blood after the Crucifixion, as per the more standard versions. Poynder rejected vessels such as the Valencia Chalice as being a reflection of the decadence of the late Roman empire. The Glastonbury Grails are also thrown out as being too dissimilar to the kind of vessels that Poynder thought Christ might have used.

The story continues with Joseph of Arimathea and his followers arriving in Britain in AD 36 and settling in Glastonbury, where the first church was built of wattle and daub. The cup, we are told, was kept at Glastonbury Abbey until the time of the Dissolution of the Monasteries. In a later edition, Poynder changed his mind and said that Joseph had built the first Christian church in Glamorgan in South Wales;[84] he blamed the medieval monks at Glastonbury for transposing the location in the tale.[85] No further evidence for this has come to light.

Henry VIII is cast as a descendant from the tribe of Judah and keeper of an ancient esoteric tradition. Henry, we are told, was under threat from the burgeoning materialistic power of the Catholic Church. This, Poynder believed, was the real reason for the dissolution – the power of the monarch was being undermined. Poynder saw the birth of the Anglican Church as an attempt to reinstitute the original Celtic Church, which he saw as being 'a church of simplicity in its dogma and practices'.[86]

In Poynder's account, with Glastonbury under threat of being sacked, three monks carried the cup from Glastonbury to Strata Florida (instead of the more usual seven). We are told that the Nanteos Cup was called 'St. Mary's Dowry' – whereas this is more usually a reference to England. The cup was kept at 'Saint Mary's Abbey' (Strata Florida) until a message was received that the place was about to be attacked. The monks from Strata Florida initially set off for Mellifont Abbey in County Meath – this detail is (as far as we can tell) original to Poynder's account, although some later versions have borrowed it. Instead of going to Ireland as planned, the monks sought refuge with a 'Catholic family' called the Powells at 'Nanteous[87] Abbey' (sic). Time passed and the last monk passed guardianship of the cup to 'the head Powell', who was to guard it 'until the Church shall claim her own'.[88]

Poynder had visited the cup's guardian and taken photographs of the cup for inclusion in his book, but was sworn to secrecy as to its location. He revealed that it was a series of 'unusual coincidences' over a period of two years that led him ultimately to go and see the cup. One of these events was a request for him to dowse at Strata Florida Abbey. He subsequently drew up his findings and these are illustrated in his book.[89]

His 'water-courses' in some ways seem to bear some relation to the geometry of the building he is dowsing; the same might be said for other diagrams in the book dealing with other abbeys and cathedrals that he had also dowsed.[90] His diagram of Strata Florida has a waterline heading up the nave towards the mysterious feature in the monks' quire which he describes as a 'running water font'.[91] This feature serves as a point of convergence for waterlines spreading out to the transepts and the presbytery and beyond the walls of the building. It is worth comparing the diagrams drawn by Poynder with the illustrations produced by Guy Underwood in *The Pattern of the Past*, especially those of Westminster Abbey and Salisbury Cathedral;[92] there are certainly points of commonality to be found. Poynder also agreed with Underwood in his belief that the patterns that he found dictated the location and geometry of the religious structures built above them. Underwood tells us that medieval churches and cathedrals were 'sited and designed according to geodetic formulae of remarkable uniformity'.[93] Some critics of Underwood suggested that the patterns he detected were more to do with the influence of the stones or stone structures around which he dowsed.[94]

As noted by Poynder, Strata Florida sits near the heart of a confluence of streams with names like Afon Glasffrwd, Afon Mwyro, Nant Egnant and Nant Rhydol. The streams have their source in the mountains to the east and meander down, merging until they feed into the River Teifi. Poynder envisaged in this landscape a gigantic humanesque figure which he termed a 'landscape angel'. The streams and rivers became the blood vessels of this angel, like the 'meridians' of oriental acupuncture. This giant figure, Poynder felt, could fit the landscape in one of two ways, either north-south or east-west. In the latter form, Strata Florida becomes the 'Solar Plexus chakra' at its centre. In similar fashion, Poynder also envisaged a regular six-pointed star or hexagram hidden in the landscape, its edges and encompassing circle marked by cairns, standing stones and other significant sites. This he labelled an 'Earth Star', centred on the cairns at Blaen Glasffrwd. The waters from this place flow past Strata Florida which is close to one of the edges that make up the star.

Poynder asserts that the Cistercians knew the secrets of Sacred Geometry and applied this knowledge when constructing their own abbey churches. One of the frequently occurring proportions in Sacred Geometry is known as the Golden Ratio, or Divine Proportion. This is an irrational number that is most often represented by the Greek letter φ (phi) and is sometimes known as the Golden Mean. The value of φ can be calculated using the following formula:

$$\phi = \frac{\sqrt{5} + 1}{2} = 1.618033988...$$

This rather special number may be found in the geometry of regular geometrical forms such as the pentagram and the Platonic solids. It is frequently linked to aesthetic beauty and occurs throughout nature.[95] Poynder's book has a diagram of the Western Arch that incorporates a figure from Sacred Geometry. This figure consists of two interlacing circles of equal size which overlap in such a way that the perimeter of one cuts through the centre of the other. The length/width ratio of these two combined circles is thus 3/2 or 1.5. The two interlacing circles are represented as fitting exactly in the doorway gap of the Western Arch.

According to a survey of 1887 by Telfer Smith,[96] the archway gap is actually 16 feet high by 9 feet 8 inches wide. The height/width ratio of this gives a value of 1.6551, which is slightly more than the true value of φ – the Golden Ratio. Thus, Poynder's diagram is inaccurate but it seems that the Golden Ratio may indeed have been intended for the dimensions of the archway gap. Working from a good photograph (though perhaps this was not entirely scientific) we found that it was relatively easy to superimpose geometry on this grand doorway in such a way that the open space fitted snugly within the bounds of a Golden Rectangle.

Poynder relates his geometrical discovery to 'Equinox Easter Sunrise', by which he must mean sunrise at the vernal equinox. He seems to have assumed that the sun would rise directly behind the altar at the equinox, which at Strata Florida is not true. To begin with, Strata Florida is off due east by around 5 degrees. At the equinox, the sun rises due east, but this only holds true if the horizon is flat. If there is a hill on the horizon the sunrise position is shifted around to the south because the sun moves clockwise towards the south as it rises. At the vernal equinox, from the perspective of someone outside the west door looking in – or even from the monks' quire – no *direct* sunlight would have been seen through the windows behind the altar. If the sunrise at Strata Florida had any significance for the monks, it would have been at the time of year when it *really did* pass behind the east windows, during the months of August and early September. There are many holy days in the Catholic Christian calendar, and one potential candidate might have been the feast day of Saint Bernard of Clairvaux – 20 August. As someone who had special importance for the Cistercians, perhaps his feast day might have been marked in some special way at Strata Florida?

Laurence Main – Druidical History

Poynder's book had an influence on other seekers of the Nanteos Cup including the author, rambler, dowser, ley-hunter and druid, Laurence Main. He was born in Oxford and graduated with a degree in History from Oxford University in 1973. Main has worked as a teacher and as a writer of over fifty books, many of them walking guides. He has travelled extensively by foot over hundreds of miles. In 2004, he walked over 1,400 miles from Callanish stone circle in Scotland to London via Carn Ingli and St David's. Main has spent over a thousand nights on top of Carn Ingli in the Preseli Hills of West Wales with the aim of attaining knowledge through dreams. He combines his rambling activities with dowsing, especially for leys, which he refers to as 'Spirit Paths'.

He has been on the council of the Vegan Society, chaired the council of British Druid Orders in 2001, and was formerly on the committee of the Society of Ley Hunters but subsequently departed to form the 'Network of Ley-Hunters'[97] in 2011. He appeared on radio and television as an expert on leys and Arthurian topics, notably with Colin Morgan and Bradley James (actors from the BBC/Shine production *Merlin*) on a BBC documentary called 'The Real Merlin and Arthur'.[98] He believes himself to be the reincarnation of Derfel Gadarn, who according to Welsh tradition[99] was one of the survivors of King Arthur's final battle – Camlann. He moved to Dinas Mawddwy in 1981 and soon came to identify the area as having been the site of Camlann.[100]

Main has investigated leys at Strata Florida, including one that was discovered by the folklorist who went by the name of 'Llowarch'. This particular ley was described[101] as running between Strata Florida Abbey and the parish church of Llanilar, crossing en route the tree under which the Welsh bard Dafydd ap Gwilym is said to be buried, a motte near the River Meurig, a hillside on which stands the fort of Ystrad Meurig, and another hill fort above Llanilar. Main dowsed three leys coming from different parts of the abbey, all of which crossed at the famous yew tree.[102]

Main has his own, very different account of the Nanteos Cup, based on dreams and other psychic experiences. This led him to believe that the Nanteos Cup was the Grail of the Last Supper of Christ, kept at Chalice Well in Glastonbury by nine maidens[103] and subsequently moved from Glastonbury after the battle of Camlann in the sixth century to 'the Strata Florida area of Ceredigion'.[104] This proposed early date for the removal of the Grail from Glastonbury is employed to explain away the absence of written evidence for the Grail at the abbey and circumvent the problem with the idea of the cup having been removed at the time of the Dissolution.[105]

Most of this is derived from a poem known as *Prieddeu Annwfyn*, attributed to the sixth-century bard Taliesin, but only surviving in a ninth-century MS, which describes Arthur and his men sailing in search of a cauldron 'warmed by the breath of nine maidens'.

Strata Florida Abbey was not built until the twelfth century, but Main took the existence of an early Celtic gravestone, situated at the east end of the church adjacent to the abbey, as evidence that a sacred site existed there during the sixth century.[106]

The cross itself may not date to the sixth century, but it is early medieval and certainly pre-dates the foundation of the Cistercian Abbey. Similar crosses have been found on Caldey Island and Llanfihangel Croesfeini Chapel.[107] The evidence from John Leland of thirty-nine yew trees in the cemetery is taken as further evidence that there was an ancient sacred site at the location:[108]

The chirch of Strateflere is larg, side ilid and crosse ilid. By is a large cloyster, the fratry and infirmitori be now mere ruines.

The coemiteri wherin the cunteri about doth buri is veri large, and meanely waullid with stoone. In it be xxxix. great hue trees.[109] [sic]

The cup, according to Laurence, was carried not by monks but by three 'warrior saints', one of whom was Main's former incarnation – Derfel.[110] The company of Derfel had brought the cup – without knowing its true significance – to a well said to be not far from where the ruin of Strata Florida now stands. It is interesting to note that Laurence subsequently discovered an ancient well, deep in the woods on a hillside above the abbey.[111] George Eyre Evans may have referred to this place:

Turn sharp to the right at the gate of the Abbey Church and follow the lane as it wends its way up the valley, with Glasffrwd, i.e. Blue Brook – babbling over its rocky course, on the right. Here you are at once in the heart of the country: – 'Alone with the Alone,' sky, water, mountains, trees, rocks and birds. The monks knew well the value of this spot, here were – nay, still are – their wells of healing waters, – iron, sulphur, chalybeate – used with benefit by the natives to-day. What more truly romantic spot can be imagined or desired than that round 'Ffynnon dyffryn tawel,' the Well of the silent grove?[112]

As with Poynder, Main emphasises the secrecy surrounding the whereabouts of the Nanteos Cup. According to his own account he was taken to see it by being driven in a number of cars, switching between one car and the next at isolated spots, to avoid being followed.[113] It was during this visit to see the cup that Laurence was shown Michael Poynder's *The Lost Magic of Christianity* and learned of the 'landscape angel', although he had intuitively felt that it must be there. Possibly the best-known New Age landscape figures are those of Katherine Maltwood's Glastonbury Zodiac. More recently, the artist Graham K. Griffiths envisaged the entire map of Britain and Ireland as being a terrestrial representation of the zodiacal signs.[114]

One difference between Maltwood's vision and these later landscape figures is that in her work, rivers and streams often delineate the boundaries of the figures[115] concerned, whereas in the works of Poynder and Griffiths the rivers are the very lifeblood of the being in question, or sometimes correspond to other bodily features. In Griffiths' zodiac, the River Dyfi becomes the womb of Virgo or Ceridwen, from whence the bard Taliesin was born.[116] It flows through Dinas Mawddwy, past his proposed site of Camlann, so that King Arthur's last battle took place at a sacred site. Main's work is influenced by both of these terrestrial zodiacs and for him they are expressions of the living landscape or Goddess. As with Poynder's 'lost' Christianity, Christian mythology, neo-druidism and New Age ideas all rub shoulders.

Replicas

We know that replicas were made of the Nanteos Cup. One was used in Margaret Powell's time to act as a decoy to confuse potential thieves; Richard Rees of Rhoserchan Isaf, Capel Seion, made this particular replica.[117] Geoffrey Bliss, who bought Nanteos Mansion in 1967, had a replica made as a tourist attraction, which sat under a glass dome. When Douglas Hague asked him about it, Mr Bliss responded that he had gotten 'the gypsy boy' to make it by working from a photograph.[118]

There was a rumour that Geoffrey Bliss had asked a local woodcarver to make a dozen copies of the Nanteos Cup based – so the story goes – on the original, which Geoffrey had somehow obtained. The woodcarver left it on his bench, where later on some children were playing and knocked it into a bin full of wood shavings which were then thrown out and burnt! If the story were true, then the original Nanteos Cup would have been destroyed in the 1960s![119]

In 2004, replicas of the Nanteos Cup were sold on Ebay.[120] These reproductions were cast in resin, based on an 'original' made from wood. These duplicates resembled the cup as it is today, with more than half of it missing and standing on a small rounded platform bearing Bligh Bond's design for the lid of Chalice Well in Glastonbury. Also available from the same seller was a reproduction of Arthur's burial cross. Today there are still many replica 'grails' for sale on the web, but most of these seem to be based on the 'Grail' either from the *Monty Python and the Holy Grail* movie or on the prop used for *Indiana Jones and the Last Crusade*.

When the Nanteos Cup was stolen in 2014 many newspaper reports used a photograph purportedly of the cup. We believe that this image shows a replica and not the real thing. Behind this cup it is just possible to make out part of the coat of arms of the Powells and we believe that the image is of the replica used by the late Revd Peter Scothern (birth name Peter Griffiths) for his 'A.D. 37' exhibition. The small cabinet in which the replica was placed had the Powell coat of arms stuck on the inside.

The 'A.D. 37' exhibition, the name of which was chosen from the supposed date on which Joseph of Arimathea arrived in Britain to found the first Christian church, first took place in Gloucestershire in 2012, and toured for a number of years. The Scothern/Griffiths connection with the Nanteos Cup is explored below.

Further replicas appear on eBay from time to time. Fans of Spielberg's *Indiana Jones and the Last Crusade* have produced replicas of both the 'Grail Diary' that appeared in the film and the cup itself. Since, in the movie, we only see a handful of the pages from the book, these creative fans have used their imaginations to fill the rest of their replica diaries with Grail-related information written in the style of Sean Connery's character, Dr Henry Jones. Some of these replicas have included pages about the Nanteos Cup, even though it was not in Spielberg's original. Nor is it true to say that the line 'that's the cup of a carpenter' had anything to do with the Nanteos Cup – John Matthews spoke to the film's producer, Robert Watts, on this matter and Watts denied the possibility in the strongest terms.[121] It has been pointed out several times that wood was not used for drinking vessels in Jewish tradition.

Adrian Wagner, Grail Composer

We have already discussed Richard Wagner – the famous German composer whose Grail opera *Parsifal* was said to have been inspired by the sight of the Nanteos Cup during a visit to Wales in the mid-nineteenth century, and have established that this story is almost certainly a myth – though a very powerful one. There are many people who still believe it today, and one who stated his belief in the story was the late Adrian Wagner (1952–2018), the great-great-grandson of Richard Wagner himself. Like his famous ancestor, Adrian Wagner was a composer and a musical innovator – he invented the world's first portable synthesizer, known as 'the Wasp'. He was also a music producer and worked with famous rock musicians such as Arthur Brown and Robert Calvert;[122] his music has been used to accompany books written by Laurence Gardner, author of *Bloodline of the Holy Grail: The Hidden Lineage of Jesus Revealed*.[123]

Adrian composed works for film and television, but two particular works from the 1990s should concern us in particular. The first of these is a recording called 'Sought and Found' which is a reading (by Tim Bowley) of the story by Ethelwyn Mary Amery[124] with music taken from parts of albums by Adrian Wagner.[125] Another of these albums was called 'The Holy Spirit and the Holy Grail'.

Adrian Wagner was influenced by Baigent, Leigh and Lincoln's *The Holy Blood and the Holy Grail*, which linked the Grail to the person of Mary Magdalene and to the village of Rennes-le-Chateau. This book had suggested that Adrian's ancestor, Richard Wagner, had visited Rennes-le-Chateau immediately prior to writing his Grail opera, *Parsifal*.[126] The parallels with the story of Richard Wagner's supposed visit to see the Welsh Grail at Nanteos (also supposedly prior to writing *Parsifal*) are fairly obvious and to Adrian they were striking because he came across the passage in *The Holy Blood and the Holy Grail* not long after his family had moved to a new home not far from Nanteos mansion. Adrian expressed his views in an essay entitled 'The Feminine Element in Mankind',[127] in which he cites passages from the Dead Sea Scrolls and the Gnostic Gospels and argues in favour of a kind of Christianity more inclusive of women, and which offered greater equality between the sexes. This, we are told, should be echoed by a mystical rebalancing within our own souls through the study of music and art. Adrian's essay bears the same title as a fragment written by his ancestor Richard Wagner; it was incomplete because the great composer died as he was writing it – the pen slipped from his fingers as he wrote the phrase '*Liebe Tragik*', meaning 'tragic love'.[128]

Rosemary Kingsland and the Grail of Caldey Island

As we have seen, in spite of the relative secrecy surrounding the whereabouts of the cup after its departure from Aberystwyth, some people seem to have found it with comparative ease. Another quester looking for the cup was the filmmaker and journalist from

Cenarth, Rosemary Kingsland. She did not discover the whereabouts of the cup in time for her intended purpose, which was a TV series called *Treasure Islands* on which she was credited as the writer.[129]

The deadline for including the cup in the programme had expired; in spite of this, Rosemary publicised her quest in the *Cambrian News* as a bit of exposure for the show.[130] The article was so riddled with factual errors that it is little wonder that she had trouble tracking down the cup! A couple of well-meaning readers wrote in correcting her errors and encouraging her to 'Talk to the local people.'[131] Neither of these addressed the most original assertion in the article, which was that the cup had been taken to the Benedictine abbey on Caldey Island, before it was transferred to Strata Florida.

This supposed link with Caldey is surprising and is not supported by the earlier sources that emanated from Nanteos. We did, however, find an allusion to this Caldey Grail tradition in a poem entitled *The Elate Island* by Raymond Garlick, dating to the 1950s and dedicated to the 'Prior and monks of Caldey':

> Seven saints looked here for heaven and lit a fire
> that warmed all Wales. Then monks built up a byre
> for beasts and praised God in a Norman choir,
>
> and hid the Glastonbury treasure-trove
> in some oblique and satin-sanded cove
> or lost green grotto, and the island wove[132]

The poet Arthur Glyn Prys-Jones (1888–1987), who knew Raymond Garlick, wrote a poem called 'A Song of Caldey' which was also dedicated to the monks of the abbey and which also mentioned the Grail: 'And on Caldey men have sought the Grail/and seen it in the West/Shining like the isles of sunset/where the heroes are at rest'.[133]

How did Caldey become connected with the Grail? Hundreds of authors have speculated about the location of the Isle of Avalon and often 'holy' islands become candidates. The important British Saint Illtud is supposed to have had a hermitage[134] on Caldey and a thirteenth-century church still stands, which is dedicated to him. Many websites and books cite a Welsh 'legend' in which Saint Illtud is described as one of three keepers of the Holy Grail. The source of this legend is most likely a Welsh triad, which says that Peredur and Cadawc fab Gwynlliw were the other two. However, this triad is from the so-called 'third series' of triads penned by the forger Iolo Morgannwg in the eighteenth century.[135] Caldey Island is situated off the West Wales Pembrokeshire coast, so it would have been a small step to connect Caldey to the Nanteos Cup legend, being sufficiently en route for monks travelling from the south-west of England. After Margaret Powell died in 1951, some suggested that the cup be handed to the monks on Caldey[136] – perhaps this might have been viewed by some as a return journey.

Reverend Peter Scothern/Griffiths and the Prayer Cloths
Back in 1997 a television celebrity priest by the name of Revd Lionel Fanthorpe hosted a bizarre late-night show called *Fortean TV*. One episode featured the Nanteos Cup and one of the guests was the Revd Peter Griffiths – better known by his adopted name, Revd Peter Scothern – who died in 2019.

Peter Scothern was a globetrotting fundamentalist evangelical preacher with strong British Israelite beliefs. He had an unshakable faith in the healing power of the Nanteos Cup and lent credence to its identity as the Chalice of the Last Supper of Christ on earth.

The literature circulated at the time of his continuing exhibition 'AD 37' was yet another rehash of the stories dating back to Ethelwyn Amery and Margaret Powell:

> When Joseph arrived in AD 37, he brought with him the Cup of the Last Supper [Holy Grail] and it is thought that it remained in the keeping of the Church in this locality. During the persecution of the Church in 1370 AD, when the Monasteries were being destroyed, six Monks and the Prior fled to a small monastery in mid Wales called Strata Florida. Eventually the Monks died and only the Prior was left. When he reached the end of his life he was looked after in a nearby large house, which had belonged to the King Henry II. Before the Prior died, he showed the owners of the house a box containing the remains of the wooden Holy Grail and asked them to look after it until 'The Lord returns for his own'.

As ever, we hear again the voices of the usual suspects loud and clear in this version. Then comes a more personal story in which we are told how, in November 1990, Scothern/Griffiths, who was apparently ignorant of the story of the Grail, had a dream in which he was told that he would 'find the Holy Chalice'. Waking, he laughed out loud at this, but on returning to sleep had the exact same dream again. This time he heard the name Strata Florida, and as he had relatives living in Florida, USA, assumed it must be connected to them. Later, he found himself ministering in North Wales and his steps were led to the ruined abbey and the museum on the site. Something moved him to recount his dream to the curator who said, at the end: 'Look, I believe every word you say, and I believe that God has spoken to you in this way.'[137] He then told Peter about the Nanteos Cup that was believed to be the Holy Grail.

Having visited the cup's guardian, the Revd Griffiths procured a replica of the cup, and this was placed in a small cabinet, which had the Powell coat of arms on the inside. Even today, there are many who believe that this photograph shows the real Nanteos Cup, but when the cup was delivered recently to the National Library of Wales it was photographed from a variety of angles and none of them bear any resemblance to the cup in this image, which was probably found on the Internet.

Scothern was supplied by the cup's guardian with water poured from it, and he used the water to anoint small rectangular pieces of cloth, which were then posted to those in need of healing. The correspondence Scothern received as a result were nothing short of astonishing: the small prayer cloths anointed by water from the cup were apparently manifesting all manner of cures, including four men cured of leprosy.[138]

The testimonies from Scothern's correspondents may seem extraordinary, but they are on a par with claims made for many other wonder-working sources such as the healing springs at Lourdes. They cannot be explained by attribution to the Placebo Effect alone.[139]

In 1883, a board of physicians was set up to scientifically examine the claims of people who believed that the waters at Lourdes had cured them.[140] Known as the *Bureau des Constatations médicales*, or Lourdes Medical Bureau, it certainly seems to have provided documented cases where pilgrims taking the waters at Lourdes have experienced remarkable cures which are hitherto inexplicable by science. Writing in the 1920s, the head of the Bureau, Dr A. Marchand, commented:

> It is not difficult to understand the resistance that reason makes to the facts of Lourdes; it is easy to grasp, also, how difficult it is for the medical profession to reject knowledge acquired by study and experience. Tumours disappear in the piscine. Unhealed fractures of long standing suddenly unite. Wounds cicatrise in a second. Phthisical cavities suddenly dry up. Lesions of the optic nerve are radically cured. Such facts as these cannot be explained, for they are contrary to all medical experience.[141]

It is now much more difficult for a Lourdes healing to be declared as miraculous, thanks to more stringent conditions (known as the 'Lambertini criteria') and the process of examining claims can take years. There is no similar scientific process for the claims made by those who were sent prayer cloths by Scothern.

Fred Stedman-Jones

Fred Stedman-Jones – the man who inspired the book you are reading and whose initial researches have been used throughout – of course went in search of the cup. He eventually succeeded in locating it and as a result had the opportunity to hold it. A memorable occasion for Fred, it was on 4 September 1985 when he found his way to the home of the Grail on the Welsh Border and was greeted by Fiona Mirylees and her 'lovely little Pekingese pups'.

Fred was welcomed in and they they talked about the cup. Fiona told Fred that she didn't want Bob Danvers-Walker to know of her whereabouts, saying he had been 'over pushing' – an intriguing reference considering the extensive accounts generated by him concerning the cup. Fred discussed the photo of the cup which shows it resting on a history book, but Fiona believed that this was not of any particular significance and probably chosen at random from the shelves at Nanteos. According to Fred, she was intrigued to learn about Lionel Smithett Lewis, his visit to Nanteos and his attempt to recover an ancient text, supposedly describing the cup's legendary journey from Glastonbury.[142]

On that occasion Fiona did not strike Fred as being a particularly religious person, although she certainly believed in the healing power of the cup; for her this was more important than its historical provenance. Her own philosophy echoed that of her mother Betty: 'if it was made in Birmingham, so what. It heals.' When Fred asked about the prophecy 'until the church shall claim its own', Fiona responded, 'Which church?', again echoing the words of Betty Mirylees.[143]

Eventually, Fred was allowed to handle the cup. We report this experience in his own words:

> Approx. 3p.m. I handled the Nanteos Cup. It was quite cold, smaller than I expected – joints were neat. ... Rim pointed out – she said silver (stopped healing). I said everything about Cup is contradictory, often said to be gold. She doubted if they would have afforded gold! I commented there was an incised pattern on inside, she agreed, too little left to judge form.

Fred's handling of the Nanteos Cup left him with a subjective impression that many who have touched the vessel will recognise, but which few could express adequately in words – although Fred did try:

> I found the Cup more impressive than I expected, knowing it well from photographs. It seemed to have its own integrity(!), a quality of being something of significance (does one project this onto it? I somehow didn't feel I was doing this).

For a man who had made a fine academic study of the cup over a number of years and for whom the cup was something of an obsession, the opportunity of being able – at long last – to see and touch it was a joy:

> I was very happy to have seen and handled it – privileged. I thanked her [Fiona] for allowing me to do so – hoped I hadn't intruded – she said not at all, 'those that seek shall find.'[144]

Fred left the home of the Grail feeling 'greatly elated'. His obsession with the cup continued unabated and he became a recognised authority, called upon by documentary makers because of his unrivalled expertise.

Fred was the chairman of the Pendragon Society, a group dedicated to exploring all aspects of the Arthurian legends, and an article written by him on the cup[145] in the *Pendragon* journal resulted in correspondence with a television producer, Colin Thomas of Teliesyn productions. Eventually, a documentary called *In Pursuit of the Holy Grail* was shot in August 2001, with an international version and a Welsh version being made. Fred's interview appeared in the international version only; the hostess was Dr Marion Loeffler, an academic in the field of Celtic Studies.

In one of his emails to Teliesyn, Fred referred to 'the attempt made to brain me by the unseen inhabitants of Nanteos'.[146] This refers to an attack on Fred made by a 'supernatural' force! The incident occurred one morning in the kitchen at Nanteos, in the company of others involved in the making of the documentary who witnessed what happened – a heavy object came crashing down, nearly hitting Fred on the head. He was unhurt by the ghoulish assault but badly shaken and never returned to Nanteos.[147]

The Nanteos Cup in Fiction

Given the stories constellating around the cup, it is hardly surprising that a number of references have appeared in contemporary fiction. We have already seen[148] how Arthur Machen alluded to the Nanteos Cup in his fictional works such as *The Secret Glory*. In more recent times Dan Brown's novel *The Da Vinci Code* has reinvigorated an interest in the Holy Grail and has inspired some authors to make it the subject of their own works. Brown's *Da Vinci Code* is not a piece of romanticism with knights in shining armour on a sacred quest but a fast-paced 'page turner' brimming with murders, conspiracies, secret societies, cyphers and treasure. It presents an alternative view of the Grail, inspired by other, earlier books such as *The Holy Blood and the Holy Grail* by Michael Baigent, Richard Leigh and Henry Lincoln, in which the Holy Grail represents the 'bloodline' of Christ and the womb of Mary Magdalene, and *The Templar Revelation* by Lynn Picknett and Clive Prince, which suggests that the stories of the Grail contained coded references to the Johannite heresy.

Most of the recent 'grail' novels are contemporary adventures, such as the novels of Keith Fauscett with allusions to English 'Templars' in possession of the Holy Grail and characters who are willing to break into churches in search of it.[149] The theft of the Nanteos Cup is also a theme in *The Unbearable Lightness of Being in Aberystwyth* by Malcolm Pryce. This novel is set in a faux version of Aberystwyth and is a humorous spoof of Raymond Chandler's novels; it is part of the series that began with *Aberystwyth Mon Amour*.

The author Tom Davies had researched the cup for his novel *Fire in the Bay*, and again it becomes the subject of theft:

> There was still that strange perfume about it though. All this fuss had merely confirmed that the cup was very valuable indeed and, if he could get it out of here, he was going to make some real money out of it.[150]

Not all of the novels are set in contemporary times. *The Grail Murders* by Michael Clynes (Paul C. Doherty) is a sixteenth-century murder mystery in which the Grail is a simple wooden cup.[151] *Flight from Glastonbury* by D. H. Davies is set at the time of the Dissolution of the Monasteries and retells Margaret Powell's story of the seven monks from Glastonbury escaping to Wales with the Grail. The author asserts a family connection to the cup, stating that his grandfather made the box in which the cup was kept.[152]

Time and circumstance have conspired to keep the story alive, and today the Nanteos Cup is familiar to many more people than in its heyday as a healing vessel with miraculous powers. Inevitably, perhaps, it drew unwanted attention, resulting in yet another spectacular story, which broke in the spring of 2014.

Theft and Recovery

Life sometimes imitates art. The fictional works that have the cup stolen actually pre-dated the occasion when it was.

In the months prior to the theft, the amount of publicity surrounding the cup was on the increase. In January 2014 the *Yesterday* channel and presenter Jamie Theakston had visited Nanteos Mansion and Fiona Mirylees for a programme on the Holy Grail; but it aired the following November, months after the cup had been taken. Also in January, on the BBC's *One Show*, there was an interview with the well-known comedian and TV presenter Griff Rhys Jones, who was due to visit Nanteos Mansion in February to film a piece for a TV series called *A Great Welsh Adventure*. A few weeks later an article appeared in the *Cambrian News*[153] about the visit and a similarly themed piece appeared in *The Guardian* a few days later.[154] The Guardian reporter wrote that it was 'considered a cover story' that the cup was kept in a bank vault.[155] A TV show from 2010, featuring Simon Armitage, *The Making of King Arthur*, had shown Fiona Mirylees' face without any concealment and she was shown removing the cup – contained in a box and a green velvet bag – from a drawer in a chest.

The increased publicity surrounding the cup made it the ideal moment for Nanteos Hotel to engage in some promotion of their own. A 'Holy Grail Bus Tour' was arranged for 1 March (St David's Day) and was promoted widely. The Nanteos chef Nigel Jones went on BBC Radio Wales' Eleri Siôn show to discuss the mansion and the cup. At the beginning of July another piece appeared in the *Cambrian News* concerning Ian Pegler's quest to discover a copy of the script of Hugh Lunt's pageant play about the cup.[156] The theft of the Nanteos Cup occurred between one and two weeks later.[157]

The theft deeply affected all those who care about the cup, especially those closest to it. Fiona Mirylees expressed her distress in an interview for *Town and Country* magazine[158] some months later. The thief had entered her own home and taken something that was not just sacred to her but also a family heirloom. She had been involved with the cup from a very young age and assisted her mother when guests came to see it.[159]

Many reports stated that the cup was taken along with a blue velvet bag in which it was said to be kept. The cup was actually kept in a box with a sliding glass lid. The only velvet bag we know of that was associated with the cup was a large green bag which was used to contain the box; this bag was made by Diane Powell from Tucson, Arizona.[160]

The cup, at any rate, had gone. Announcements were made by West Mercia Police and on the BBC's *Crimewatch*. Some elements of the press seemed to find it amusing that the police were now on a 'quest for the Holy Grail' and syndicated news stories circulated worldwide. Rather irrelevant references were made to *Monty Python and the Holy Grail* and of course to *Indiana Jones and the Last Crusade*; at times it seemed that the human element of the story had been lost. Even more bizarre headlines appeared when the police raided a pub on the Welsh Border after a tip-off that someone had been drinking from the Nanteos Cup at the bar (a near physical impossibility). The raid proved fruitless, but the news stories spread around the world and the Wikipedia page for the Nanteos Cup was visited heavily for two days running.[161]

The hunt for the missing cup became part of Operation Icarus – an investigation set up by West Mercia Police aimed at retrieving religious artefacts stolen from churches and other religious buildings. Months passed with no sign of the cup; the offer of a £2,000 reward by the Mirylees family and West Mercia Police yielded no leads.

Then, on 11 June 2015 – nearly a year after the theft – an appeal was made on the BBC *Crimewatch Roadshow* (*Crimewatch Live* from 2021). At last progress was made. A number of phone calls led to a clandestine meeting 'on neutral ground' at a lay-by on a Welsh road. A shadowy figure appeared and handed over the cup, thankfully none the worse for its adventure in the hands of thieves who, at the time of writing, are still at large.

The cup had been retrieved but the male who handed it over was not arrested; the police were confident that he had not stolen it. The announcement of the recovery was made on the BBC *Crimewatch Roadshow* on 25 June 2015, with most news reports emerging the following day.

A New Home for the Cup

The return of the cup was a cause for great relief and joy for all those who cared about it; however, its future needed to be decided upon. Clearly, it needed to be stored in a more secure location. Thanks to the publicity both before and after the robbery, Fiona's cover had been completely blown; it was already a poorly kept secret even before that time. It would not have taken much detective work to trace her location.

Months passed with no word of the cup. Then in December 2015 it was leaked on the Internet that negotiations were ongoing with the National Library of Wales to rehouse the cup there.[162] This rumour turned out to be true, but another six months passed before the announcement was made official. A specially made burglar-proof display case was manufactured, along with illustrated boards detailing the cup's 'history'. The cup was placed in the case along with the glass bowl used to hold it and a few of the nineteenth-century receipts that recorded the loans.[163] The cup was already in place before the official announcement was made and a few weeks later, on 9 July 2016, there was an official opening event.

Immediately before the opening, Professor David Austin, chairman of the Strata Florida Trust, gave a talk entitled 'Strata Florida and Its Sacred Landscape: a Context for the Nanteos Cup'. It was divulged during this talk that the cup would be taken once a year to Strata Florida, where its traditions would be celebrated.

Professor Austin pointed out that Strata Florida, at 126 acres, was once possibly the largest monastic site in Britain. It must have been very culturally important to the Welsh as the place where Llewelyn the Great summoned the princes of Wales to swear allegiance to his son, and there must have been a reason for this being done there rather than anywhere else. The production of Welsh manuscripts at Strata Florida also points to the cultural importance of the place, as does the decidedly Celtic architecture on the beautiful Western Arch.

Professor Austin speculated that the strange architectural feature at the crossing of the church of Strata Florida was once an ancient holy well and that perhaps water used for healing was drawn from it using the Nanteos Cup. We were told that water from the River Glasffrwd was diverted through this holy well and out to the Teifi. Professor Austin mentioned that a similar feature to the Strata Florida holy well had been discovered at Landévennec Abbey in Brittany.

Regarding the cup, Professor Austin speculated on the possibility of performing spectrometry analysis on the foot, to see if it was ever encased in silver. The President of the National Library of Wales, Rhodri Glyn Thomas, officially opened the exhibition and different speakers, including Welsh Assembly member Elin Jones, made a variety of speeches. Fiona Mirylees was present with her sister Clementina. Fiona was presented with a framed photograph of the cup and said a few words; she expressed her desire for the healing tradition to continue and this was greeted with applause. A member of the library staff filmed the event for posterity.[164]

The cup is still formally the possession of the Mirylees family, but the National Library were very pleased to acquire it as a permanent exhibit. In a press release, Pedr ap Llwyd, Director of Collections and Public Programmes, said:

At last this much revered ancient relic has returned home to Ceredigion and Wales and placing it on permanent display will allow visitors to the Library to view this mysterious object. Whether the vessel is the Holy Grail or a piece of the True Cross or a communion cup which belonged at one time to the abbey at Strata Florida Abbey, visitors have to decide the truth for themselves. This is truly a remarkable object and a very interesting addition to the National collections. We are grateful to the Mirylees family for entrusting the safekeeping of the Cup to the National Library.[165]

Large banners were manufactured and placed around the town of Aberystwyth – the photo used was one taken[166] in 1904 by Robert Smith, the draper from Harrow whose visit with the British Chautauquans and magic lantern show we discussed in Chapter 4. Reports on the exhibition appeared on the BBC Wales News[167] and in the *Cambrian News*.[168]

Magnificent photographs were taken of the cup and the cup's Wikipedia page was updated, displaying it in glorious colour, for all the world to see. [Plates 1–4]

On 16 July 2017, as part of a celebratory event, the cup was taken to Strata Florida Abbey where it was displayed in a glass case (closely watched by two security guards). On the same day a special service led by Father Brendan O'Malley (a former Cistercian monk) took place to consecrate the 'holy well' at the heart of the abbey church. Two Mirylees sisters, Fiona and Clementina, were also present and a number of attendees were in medieval costume.

The cup returned to Strata Florida a few weeks later, when HRH Prince Charles was making his annual tour of Wales. The Prince, accompanied by Prof. David Austin, was told about the history of the cup and was allowed to handle it with white-gloved hands.[169]

The Nanteos Grail now spends most of its time in its display case in the National Library and anyone can go and see it. Questions remain about the healing tradition, but the cup is at least safe and well looked after and accessible to the many rather than the few.

The long and complex history of the Nanteos Cup remains what must surely be seen as one of the most fascinating accounts concerning the evolution of a sacred relic. We have tried to uncover the many and various secrets surrounding the cup, and to trace some of the misunderstood accounts that have continued to be passed on to the present.

We have been able to posit a reasonable argument for its origins as a medieval mazer and have uncovered virtually every detail of the story that began to circulate from the nineteenth century onwards. The evidence we have uncovered concerning the origins of the Stedman family and its connection with the relic push back the history of the cup into a more satisfactory medieval period. The story of the journey from Glastonbury to Strata Florida and thence to Nanteos House remains mysterious – perhaps no more than legends seen in retrospect. Against this we must place the very real, and deeply felt, accounts of miraculous healings, and of the sometimes mystical experiences of those who have come into the presence of the cup.

This is not the place to question the validity, one way or the other, of such claims. Like many other such objects, some of which the authors have examined, it is better to say that none of these are 'the' Grail (assuming it to have existed at all) but that they may, in some sense, be seen as 'a' grail or grails, infused with power by the many thousands of believers who have stood before them.

To this end, we return to the story from the thirteenth-century romance of *Perlesvaus*, concerning the two young knights who, learning of a strange ruined castle that many years previously was believed to have held the Grail, set off to explore. They were gone for some time, and when they eventually returned, they were much changed. Asked what had happened to them they replied: 'Go where we went, and you will see.'

Perhaps we are all King Arthur's knights now, and must take up the quest for ourselves, following in the footsteps of earlier seekers. What we may find remains as mysterious as the ultimate origins of the wooden vessel known as the Nanteos Cup.

APPENDIX 1

'Hunangofiant Cwpan Nanteos' by Mary Jones, Translated by Anne Pegler

We include this curious document as an example of the kind of response elicited by the Nanteos Cup as recently as the early twentieth century. 'Hunangofiant Cwpan Nanteos' was written by Mary Jones of Pennant, in the voice of the cup itself. A Prize-winning essay at the National Eisteddfod at Aberystwyth in 1952, it was written in Welsh and is here translated for the first time into English by Ellen Anne Pegler.

*

It is interesting for an old holy relic like me to slip back from the tottering present days, to reminisce and remember the times that have been. It would seem that the experience of the old hymnist is also appropriate for me now: -

"More has already been spent
Than remains of this old wilderness"

As I meditate today on the past, many emotions and feelings frequent my heart. I have known better times when my condition was bright and lustrous. But if the glory of my previous times are past and I am now worn and broken, then I must seek comfort in the fact that for centuries I have sought to serve mankind – a sacred role in this world – a service of dignity. I know that many a weary soul suffering tribulation and affliction have had help and been boosted on their way.

It is true that I have lost my lustrous, glorious days but do not scorn me in my old days for the past spreads its enchanting wings around me.

I do not boast when I say that I shall still be known and talked about even when the rivers run dry as I possess this mysterious secret. I have had many experiences that have enriched my life, as I, too, have enriched the lives of many others.

Like civilization, I have travelled from east to west. I was formed from the wood of the olive tree by an able craftsman in the middle east. Some carpenter from Jerusalem ably created me with his saw and chisel. Perhaps these same strong arms carved strong wooden ploughs or perhaps the rafters for the roof of some important person's house, and I dare say many would have thought of me as being something quite insignificant in comparison.

But my Golden Hour came! – and I can quote the words of that notable donkey saying, "Idiots I too had my hour"! I had the privilege and honour of being used by The Saviour of the World as he shared The Last Supper in that Upper Room. I have never felt the same since that memorable night and even though it is now nigh two thousand years the mists of time have failed to dim my memories.

I remember well the long table in the room, and I remember the young man, the pure face, the grave and solemn appearance and the strong but gentle voice saying: -

"This is my Blood, do this
in Remembrance of me."

These words hooked on to my mind, echoing eternity, and time can never obliterate them. Each disciple, in turn, held and drank of me and I felt a great respect in their touch. This was a thrilling experience and I felt, in Joseph's words, that this was indeed "the gateway to Heaven".

Such delight, such bliss does not last. The company dispersed one by one and I was left alone in the upper room where they had eaten. After some time, a Jew came and picked me up and I was uneasy in his company. However, I did not have to worry for long as he presented me to a man by the name of Joseph of Arimathea as payment for his faithfulness over the years. Joseph was a Jewish counsellor, a secret disciple of Christ. I was instantly happy in his presence and he spent time setting me at my ease. Then he started on the long, narrow, lonely road leading to Calvary or Golgotha. The pain of seeing the man, who had drunk the wine held by me, hanging on the cross was like spears being hammered into my heart. Seeing the iron nails forced into his hands and feet and the crown of thorns on his forehead, then the throng shouting: "Crucify him".

No one on his own would have shouted – but the crowd together persisted. And each and every one was as guilty as the other.

I heard my master asking for the corpse but from the derision and mockery of the soldiers it was evident that they would not comply. Amidst the derisive laughter my master turned away.

Later, and in the company of a man named Nicodemus, one of the Jewish statesmen, Joseph turned into a shop to buy a white robe to wrap the body of Jesus in.

On their ponderous and sad return to Golgotha and in their distress, I noticed a thick mist and intense darkness befalling, not a sound anywhere, but I do believe I heard a soul sighing in intense distress.

They found the soldiers had disappeared on their return, so Joseph set about bringing down the body, gently washing it and wrapping it in the white robe, cleaning the lashings of the whip and the blood seeping from the wounds. Joseph remembered me and I had the honour of catching the sacred blood oozing from the body of Jesus Christ. As Moses of old I felt as if I was walking on Holy Ground. After anointing the body with myrrh and aloes, they interred the body in a tomb in the vicinity.

I remember nothing more until a huge crowd came and arrested Joseph, Nicodemus fleeing for his life, and Joseph in prison. Like Paul and Silas, I, too, was imprisoned and even though I can't say I liked the place, there for the first time, I came face to face with an angel. I heard him uttering comfortable words to my master, advising him to take care of me so that he would never want for anything.

We were there for a long time and at times I felt as if the darkness of the world was encircling me. But as the saying goes:

"The darker be the hour
The nearer we are to the dawn"

The hour of our freedom arrived. There were tools to knock down the prison tower – pickaxes and spades, axes and hammers, mallets, sledgehammers and crowbars. With our feet unfettered we were so pleased to see the Sun and daylight again. We had a long journey to make but before starting off, Joseph gathered together seventy-five disciples of Jesus to help him spread the gospel. Then we commenced on our journey in the direction of Bethany, a small village at the foothills of the Mount of Olives.

Soon they made for me a chest to keep me secure and I felt happier to be kept in this. Then I learnt that Josephus the son of Joseph who had taken such tender care of me, had been designated as my guardian to look after and keep me safe. On that journey I was able to heal and convert to Christianity many fellow travellers.

One day when Josephus was not actually on the spot, someone came along and lifted the lid of my chest and he was immediately blinded. Until that very day I had never realized the powers I possessed. But mercifully the angel returned and fully restored and healed the man who had lifted the lid of the chest.

Travelling in many foreign lands and deserts many trials and tribulations came upon us, but with gladness in our hearts my companions and I surmounted these trials unharmed. Following every woe, a new dawn broke and we realized that following every difficulty a new opportunity arose.

One day we landed in a country called Britain, and for a long period I spent my time in my chest in a place called Avalon [Somerset]. My masters one day prepared a feast as they wanted to see which and how many of the disciples were worthy of the work allocated to them. One scoundrel pushed himself forward and sat next to Joseph from where he started praising himself unceasingly and bragging of all the good works he had done. Quite soon, all present became somewhat bored with all this distasteful rhetoric and suddenly all became very dark within, with black clouds above (seeming like mourners in a funeral) and a deafening clap of thunder. When daylight reappeared, there was no sign of the rascal and the seat next to Joseph was empty.

One day I had the honour of accompanying my master on a journey to Scotland but alas there, to my great and absolute distress, my master, reaching the end of his travels, passed away.

His body was carried back amidst great heartbreak, to Avalon where it was buried. A distressing, heartbreaking day in my history.

I was then installed in a small church near to our cell, and many pilgrims and travellers came and paid tribute, in the words of the bard Alun:

"How many Ave, creeds and prayers
Were uttered amidst these walls?"

I heard that the knights of Arthur came searching for me, and it was said that Lancelot was amongst those blinded by my shining splendour. I can only say that it is the "Pure of Heart that see God".

Following this I spent a quiet period of time. It is said that such quiet times are important times in everyone's existence, making history possible. Life is barren and poor unless you have a quiet room to return to at times, to meditate and rebuild.

However, to break on my peaceful time a great disaster occurred where there had been only prayer and peace. In the history of the Church and the Abbey a great upheaval occurred – a great dispersal. By some great miracle I was carried safely away from Somerset across the mountains to Strata Florida – a Cistercian abbey in Ceredigion in Wales. You will see therefore that my life, like the rest of you, has been somewhat black and white.

I was happy in my new home from the beginning.

Strata Florida had set deep roots here. There was a quietness and peace here, a place for meditation and prayer set amongst the distant hills. I came to like the place for its silence and solitude – solitude and God near at hand. I developed a longing to stay here away from the world's noise and bustle.

In the nearby church close to the abbey was my Honourable Seat and on a quiet day I could hear the River Teifi murmuring its way to the sea. People from far and wide came flocking their way to come and see me, to fondle and cherish. The monks used me during their Communion Services and often they carried me to the sick beds of the poor in health as whomsoever drank out of me were cured of whatever illness. I never failed to complete this miraculous cure.

This for many was not enough as they took bites out of me, but this did not bother me. Oddly enough, no-one ever called for me until they had first tried all other remedies. Like the preacher, I was called upon by the nobility, the rich and the poor, the learned and the illiterate, the genial and the arrogant. I saw their facial expressions changing as they drank of me. Some glowing, the eyes of others shining and glistening. Some healing to their very depths.

Life at the abbey was familiar to me. From time to time many pilgrims called on their way from Bardsey to St. David's in Pembrokeshire. They believed that two pilgrimages to St. David's was equivalent to one to Rome. Many times I heard their footsteps through the field known as the Holy Gateway. Before leaving on their pilgrimage many went to the old yew tree in the nearby churchyard, where, it is said, lies buried the Welsh poet Dafydd ap Gwilym, then they visited the church to give their offerings to boost the Church's coffers.

By now the paths are grassed over again but I feel sure that pilgrims will once more be flocking to Strata Florida to see what remains of the noble abbey that guarded the hearts of the Welsh nation, and the graves of equally noble Welshmen. Perhaps also they might see on the Church wall a strange gravestone on which is inscribed in English the following:

> *"The left leg and part of the thigh of*
> *HENRY HUGHES, COOPER,*
> *was cut off and interred here*
> *June 18th, 1756"*

W. J. Gruffydd, the Welsh bard wrote:

> *Who was the one-legged cooper*
> *Knowing nothing but woe and pain*
> *Yielding his leg and his thigh*
> *To the earth, at Ystrad Fflur*

I too saw many noble funerals making their way towards the abbey, the monks endlessly persisting in their prayers, the prior, guests and visiting monks, each one with his fingers on his rosary. I remember their mantles of white, undyed wool.

Punctually, between midnight and one thirty, the Cistercians would come for their nightly service (or Matins). They would rise very early for the Prime, and late for the last service of the day – the Compline. I heard the quiet whispering of their Creed from dawn to dusk. There was the constant lighting of candles and the air was heavy with the aroma of candlewax.

The sound of the kissing from the shelter of the trees bothered them not, and they enjoyed Paradise without any daughter of Eve being anywhere near. There would be music and litany, devotion and sacrament; the sound of their sandals clap, clang back and forth, then a short break when they all took a few hours rest. There were times when they all feasted regally on shoals of fish and locally reared venison when important people and visitors were at Strata Florida.

Just like the monks at Strata Florida, there was to be no Eternal City, neither for them nor for me. Around the year 1536, the enemies from without came and there was to be no more peace and tranquility at the abbey. They rampaged, savaged, destroyed and stole everything. By 1539 Henry VIII with his destructive hand came and left Strata Florida in ruins, as he had all other abbeys in the country – like drunks on the wine.

By some miraculous deed I managed to escape from their vicious grasp, and I am to this day eternally gratefully for that. I know little of what happened to the treasures at the abbey. I heard that the parishioners claimed the bells and that they do indeed still ring at the tower of Tregaron church. Only a small handful of monks had survived at the abbey by this time and I know that seven of them escaped taking me with them.

We were given succour and shelter by the Lord Lieutenant of Vaenor in a mansion called Nanteos – one of the grand mansions in Ceredigion, which stood some three miles to the south-east of the town of Aberystwyth in the wooded valley called Paith.

I had many a pang of sorrow and distress after the loss of my friend the Abbot Richard Talley, but eventually, on seeing the gracious and kind face of my new guardian, a man by the name of Powell, I became happier and more settled with my lot. One by one as the old monks died, the last survivor handed me over to the care of Mr. Powell – as all the abbeys had disappeared by then.

Having told Mr. Powell all he knew of my history, he implored him to take care of me. Over the years Mr. Powell and his descendants took great care of me, treating me as a precious jewel.

I felt justly proud of my regal home even though it differed greatly to the old abbey. Magic and Romance seemed thickly embedded in the place, and every Christmas Day the talented old harpist Gruffydd Ifan came to play his harp. This he had done, apparently, for sixty-nine years. I enjoyed his playing very much.

Swinburne visited from time to time to meet up with his old friend George Powell and it is quite likely that this is where he wrote "The Garden of Prosperine". I met many other men of renown from time to time, men like Richard Wagner, Rossetti and Longfellow.

I was ensconced for safety in the library – far from the noise and bustle of the world and there, – there was nothing to disturb me save the monotonous tedium of the old clock, tick-tock! I was kept in a glass case, finely lined with silk.

Very often requests were made for me to visit the sick and I travelled far and wide within Ceredigion and far beyond. I'm pleased to say that I was able to do much goodness. Lest you should think that I brag and am just trying to boost my autobiography, take a trip to Nanteos where you will find dozens of letters, from far and wide, thanking them for the loan of me and for my healing powers.

It became customary for the borrowers to leave a pledge ensuring my safe return. A request came from as far afield as Monmouthshire and my master was somewhat reluctant for me to go so far. The pleading for help was such, and the offer of a pledge to leave his watch valued at seven pounds, he succumbed and let me go. On the journey, the man kept checking the bag for my safety. As his wife kept drinking water from me within days she was healed. I was carried back to Nanteos with more reverence and more famous than ever. I was so proud and pleased to have seen a wonderful smile on such a sad face.

Every year until 1862 there were regular and constant demands for my help. I carried on until 1865 but unfortunately, I started deteriorating because of the constant use I was put to. My body cracked and I was taken on a long journey to London to have a band put around me to try and prolong my life. This was a mistake – my healing powers disappeared completely. On my return to Nanteos the band was removed – the marks it left on me remain to this day. On its removal my healing powers (even though part of my body has broken off) are now fully restored.

I remember the year 1887. During May the Welsh harpist John Roberts was staying in Aberystwyth as he was about to give a concert there. He took a walk to Nanteos Mansion where he greatly admired the architecture and furnishings there. He arrived in the library where I was kept. He took one look at me and started laughing out loud. "This thing healing – what utter nonsense." I felt a cold shiver as he derided me, I was not accustomed to such ridicule. It is no good to measure life amidst disappointments so I kept my peace whilst feeling at the same time that things would be put to right, and so it came to be. On returning to Aberystwyth and taking to his bed for the night, he completely failed to sleep a wink. Conscience indeed has its teeth. He made his way back to Nanteos the following morning and implored the chief butler that he be allowed to see me again. The request was granted and when Mrs. Powell came to the library, he had lifted me to fondle and cherish me and she heard nothing but praise for me. She saw a man whose heart of stone had turned to dust – and yet the man was not destroyed.

In the year 1932 I was allowed to go on my last journey from Nanteos. As this request had come from Fishguard I was extremely pleased to have the opportunity once more of seeing the county of Gerald of Wales and Saint David. An elderly man in his eighties was seriously ill, barely walking and with dimmed eyes. His testimony at the time was that I had been of great benefit to him with his eyes now again bright and shining and I too saw the definite proof that faith can bring back health and well-being to a man's body.

Soon after my return to Nanteos, a lady from London came and left five pounds in me. Very often people from all over the world came to see me, some asking that I be filled with water which they then poured into a bottle for taking with them to America, Africa and the far corners of the globe.

In 1951, the last of the Powell family died and this made me very sad, realizing that life for all mankind has its black side, and that each man in his turn is called upon to walk the last path. The day of the funeral I was very sad – the end of a happy time for me – I somehow sensed that the days of the large country mansions were coming to an end also.

I suppose that I shall be kept in some museum or the National Library of Wales, where many of the Treasures of Wales are kept.

I am facing a bleak, blank future but I have a treasure-chest full of memories and recollections defending me against this future. I shall seek comfort as I recede into the blessed past and re-live some of my rich experiences and happy memories.

In the words of the Welsh poet Ceiriog:

"The old ways of Wales are over
Change comes with the water wheels
Turning, turning."

It is difficult to compare the olden times with that of the present generation. Now is the age of doctors and free national health. Science has taken a giant leap forward.

Man has become clever enough to transplant body parts from one person to another. Charity can now help with clothing and feeding the poor and needy.

However, there is danger also for mankind in that it has to face and overcome the moral hurdle of the nuclear age. Perhaps there will be occasions when the Nation will be glad that they have the chance to turn back to an old Sacred Relic like me once again. It is true that we have heard of no one finding honey in the skeleton of Solomon, but my healing powers remain.

If my body starts deteriorating then I find glory in the fact that I have dedicated my whole life to the service of our Saviour of the world, Jesus Christ.

From the Gospel I would like to invite you as follows:

"Come unto me all ye who travail and are heavily laden
and I will refresh thee."

Then you will see the glimmer of hope that is never-ending.

APPENDIX 2

Particulars from original receipts &c. kept with the Healing Cup at Nanteos: 6 July 1909, Cardiganshire Antiquarian Society M.S.S. Autographs, Plates A.D. 1910-1911, held at Ceredigion Archive, DSO/100. Compiled by George Ewart Evans

Particulars from original receipts &c. kept with the Healing Cup at
Nanteos: 6 July 1909
   21 Sept. 1857
   15 Oct. 1857 27 Nov. 1857
   3 Jan. 1858
   8 Feb. 1858
   28 March 1858 5 April 1858 31 May 1858
   3 June 1858
   26 July 1858 13 Sept 1858
   5 Feb. 1859
   13 Aug 1862 12 June 1873 23 Jany, 1882
   Cup lent this day to Ebenezer Vaughan Gwaneiom Llwyniouserth
ucha for use of his wife – Left £1.00. Cup returned 5 October 1858.
Cured.
   to Thomas Jenkins, Joiner, Llwynfwy-ucha for wife left £1.0.0.
Cured

to Wm. Rowlands, Ystrad, Tregaron; use of his sister Mrs. Jones. Maesllyn, wholly cured, left £1.00. returned 2 Jan 1858.

John Edwards, Lluestfawr nr. Goginan, use of wife who has miscarried; left a watch. Cured. Returned 13 Feb. 1858.

Isaac Hughes, Ffynnon huinant, for wife, left £1.0.0. Cured. Cup returned 6 of March 1858.

to Griffith Daniel Jr. Leuel fawr for Elizabeth Edwards, mother in law of above Grif. Daniel, left £1. Cup returned 5 Ap. 1858. Cured.

Cup lent to Evan Evans, Pantyffy[n]non, Ystumtuen for Sarah his wife. Left a watch. Retd May 1858 pw John Jones Caiman, Aberystwyth.

Lent to Griffith Jones, Dyffryn Ceilog behewyd [??dihewyd??] for use of wife of James Morgan, Drewen, behewyd [?]. Retd 26 June 1858 Cured.

Mr. Evans Jones, Trecoll, Llanbadarn Ddwyn, for use of his dau. Mary, the wife of the Rev. Herbert Jones, Blaenpennal. A note was given this day to the Mr. Evan Jones to go Griffith Jones, Dyffryn Ceilog for the cup if done with, which was given to him for 4 or 5 days when his dau. was wholly cured, consequently the cup was returned by him to Griffith Jones, Dyffryn Ceilog & brought back by G. J. on the 26 June 1858.

to James Morgan Drewen Dehewyd [??dihewyd??]. left a sovereign.

to Elizabeth Humphreys, widow, Pier Street, bleeding stopped, returned 29 Oct. 1858.

to Wm Lloyd, Cornwall, henMynachlog for use of wife, left a watch, retd. 7 March 1859. Cured.

to Wm. Jones, Llanbadarn, left a silver watch. retd. 4 Sept 1862. Case cured. to John Edwards, Castle Hill, Watch left, Venna Edward[s] his wife.

to John Herbert, Hendre, Blaenpennal, for use of his mother-in-law Mary Jones, Felinfach, Blaen penal. 2 half sovereigns deposited in the drawer, library table. S. H. Lewis. retd. 27 Feby 1882.

17 Dec 1883

19 May 1884 20 April 1886

14 Sept [?]

to Dr. Jones, Esgeihen for use of his sister. The Cup to be fetched & had from Richard Jones, Cifngar, Strata Florida. £1 left.

to Thomas Davies, New Quay, Cardiganshire, watch left, retd. 2 June 1884.

to Thomas Jones, for use of mother, watch left "retd. cured." Tynfynon, Talybont.

to Wm. Jenkins for use of sister Catherine Jones. £1 left.

"The Cup was seen – handled by me John Roberts, Telynor Cymru on the morning of the 4th May 1887. Mind completely at ease."

[Note: J.R. father of the seven sons, all of whom were harpists. He performed before Queen Victoria, at Portsmouth, in 1834, & twice at Winchester 1835]

24 Nov 1887 29 March 1889

12 Sept 1901

lent to Charles Edwards, for use of his dau. Mary Edwards. One pound left, retd. 13 Dec. 1887. "A wonderfull [sic] cure"

to Mary Jones, Velin, Blaenpenal, near Tregaron "in charge of a person named Stephen Owens". "One pound left as a guarantee of its return". Retd 10 April 1889.

lent to Evan Parry, for use of his Cousin Jenkin Evans, Penlan, Blaenpennal. "a sov. left"

Notes

Introduction

1. https://www.unexplained-mysteries.com/column.php?id=96373

1 The Great Quest

1. Primary sources are Chretien de Troyes' *le Conte del Graal. The Lancelot Grail Cycle, Le Morte d'Arthur* by Sir Thomas Malory and *Parsifal* by Wolfram von Eschenbach. For details see the bibliography on **pp00-00.**
2. 'Prieddeu Annwn', trans. Caitlin Matthews in *King Arthur's Raid on the Otherworld* (Glastonbury: Gothic Image Press, 2000)
3. *Taliesin: The Last Celtic Shaman* by John Matthews (Inner Traditions, 2002)
4. *The Mabinogion*, translated by Sioned Davies (Oxford University Press, 2008)
5. Trans. Caitlín Matthews, *King Arthur's Raid on the Otherworld* (Glastonbury, Gothic Image Press, 2000)
6. See *Temples of the Grail* by John Matthews (Llewellyn Publishers, 2019)
7. Estoire de Saint Graal. *The Lancelot-Grail Cycle (vol 6.) The Quest for the Holy Grail: The Old French Arthurian Vulgate and Post-Vulgate in Translation*, ed. Norris J. Lacey (D. S. Brewer, 2010)
8. Chretien de Troyes, *The Complete Story of the Grail: Chrétien de Troyes' Perceval and Its Continuations*, trans. Nigel Bryant (D. S. Brewer, 2018)
9. Robert de Boron, *Perceval*, trans. N. Bryant in *Merlin and the Grail* (D. S. Brewer, 2008)
10. Wolfram von Eschenbach, *Parzival and Titurel*, trans. Cyril Edwards (Oxford UP, 2009)
11. See Caitlin and John Matthews: *The Lost Book of the Grail* (Inner Traditions, 2019) for a translation of this text.
12. *Didot Perceval (The Romance of Perceval in Prose)* Trans D. Skeels (University of Washington Press, 1960)
13. *Perlesvaus (The High Book of the Grail)*, trans. N. Bryant (D. S. Brewer, 1978)

14. Robert de Boron, *Merlin and the Grail*, trans. N. Bryant (D. S. Brewer, 2008)
15. *The Voyage of Saint Brendan: Journey to the Promised Land*, trans. J. J. O'Meara (Colin Smythe, 1991)
16. *Sone de Nansay*, trans. in part by Gareth Knight in *Temples of the Grail* by John Matthews (Llywellyn Publishing, 2019)
17. Robert de Boron *Merlin and the Grail*, trans N. Bryant (D. S. Brewer, 2008)
18. See Matthews, J. *Temples of the Grail* (Llewellyn Publishing, 2019)
19. Wolfram von Eschenbach *Parzival*, trans. A. T. Hatto (Penguin Books,1980)

2 Strata Florida, the Mazers and a Prince of Arabia

1. Report on the Lampeter Meeting, *Archaeologia Cambrensis*, Fourth Series, No. XXXVI October 1878, p.336.
2. Henderson, George, *Early Medieval* (Penguin books, 1977 edn, p.219).
3. Bernard, J. H., *The Pilgrimage of S. Silvia of Aquitania to the Holy Places, circa 385 A. D.* translated with introduction and notes (Palestine Pilgrims Text Society, 1891), pp.63-64.
4. Wilkinson, John, *Egeria's Travels* (London: SPCK, 1971), p.7.
5. Bernard, J. H., *The Pilgrimage of S. Silvia of Aquitania to the Holy Places, circa 385 A. D.* translated with introduction and notes (Palestine Pilgrims Text Society, 1891)
6. Report on the Lampeter Meeting, *Archaeologia Cambrensis*, Fourth Series, No. XXXVI October 1878, p.336.
7. Bede, *The Ecclesiastical History of the English Nation* (London: J. M. Dent, 1903, Book 3, Chapter 2), p.140.
8. Tennant, Winifred Coombe, 'Croes Naid', *National Library of Wales Journal*, Cyf. 7, rh. 2 (Gaeaf 1951), pp. 102-115.
9. Shoesmith, Ron & Richardson, Ruth (eds), *A Definitive History of Dore Abbey* (Logaston Press, 1997), p.209.
10. MS Penrice and Margam 106, kept at the National Library of Wales.
11. Burton, Jane & Stöber, Karen, *Monastic Wales – New Approaches* (Cardiff: University of Wales Press), p.120.
12. Augustine, Saint, Bishop of Hippo, *The City of God (De civitate Dei)* translated by the Revd Marcus Dods MA (Edinburgh: T & T Clark, 1884, Vol. 2), p.484.
13. Augustine, ibid.
14. Augustine, ibid.
15. Pick, Bernard, *The Apocryphal Acts of Paul, Peter, John, Andrew and Thomas* (Chicago: The Open Court Publishing Co., 1909), p.270.
16. Rubin, *Corpus Christi – the Eucharist in Late Medieval Culture* (Cambridge University Press, 1991), p.149.
17. Rubin, *Corpus Christi – the Eucharist in Late Medieval Culture* (Cambridge University Press, 1991), pp.338-339.
18. Jones, G. Hartwell, 'Celtic Britain and the Pilgrim Movement', *Y Cymmrodor*, Vol. 23, 1912, pp. 379-380, footnote 3.
19. Robinson, David M. *Strata Florida Abbey, Talley Abbey* Cadw Welsh Historic Monuments, 2007.

20. 'The Novice-master in the Cistercian Order', *Generations in the Cloister – Youth and Age in Medieval Religious Life*, eds Sabine von Heusinger / Annette Kehnel (Vita regularis. Abhandlungen 36) (Berlin, 2008), pp 145-155

21. https://www.dhi.ac.uk/cistercians/cistercian_life/monastic_life/death_&_burial/appendix1.php

22. *Brut y Tywysogion*, ed. and Trans. Thomas Jones (University of Wales Press, 2000)

23. Saunders Lewis, *Meistri'r canrifoedd: ysgrifau ar hanes llenyddiaeth Gymraeg*, Gwasg Prifysgol Cymru, 1982, p. 33. Os un awdur a fu i'r Pedair Cainc, ac at hynny y mae'r dystiolaeth yn tueddu, ai damcaniaethu ormod yw awgrymu mai brodor o wlad Dyfed a oedd yn fynach yn Ystrad Fflur, un wedi teithio yng Nghymru a Lloegr ac efallai yn neau Iwerddon, a sgrifennodd y Mabinogi yn ystod y ..." 'If the Four Branches was written by a single author, and the evidence tends to it, is it to speculate too much to suggest that a native of Dyfed was a monk in Strata Florida, having travelled in England and Wales and perhaps in Ireland, who wrote the Mabinogi...'

24. T. Jones Pierce: Strata Florida Abbey. *Ceredigion: Journal of the Cardiganshire Antiquarian Society* Vol. 1, nos. 1-2 1950-1951

25. Williams, Stephen W., Report on excavations at Strata Florida Abbey, Cardiganshire, *Archaeologia Cambrensis*, Vol. IV, Fifth Series, 1887, pp.290-299.

26. D. and A. Matthew *The Dublin Review*, January 1929

27. F. Stedman-Jones Archive: *Strata Florida Chronology*

28. *The British Genealogist: A collection of the Pedigrees and Arms of the families inhabiting the counties of Monmouthshire, Glamorganshire, Carmarthenshire, Pembrokeshire and Cardiganshire. To which is added Fragmenta Geneologica. The whole compiled from the best authorities and assistance of the best Herald*, by Edward Llwyd, Keeper of the Ashmolean Museum in Oxford 1693. Copied from the original and augmented from later manuscripts and information by Samuel Rush Meyrick, AB of Queen's College Oxford 1807. (Vol V: Of the gentry of Cardiganshire Strataflorida or Ystradflur).

29. https://www.sanctisepulchri.org/home/?lang=en

30. Sir Samuel Rush Meyrick, *The History and Antiquities of the County of Cardigan* (T. Bensley for Longman, 1808) pp230-1

31. Nicholas, Thomas, *Annals and Antiquities of the Counties and Country Families of Wales* vol I, 1872, pp168-9.

32. Most of the material presented here is from the archive of the late Fred Stedman-Jones, who had researched his family over many years. We have not been able to trace all of his sources, so that all of the following should be considered as part of the archive.

33. Personal information from John Matthews who visited Downside in 1988 to view the papers, only to be told they were no longer to be found.

34. *Downside Abbey Guidebook* (Downside Abbey Books, 17th edn, 2017)

35. See, for example, *The Academy*, Jan 4, 1896, No.1235.

36. First Meeting of the Cambrian Archaeological Association, *Archaeologia Cambrensis*, First Series, Vol. II, 1847, pp.361-2.

37. Fenn, R. W. D., Sinclair, J. B., Our Ubiquitous Friend, *Transactions of the Radnorshire Society*, Vol. 59, 1989, pp.116-133.

38. Williams, Stephen W., *The Cistercian abbey of Strata Florida: its history, and an account of the recent excavations made on its site* (London: Whiting & Co., 1889), p.190.

39. Williams, Stephen W., Report on excavations at Strata Florida Abbey, Cardiganshire, *Archaeologia Cambrensis*, Vol. IV, Fifth Series, 1887, pp.290-299.

40. Willis-Bund, J.W., Strata Florida, *Proceedings of the Society of Antiquaries of London*, Second Series, Vol. XII (London: Nichols & Sons), p.21.

41. Williams, Stephen W., *Archaeologia Cambrensis*, Vol. VII, Fifth Series (London: Pickering & Chatto, 1890), pp.242-3.

42. Williams, Stephen W., On further excavations at Strata Florida Abbey, *Archaeologia Cambrensis*, Vol. VI, Fifth Series (London: Pickering & Chatto, 1889), pp.24-58.

43. Williams, Stephen W., *The Cistercian abbey of Strata Florida: its history, and an account of the recent excavations made on its site* (London: Whiting & Co., 1889).

44. Letter by Stephen Williams to Mr. Venables, dated 22 March 1889, Llysdinam B1198, held at the National Library of Wales.

45. Fenn, R. W. D., Sinclair, J. B., Our Ubiquitous Friend, *Transactions of the Radnorshire Society*, Vol. 59, 1989, p.127.

46. See letters from Sir Henry Ponsonby and Arthur Biggs, Balmoral Castle, and a letter from Ralph Walpole, Penralley 682, held at the National Library of Wales.

47. Williams, David H., *An Appreciation of the Life and Work of Stephen William Williams* (1837-99), p.75.

48. *The Tablet*, 4 October 1889.

49. Tout, J. F., Review of The Cistercian Abbey of Strata Florida, *The Archaeological Review*, Vol. III (March–July 1889) (London: David Nutt), p.292.

50. Williams, Stephen W., Archaeological Notes and Queries, *Archaeologia Cambrensis*, Vol.5, Fifth Series (London: Pickering & Chatto, 1888), opposite p.170.

51. Williams, Stephen W., *The Cistercian abbey of Strata Florida: its history, and an account of the recent excavations made on its site* (London: Whiting & Co., 1889), p.188.

52. Williams, Stephen W., Archaeological Notes and Queries, *Archaeologia Cambrensis*, Vol. 5, Fifth Series (London: Pickering & Chatto, 1888), p.171.

53. *Lleuad yr Oes, Chwefror* 1828, p.107.

54. St. John Hope, William, *On the English medieval drinking bowls called Mazers, Archaeologia, or, Miscellaneous tracts relating to antiquity*, Society of Antiquaries of London, Vol. 50, 1887, pp.129-193.

55. ibid. pp 130-32.

56. ibid. pp 162-3.

57. Gilchrist, Roberta, *Medieval Life: Archaeology and the Life Course* Boydell Press, 2012

58. ibid p 179.

59. Somner, William, *Dictionarium Saxonico-Latino-Anglicum, voces, phrasesque praecipuas Anglo-Saxonicas . . . cum Latina et Anglica vocum interpretatione complectens . . . Aecesserunt Aelfrici Abbatis Grammatica Latino-Saxonica cum glossario suo ejusdem generis,'* 2 parts, Oxford, 1659; 2nd edition, with additions by Thomas Benson, 1701.
60. Lucan: Pharsalia, ed. and trans. Jane Wilson Joyce (Cornell University Press, 1993), p 125.
61. St. John Hope, William, *On the English medieval drinking bowls called Mazers, Archaeologia, or, Miscellaneous tracts relating to antiquity*, Society of Antiquaries of London, Vol. 50, 1887, pp.184.
62. Spencer, Edmund, The Complete Works, ed. T. Hughes, 1715. 4:1086-92
63. Gilchrist, Roberta, *Medieval Life: Archaeology and the Life Course* Boydell Press, 2012, p18.
64. Hope, Sir William Henry John, et al. Ed. *Rites of Durham, being a description or brief declaration of all the ancient monuments, rites, & customs belonging or being within the monastical church of Durham before the suppression.* Facsimile Publisher (2015) p133
65. Williams, David Henry, *Atlas of Cistercian Lands in Wales* (University of Wales Press, 1990), P12
66. *The Role of the Hospital in Medieval England: Gift-Giving and the Spiritual Economy* (Dublin: Four Courts Press, 2010), p264.
67. Davies, John, The Antiquities of the Abbey or Cathedral Church of Durham: Also, a Particular Description of the County Palatine of Durham, compiled from the Best ... and Original Manuscripts (Forgotten Books, 2018)
68. Report on the Lampeter Meeting, *Archaeologia Cambrensis*, Fourth Series, No. XXXVI October 1878, p.337.
69. F. Stedman-Jones Archive.
70. Williams, Stephen W., *The Cistercian abbey of Strata Florida: its history, and an account of the recent excavations made on its site* (London: Whiting & Co., 1889), p.175.
71. Cripps, Wilfred Josephs, *Old English Plate, Ecclesiastical, Decorative, and Domestic, Its Makers and Marks* (London: Spring Books, 1967; original edition, 1878).

3 *The Legend Begins*

1. Green, Francis, *Genealogies of Cardiganshire, Carmarthenshire and Pembrokeshire families*, A Reprint of Peniarth MS No. 156, 1912, p.44.
2. *Cwrtmawr Deeds 1624 – Covenant to levy a fine on a third part of a capital m. heretofore called Neyadd Lowdden and now called Nanteos ... 1690, March 26.* Held at the National Library of Wales.
3. Horsfall-Turner, E. R., *Walks and Wanderings in County Cardigan* (Bingley: Thomas Harrison & sons, 1902), p.75 & 85.
4. Horsfall-Turner, ibid., p. 274.
5. *Cwrtmawr Deeds 1626 – Settlement on the proposed marriage of the said William Powell and Avarina, eldest daughter of Cornelius Le Brun and Anne ... 1690, April 1st.* Held at the National Library of Wales.

6. *Nanteos 76 031/3, Plan of Intended Improvements at Nanteos,* John Davenport, 1791.
7. Meyrick, Samuel Rush, *The History of Cardiganshire,* new edn, 2000, S. A. Collard, p.373.
8. Evans, J. T., *The Church Plate of Cardiganshire* (Stow-on-the-Wold: James H. Alden, 1914), p.94, footnote 4.
9. Wolff, Robert Lee, *Strange Stories and other explorations in Victorian Fiction* (Boston: Gambit Incorporated, 1971), pp.36-7.
10. University of Texas website, http://www.hrc.utexas.edu/collections/books/ holdings/wolff/accessed 2 November 2015.
11. Algernon Charles Swinburn, *Tristram of Lyonesse* (Chatto & Windus, 1882)
12. Letters from Swinburne to George E. J. Powell 1864-1874, transcribed by George Eyre Evans, Minor deposit 1406 A, p.3. – letter to G. Eyre Evans from T. Witton Davies, 25 February 1921.
13. Letters from Swinburne to George E. J. Powell 1864-1874, transcribed by George Eyre Evans. Minor deposit 1406 A, held at the National Library of Wales, p.41.
14. Affidavits and correspondence in a cause in Chancery between George Ernest John Powell, plaintiff, and William Thomas Rowland Powell et al, 1867-69, CM22/68. Held at the National Library of Wales.
15. Lang, Cecil Y. (ed.), *The Swinburne Letters,* Vol. 1 (New Haven: Yale University Press, 1959), p.305.
16. Letters from Swinburne to George E. J. Powell 1864-1874, transcribed by George Eyre Evans. Minor deposit 1406 A, page 104. A note by G. Eyre. Evans reads: 'In G. E. J. P.'s scrapbook marked "Gleanings" ... is a printed copy of Swinburne's verses headed "Ex-Voto": to the seventh beginning "when thy salt lips well ough[sic] Sucked in my mouth's last sigh", G.E.J.P. has affixed this M.S. note:-".
17. Steegmuller, Francis, *Maupassant* (London: Collins, 1950), p.37.
18. Edel, Leon (ed.), *Henry James Letters,* Vol IV 1895-1916 (London: Belknap, 1984), p.631.
19. Barnes, Julian, *Brits Abroad, The Guardian,* 18.10.08.
20. Edel, ibid, p.631, footnote 2.
21. Gosse, Edmund, *Portraits and Sketches,* London: William Heinemann, 1912, pp.29-30.
22. *Aberystwyth:* University College of Wales, George Powell – an early benefactor of the College Library, 1971, p.2.
23. *Cambrian News,* Aberystwyth edn, 31 May 1878, p.8.
24. *Cambrian News,* 21 June 1878, p.5, under 'Tregaron'.
25. Evans, George Eyre, *Cardiganshire Notes 1900-1903,* NLW MS 13483C, p.24.
26. *Archaeologia Cambrensis,* vol. IX, 4th series, 1878, pp.320-354.
27. *Lleuad yr Oes, Chwefror* 1828, p.107. Translated by Ian Pegler.
28. *Lleuad yr Oes, Chwefror* 1828, p.107. Translated by Ian Pegler.
29. *Lleuad yr Oes, Ebrill* 1828, p.220. Translated by Ian Pegler.
30. First County Gathering at Strata Florida, Transactions and archaeological record, *Cardiganshire Antiquarian Society,* Volume 1, No. 1, 1911, p.1.

31. Nanteos Cup: No Evidence for certainty, *Cambrian News*, Friday 15 November 1991, p.4.

32. E-mail from Fred Stedman-Jones to Ian Pegler and John Matthews, dated 28 October 2015.

33. Lewis, David, Three Ancient Drinking Vessels: 1. – The Cup of Nanteos, *Wales – A national magazine for the English-speaking parts of Wales*, edited by Owen M. Edwards MA, Volume 2, No. 19, November 1895, pp.504-506.

34. Evans, George Eyre, NLW MS 13483C *Cardiganshire Notes 1900-1903*, page 24.

35. Silvan Evans, Daniel, Jones, John, *Ysten Sioned: neu y Gronfa Gymmysg*, 1882. Translated by E. A. Pegler.

36. Silvan Evans, Daniel, Jones, John, *Ysten Sioned: neu y Gronfa Gymmysg*, 1882.

37. Lewis, David, Three Ancient Drinking Vessels: 1. – The Cup of Nanteos, *Wales – A national magazine for the English-speaking parts of Wales*, edited by Owen M. Edwards MA, Volume 2, No. 19, November 1895, pp.504-506.

38. *Cymru Fu*, Geo. H. Brierley (ed.) (London: Elliot Stock, 7 Sept 1889), pp.40-41.

39. Mackay, Christopher S., *Malleus Maleficarum* (Cambridge University Press, 2006), Volume II, p.116.

40. Trzebiatowska, Marta & Bruce, Steve, *Why are women more religious than men?* (Oxford University Press, 2012).

41. Harris, Ruth, *Lourdes: Body and Spirit in the Secular Age* (Penguin, 2008 edn), p.18.

42. Lewes, Mary L., The Healing Cup of Nanteos, *Occult Review*, August 1910, p.85.

43. Lewes, Mary L., The Healing Cup of Nanteos, *Occult Review*, August 1910, p.85.

44. *The Cup of Healing – a mysterious Cardiganshire relic*, A. G. Prys-Jones, MS 956, held at the National Library of Wales. Undated.

45. Jowett, B., *The Dialogues of Plato* translated into English (Oxford: Clarendon Press, 1892), Vol. 1, p. 13.

46. Brooks, Michael, *13 Things That Don't Make Sense* (Profile Books, 2009), p.164.

47. Brooks, Michael, *13 Things That Don't Make Sense* (Profile Books, 2009), p.169.

48. Bourdillon, Hilary, *Women As Healers – A History of Women and Medicine* (Cambridge University Press, 1988), pp.6-9.

49. Bourdillon, ibid., pp.33-35.

50. Lewes, Mary L., *Stranger Than Fiction: Being Tales from the Byeways of Ghosts and Folklore* (W. Rider, 1911), p.183.

51. Williams, W. Roland, Welsh Physicians and the Renaissance, *British Medical Journal*, 22 December 1928, p.1133.

52. Harte, Negley, *The University of London 1836-1986: An Illustrated History* (Athlone Press Ltd, 1986), p.25.

53. Harte, ibid, p.128.

54. Brock, M. G., Curthoys, M. C. (eds), *The History of the University of Oxford, Vol. VII Nineteenth-Century Oxford, Part 2* (Oxford: Clarendon Press, 2000), p.875.

55. See http://www.cam.ac.uk/about-the-university/history/nineteenth-and-twentieth-centuries. Accessed 27.8.2015.

56. Evans, D. I., Hospital services in Aberystwyth before 1948, Ceredigion: Journal of the Cardiganshire Antiquarian Society, Vol. 5, no.2, 1965, p.168.

57. Oliver, Richard, Doctor Rice Williams of Aberystwyth (1755–1842), Dyfed Family History Journal/Cylchgrawn Hanes Teuluoedd Dyfed, Vol. 10, No. 1, Dec. 2008, pp.24-27. p.22.

58. Jeffreys, Diarmud, Asprin – the remarkable story of a wonder drug. Bloomsbury, 2005, p.74.

59. Rainsford, K. D., *Aspirin and related drugs* (CRC Press, 2002), p.1.

60. All the remedies named here were advertised in *The Cambrian* in 1821 and continued to be advertised for many years after.

61. *The Cambrian*, 31 March 1821, p.1.

62. *The Times* [London England] 4 Mar 1793:4. The Times Digital Archive. Web. 15 July 2015.

63. Two manuscript volumes of 'Rural Lore, Capel Seion', prepared by Bridget Roberts, headmistress of Capel Seion school, 1921–1925, MUS/103, held at Ceredigion Archive.

64. Richards family transcripts, 277B, p.21, held at the National Library of Wales.

65. *Pharmacopaeia Chirurgica, Henricus Atkinson*, Nanteos Miscellaneous manuscripts, National Library of Wales.

66. Bellamy's recipes for the cure of scouring in Cattle and Sheep, Nanteos Miscellaneous manuscripts, National Library of Wales.

67. Owen, Morfydd E., *The Medical Books of Mediaeval Wales and the Physicians of Myddfai*, Carmarthenshire Antiquary, Vol. 31, 1995, p.43.

68. Jones, Emyr Wyn, Medical glimpse of nineteenth century Cardiganshire, *National Library of Wales journal*, Cyf. 14, rh 3, Haf 1966, p.260.

69. The Aberystwyth Infirmary and Cardiganshire General Hospital: a grand bazaar ... 1920, *Aberystwyth: Cambrian News*, 1920, p.7.

70. Evans, George Eyre, Aberystwyth miscellanea, 1821-1909, NLW MS 7963E, p.14.

71. Evans, George Eyre, *Aberystwyth miscellanea*, 1821-1909, NLW MS 7963E, p.15.

72. Evans, George Eyre, Aberystwyth and its Court Leet, *Welsh Gazette*, 1902, p.119.

73. The Aberystwyth Infirmary and Cardiganshire General Hospital: a grand bazaar ... 1920, *Aberystwyth: Cambrian News*, 1920, p.7.

74. The Aberystwyth Infirmary and Cardiganshire General Hospital: a grand bazaar ... 1920, *Aberystwyth: Cambrian News*, 1920, p.7.

75. Evans, George Eyre, *Aberystwyth miscellanea*, 1821-1909, NLW MS 7963E, p.15.

76. Evans, George Eyre, Aberystwyth and its Court Leet, *Welsh Gazette*, 1902, p.120.
77. The Aberystwyth Infirmary and Cardiganshire General Hospital: a grand bazaar ... 1920, *Aberystwyth: Cambrian News*, 1920, p.7.
78. Silvan Evans, Daniel, Jones, John, *Ysten Sioned: neu y Gronfa Gymmysg*, 1882. Translated by E. A. Pegler.
79. Dunning, R. W. (ed.), *The Victoria History of the Counties of England, Vol. 9, Glastonbury and Street* (Boydell & Brewer), 2006, p.16.
80. Ashe, Geoffrey, *Avalonian Quest* (Fontana, 1984), p.117.
81. Anon, John v. 6. *Wilt thou be made whole, or, The virtues and efficacy of the water of Glastonbury in the county of Somerset* (London: Benjamin Matthews, 1751), pp.17-18.
82. Rahtz, P., Watts, L., *Glastonbury – Mythology and Archaeology* (Tempus, 2003), pp.134-138.
83. Benham, Patrick, *The Avalonians* (Gothic Image, 2nd edn, 2006), pp.7-140.
84. Miller, Hamish and Broadhurst, Paul, *The Sun and the Serpent* (Pendragon Press, 1990), p.157.
85. Twinn, Nigel, *Hamish Miller – A Life Divined* (Penwith Press, 2010), p.236.
86. Hall, W. R., *Aberystwyth: What to See and How to See It – a guide to walks, excursions and places of interest* (Aberystwyth: J. Gibson, 1880). Copy at NLW, XDA 1345, box 1, (uncatalogued).
87. Hall, William Robert, 'School is a Pleasure', *Reminiscences of a Journalist*, NLW MS 7194B. p.19.
88. NLW MS 4629C, Biographical material relating to Samuel Evans 20 cent. Letter to Dr Samuel Evans from W. R. Hall, 21 Queen's Road, Aberystwyth, 8.1.33.
89. Hall, W. R., *West Wales Historical Autobiography*, NLW Deposit 292A, 1936.
90. Hall, W. R., *Cardiganshire Traditions*, NLW MS 10824C, 1935.
91. 'W. R. H.' (William Robert Hall) in *Bye-gones*, March 1876, p.31.
92. *Dictionary of Welsh Biography* (online resource), accessed 26.1.16.
93. Hall, W. R., Readings to a set of lantern slides illustrating Aberystwyth and Cardigan, Aberystwyth: *Cambrian News,* 1911, XDA 1345 (uncatalogued).
94. Guto'r Glyn, translated by Ian Pegler, *Valle Crucis and the Grail* (Llanerch Press), 2010, pp.125-6.
95. Rhys, John, *Studies in the Arthurian Legend* (Oxford: Clarendon Press, 1891), p.346.
96. Hall, W. R. (alias 'Amicus'), *University College of Wales magazine*, Vol. IX No. 2, 17 December 1886, p.52. The quoted words of Sir John Rhys are a paraphrase of some remarks more specifically about Wessex, from *Celtic Britain.*
97. Hall, W. R. (alias 'Amicus'), *University College of Wales magazine*, Vol. IX No. 2, 17 December 1886, p.50.
98. The quote is actually a paraphrase, based on Freeman, Edward A., King Ine Part II, *Proceedings of the Somersetshire Archaeological and Natural History Society*, Vol. XX (1874), part ii, p.39.

99. Letter from W. R. Hall (William Robert Hall) to George Gilbert Treherne (1837–1923), NLW MSS 10127C, dated 26 July 1917.

100. W. R. Hall's application for the post of Librarian of the Municipal Library, dated 21 September 1918, contained within Evans, George Eyre, *Cardiganshire Notes 1916-1920*, NLW MS 13493C.

101. Transactions and archaeological record, *Cardiganshire Antiquarian Society*, Vol. 8, 1931.p.44, footnote 4.

102. *Aberystwyth Guide*, 1925, p.80. Also, other editions.

103. Letter from W. R. Hall (William Robert Hall) to E. Morgan Humphreys, NLW MS A/1282 dated 8.10.36.

4 *The Legend Grows*

1. Diaries of George Eyre Evans, 31 January 1901, NLW MS 13385A.

2. Evans, George Eyre, NLW MS 13483C, Cardiganshire Notes 1900-1903, page 24.

3. ibid.

4. *Welsh Gazette*, 30 May 1901, page 7.

5. Evans, George Eyre, NLW MS 13482C, p.54.

6. ibid.

7. Diaries of George Eyre Evans, 21 May 1901, NLW MS 13385A.

8. Owen, Janet, Hornsey, the 1902 Education Act and Passive Resistance, *Bulletin 54, Hornsey Historical Society, 2013*, p.33, footnote 28.

9. Evans, George Eyre, NLW MS 13482C, p.72.

10. *The British Chautauquan*, 19 July 1897, p.11.

11. Letter to George Eyre Evans from Percy C. Webb, dated 10 July 1901, in NLW MS 13482C, page 73.

12. *Welsh Gazette* Articles by 'Philip Sidney' (George Eyre Evans), NLW MS 4292D, Volume 2, 24 July 1902.

13. Evans, George Eyre, NLW MS 13482C, p.72.

14. *Welsh Gazette*, 'Reception at Nanteos', 22 August 1901, p.8.

15. Hall, W. R., *Aberystwyth: What to See and How to See It*, first printed *c*. 1879. See Chapter 3.

16. *Welsh Gazette*, 'Philip Sidney' (aka George Eyre Evans) 'On Tramp', No 2, 29 August 1901, p.7.

17. 1901 copy held in uncatalogued box, XDA 1345, National Library of Wales.

18. See, for example, the diary of George Eyre Evans for 1904, 10 August, NLW MS 13388A.

19. See NLW MS 13482C pp.86, 90, 98, 99.

20. See NLW MS 13483C, p.81 and NLW MS 13485C, p.49.

21. *Welsh Gazette*, 'Reception at Nanteos', 22 August 1901, p.8.

22. *The British Chautauquan*, 1897, 19 August, p.52.

23. Evans, George Eyre, NLW MS 13482C, p.81.

24. *The International Theosophical Yearbook 1938*, The Theosophical Publishing House, Adyar, Madras, India, p.165.

25. 'University Intelligence', *Times* [London, England] 20 Nov. 1894:8. *The Times Digital Archive* Web. 4 Feb. 2015. [stet]

26. *The British Chautauquan*, 1897 17 August, p.42.
27. Evans, George Eyre, NLW MS 13483C, p.83.
28. ibid., p.81.
29. Letter from Ethelwyn Mary Amery to George Eyre Evans, in Evans, George Eyre, Cardiganshire Notes, NLW MS 13492C, p.73.
30. University of London, *The Historical Record* (1836–1912) being a supplement to the Calendar, p.290.
31. *Whitaker, Joseph, An Almanack for the Year of Our Lord 1913*, p.902.
32. *The International Theosophical Yearbook 1938*, The Theosophical Publishing House, Adyar, Madras, India, p.165.
33. Census of Manitoba, Saskatchewan and Alberta, 1916.
34. The Poona guide and directory, 1922, p.35.
35. *The General Report of the Theosophical Society*, 1927, p.18.
36. NLW MS 13483C, Cardiganshire Notes 1900–1903, George Eyre Evans, p.81, British Chautauqua Summer Programme for 1902. The date of the excursion was moved to the 15th.
37. Amery, Ethelwyn Mary, 'Reminiscences of An Ideal Holiday', *Ferme Park Magazine*, 1902.
38. *Welsh Gazette* Articles by Philip Sidney (George Eyre Evans) NLW MS 4292D, 4 December 1902, 'Through other Glasses'. p.7.
39. Evans, George Eyre, *CARDIGANSHIRE: A Personal Survey of Some of Its Antiquities, Chapels, Forts, Plate and Registers*, Chapter 3 'Through Other Glasses', pp.65-67.
40. Amery, Ethelwyn Mary, A Twentieth Century Quest of the Graal, Central Foundation Girls' School, Tower Hamlets, School Magazine: Vol. 1 No 3, March 1904, pp.69-71.
41. Amery, Ethelwyn Mary, *Sought and Found – A Story of the Holy Graal* (Aberystwyth: William Jones, 1905), p.3.
42. Amery, Ethelwyn Mary, *Sought and Found – A Story of the Holy Graal* (Aberystwyth: William Jones, 1905), p.4.
43. Chase, Carol J. (trans.), Lacy, Norris J. (ed.), *Lancelot-Grail – The Old French Arthurian Vulgate and Post-Vulgate in Translation*, Volume 1, The History of the Holy Grail (D. S. Brewer, 2010), p.296.
44. Amery, Ethelwyn Mary, *Sought and Found – A Story of the Holy Graal* (Aberystwyth: William Jones, 1905), p.20.
45. Amery, ibid., pp.25-26.
46. Amery, ibid., p.26.
47. Amery, Ethelwyn Mary, A Twentieth Century Quest of the Graal, *Central Foundation Girls' School, Tower Hamlets, School Magazine*: Vol. 1 No 3, March 1904, p.69.
48. Amery *Sought and Found*, ibid., p.27.
49. ibid.
50. Amery *Sought and Found*, ibid., p.28.
51. ibid.
52. Amery, ibid., p.2. Compare with Tennyson's Idylls of The King, The Holy Grail, lines 47-48.
53. Amery, Ethelwyn Mary, *Sought and Found – A Story of the Holy Graal* (Aberystwyth: William Jones, 1905), p.28.

54. Amery, ibid., pp.28-29.
55. ibid.
56. The word 'And' is fairly consistently eliminated from the beginning of sentences.
57. Amery, Ethelwyn Mary, *The Theosophist*, Volume 71, October 1949, p.52.
58. *The British Chautauquan*, 28 August 1897, p.84.
59. *The British Chautauquan*, 29 March 1897, p.3.
60. ibid., p.6.
61. ibid., p.3.
62. *The British Chautauquan*, 26 August 1897, p.75.
63. The British Chautauqua, *Cambrian News*, 22 August 1902, p. 8.
64. The Holy Grail, *Harrow Gazette*, 1 April 1905.
65. See section below: The American Writer.
66. Llyfr Ffoto G. E. Evans, Album 4 [graphic] 240 A. Held at the National Library of Wales.
67. Jeffs, H., 'J. B.' – *J. Brierley, His Life and Work* (London: James Clarke & Co., 1916).
68. Brierley, J. J., *Church Times*, 16 February 1906, A Welsh Relic – The Nanteos Healing Cup.
69. ibid.
70. See Chapter Six, Douglas Hague.
71. Brierley, J. J., ibid.
72. *Church Times*, 23 February, 1906.
73. Davies, Jonathan Ceredig, *Folklore of West and Mid-Wales*, Welsh Gazette Offices, Aberystwyth 1911, pp.293-297.
74. The term *Phiol* was used in *Lleuad yr Oes* in 1828, see Chapter 3.
75. Davies, Jonathan Ceredig, *Folklore of West and Mid-Wales*, Welsh Gazette Offices, Aberystwyth 1911, p.294.
76. Evans, George Eyre, NLW 13485C, p.49. – British Chautauqua Summer Programme for 1904.
77. Evans, George Eyre, diary entry for 10 August 1904.
78. Evans, George Eyre, NLW 13485C, pp.60-64.
79. Evans, ibid., p.65.
80. Evans, George Eyre, NLW 13435B, 10 August 1904.
81. Evans, George Eyre, NLW 13486C, p.168 – British Chautauqua Summer Programme for 1905, p.17.
82. *Welsh Gazette*, 18 August 1904, p.8.
83. Howells, W. D., *Seven English Cities* (Harper & Brothers, 1909), pp.130-132.
84. Howells, W. D., ibid., p.130.
85. ibid.
86. *Welsh Gazette*, 18 August 1904, p.8.
87. A document by E. A. L. Powell – NANTEOS 4542(d). Held at the National Library of Wales.
88. See the discussion on the Lionel Lewis letters in Chapter Five.
89. Ward, C. H. Dudley, *History of the Welsh Guards* (London: John Murray, 1920), p.284.
90. Griffiths, Niall, *Real Aberystwyth* (Seren, 2008), p.53.

91. Ward, C. H. Dudley, *History of the Welsh Guards* (London: John Murray, 1920), p.280.
92. Ward, ibid., pp.280-1.
93. Ward, ibid., p.281.
94. Ward, ibid., p.279.
95. Ward, ibid., p.282.
96. Ward, ibid., p.280.
97. Ward, ibid., p.284.
98. *Cambrian News*, 27 January 1922, p.5.
99. *Welsh Gazette*, 1 June 1922, p.8.
100. Lewes, Mary L., The Healing Cup of Nanteos, *Occult Review*, August 1910.
101. See discussion in Chapter Five.
102. Lewes, Mary L., *Stranger than Fiction: Being Tales from the Byways of Ghosts and Folklore* (W. Rider, 1911).
103. Lewes, Mary L., *The Queer Side of Things* (Selwyn & Blorent, 1923).
104. Lewes, Mary L., The Healing Cup of Nanteos, *Occult Review*, Vol 12 (W. Rider & Son Ltd, August 1910), p.85.
105. Lewes, ibid., p.82.
106. Lewes, Mary L., *The Queer Side of Things* (Selwyn & Blorent, 1923), p.170.
107. Waite, A. E., *The Hidden Church of the Holy Grail* (London: Rebman Ltd, 1909), p.441.
108. Machen, Arthur, *The Great Return* (London: Faith Press, 1915), p.69.
109. Machen, Arthur, *The Shining Pyramid* (London: Martin Secker, 1925), p.111.
110. Waite, ibid., p.461.
111. Llangibby Letters, NLW MS 17105D/63, Letter to Mr Wood, dated 11 December 1916.
112. Machen, Arthur, *Selected Letters*, ed. Dobson, Roger, Brangham, Godfrey & Gilbert RA (Aquarian Press, 1998), p.221.
113. Machen, Arthur, *The Secret Glory* (London: Martin Secker), p.213.
114. Machen, Arthur, The Holy Graal – A New Theory, *T.P.'s Weekly*, Vol. 13, Feb. 12th, 1909, p.212.
115. Hall, W. R., Application for the post of Librarian of the Municipal Library, 21 September 1918, in Evans, George Eyre, Cardiganshire Notes, 1916-1920, NLW MS 13493C, held at the National Library of Wales.
116. *Official guide and souvenir of Aberystwyth*, The Corporation of Aberystwyth, 1923, p.80.
117. *Official guide and souvenir of Aberystwyth*, The Corporation of Aberystwyth, 1932, pp.47-48.
118. *Transactions and archaeological record*, Cardiganshire Antiquarian Society. Vol. 7 (1930), p.8.
119. http://www.ceredigion.gov.uk/index.cfm?articleid=4944
120. *Transactions and archaeological record*, Cardiganshire Antiquarian Society. Vol. 8 (1931), pp.9-24.
121. *Welsh Gazette*, 5 July 1900, p.6.

122. *Cambrian News*, 13 July 1934.
123. Casgliad Arthur Lewis, Vol. 1394, AL/D112, AL/D113, AL/D114. In addition, there is a photo of the finale in Vol. 1387, AL/032B showing the monks with their backs to us.
124. *Cambrian News*, 17 July 1932, p.8.
125. *Transactions and archaeological record*, Cardiganshire Antiquarian Society. Vol. 12 (1937), p.11.
126. *Welsh Gazette*, 30 June 1932, p.5.
127. Casgliad Arthur Lewis, Vol. 1394, AL/D112, AL/D113, AL/D114.
128. *Cambrian News*, 13 July 1934.
129. Pontrhydfendigaid column, *Welsh Gazette*, 19 May 1932, p.6.
130. *Cambrian News*, 13 July 1934.
131. *Cambrian News*, 1 July 1932, p.5.
132. Lunt, Hugh (alias 'Gwynodl'), *'Cwmcynfelin' - I ddathlu Can mlwyddiant mudiad Rhydychen 1833 – 1933*, NLW ex 2434, 1933.
133. *Caernarfon & Denbigh Herald and North Wales Observer*, Friday 6 November 1942, p.4.
134. Lane, Cecily, & Shannon Jr, Edgar F. (eds), *The Letters of Alfred Lord Tennyson*, Volume 1, 1821-1850 (Clarendon Press, 1982), pp. 171-172.
135. Evans, George Eyre, *Aberystwyth: It's Court Leet*, Aberystwyth: Welsh Gazette, 1902, p.123.
136. Lewis, W. J., *Born on a Perilous Rock – Aberystwyth Past and Present* (Aberystwyth: Cambrian News, 1980), p.175.
137. MacDonald, Tom, The Treasure House in a Cardigan Glen, *Western Mail*, 4 July 1934, p.11. Part two was called 'The Treasure House of a Cardigan Glen', *Western Mail* on 5 July 1934, p.7.
138. MacDonald, Tom, The Treasure House in a Cardigan Glen, *Western Mail*, 4 July 1934, p.11.
139. 'The Holy Grail in Music', *Cambrian News* (Aberystwyth Edition), 12 March 1965, p.4.
140. For example: De Saint-Simone, Ysatis, My Quest for the True Holy Grail, on http://www.biblicalcatholic.com/apologetics/HolyGrail.htm accessed 18.2.15.
141. For example: Manchester, Sean, *The Grail Church – Its Ancient Tradition and Renewed Flowering*, 'Holy Grail' (Gwynedd, 1995), p.119.
142. For example: Kannard, Brian, The Nanteos Cup, on http://www.unexplained-mysteries.com/column.php?id=96373 accessed 13.2.15.
143. Wagner, Richard, *Mein Leben* (München: F. Bruckmann A-G), 1911.
144. Wagner, Richard, *My Life* (Constable & Co. Ltd, London, 1911) (1994 reprint).
145. In relation to his stay at a house in Portland Terrace in 1855 he writes of 'former visits' ('von meinem früheren Besuche'). This is ambiguous but ultimately irrelevant as even 1855 is still too early.
146. Wagner, Richard, *My Life* (Constable & Co. Ltd), p.365.
147. Gregor-Dellin, Martin and Mack, Dietrich, Cosima Wagner's *Diaries*, Translated with an Introduction by Geoffrey Skelton, Volume II 1878-1883 (London: Collins, 1980), p.295.

148. Wagner, Richard, *My Life* (Constable & Co. Ltd), pp.661-662.

149. Gregor-Dellin, Martin and Mack, Dietrich, *Cosima Wagner's Diaries*, Translated with an Introduction by Geoffrey Skelton, Volume I 1869-1877 (London: Collins, 1980), pp.961-966.

150. Gregor-Dellin, Martin and Mack, Dietrich, *Cosima Wagner's Diaries*, Translated with an Introduction by Geoffrey Skelton, Volume I 1869-1877 (London: Collins, 1980), p.976.

151. See for example: Evans, David R. A., Wagner a Nanteos [stet], *Taliesin*, May 1988, p

5 The Struggle for the Cup

1. MacDonald, Tom, 'The Treasure House of a Cardigan Glen', *Western Mail* on 5 July 1934, p.7.

2. Joel, Janet, *Nanteos*, published by Janet Joel, 1996, pp. 6-7.

3. For an example see Nanteos Letter 4579 from E. Allen to Margaret Powell, held at the National Library of Wales.

4. See Chapter 4, The Last Generation.

5. MacDonald, Tom, 'The Treasure House of a Cardigan Glen', *Western Mail* on 5 July 1934, p.7.

6. Joel, Janet, *Nanteos*, self-published, 1996, p.16.

7. *Cambrian News*, Friday 4 August 1916, p.8. 'Penparke' is an old spelling of Penparcau, Aberystwyth.

8. *Ceredigion: Journal of the Cardiganshire Antiquarian Society*, Vol. 13, no. 3, 1999, p.70.

9. Our own chosen alias, for readability.

10. The earliest hand-list of Manuscripts in the National Library of Wales (Vol. 1) dates to 1943 – years after the manuscript was submitted. The entry reads: '3297B THE NANTEOS HEALING CUP. A note on "Cwpan Nanteos", the healing cup kept at Nanteos, near Aberystwyth. English XX cent.'

11. For comparison see NLW Nanteos Estate collection, L5126-5245, Personal letters from E. A. L. Powell to his wife, 1910-18. Ceredigion archive have examples of Margaret Powell's handwriting, see ADX/415, letters from Margaret Powell to Florie Hamer.

12. See for example NLW MS 7951C, p.205. Letter to Mr Eyre Evans from Margaret Powell. The handwriting is not Margaret Powell's except for the signature.

13. Statement by Margaret Powell, Aberystwyth: What to See and How to See It, *Cambrian News*, p. 42. no date given.

14. Cwpan Nanteos, NLW MS 3297B.

15. Nanteos L4655, Letter to Margaret Powell, from W. H. Davies, held at the National Library of Wales.

16. Amery, Ethelwyn Mary, *Sought and Found – A Story of the Holy Graal* (Aberystwyth: William Jones, 1905), p.28.

17. Apperley, Newton Wynne, *A Hunting Diary* (Nisbet & Co. Ltd, 1926), Introduction by E. W. Cuming, pp. 32-33.

18. Apperley, Newton Wynne, *A Hunting Diary* (Nisbet & Co. Ltd, 1926), p.157.

19. Apperley, Newton Wynne, *A Hunting Diary* (Nisbet & Co. Ltd, 1926), p.x.
20. National Museum of Wales, Fifth Annual Report (1911-12), p.23.
21. National Museum of Wales, Third Annual Report (1910), pp.13-14.
22. National Museum of Wales, Fifth Annual Report (1911-12), p.16.
23. Ashdown, Paul, *The Lord was at Glastonbury* (Squeeze Press, 2010), p.69.
24. Hopkinson-Ball, Tim, *The Rediscovery of Glastonbury* (Sutton Publishing 2007), p147.
25. Ashdown, Paul, *The Lord was at Glastonbury* (Squeeze Press, 2010), p.72.
26. Ussher, James, *The Annals of the World, deduced from the Origin of Time, and continued to the beginning of the Emperour [stet] Vespasians Reign* (London, 1658).
27. In one letter (no. 4784, dated 31 October 1938) Lewis writes '...when you first wrote to me years ago'.
28. Letter to Sir George Fossett-Roberts from Revd Lionel Lewis, kept with FACS 202, National Library of Wales.
29. Revd Warrilow is not mentioned in the Lewis correspondence, but his presence is confirmed by a letter from Sir Charles Marston to Mrs Powell, no. 4812; also, by NLW Facs 202 (both at the National Library of Wales).
30. Document held at National Library of Wales, NLW Facs 202.
31. Letter 4781 from Lionel Lewis dated 30 September 1938 refers to '8 smallish volumes' but this has been crossed out in pencil and the words 'very big' inserted above the line, together with the initials M. P. in brackets.
32. Document held at National Library of Wales, NLW Facs 202, p.1. Elsewhere the phrase 'impassable mountains' may refer to the trek of the monks from Strata Florida to Nanteos.
33. NLW Facs 202, op. cit.
34. An entry for John Maunsell Bacon appears in *Alumni Cantabrigienses*, J. & J.A. Venn, Part II, 1752-1900, Volume I (Abbey – Challis) on p.110. This reveals his role as headmaster of a military prep school called Winton House in Cargate, Aldershot. In a letter to Mrs Powell held at the National Library of Wales, Bacon wrote: 'Yes, I am John Bacon of Winton House', confirming that he was headmaster there and remembered Billy Powell. See Powell Correspondence at National Library of Wales, Letter 4582 from John M Bacon to Mrs Powell of Nanteos, dated 1 November 1938.
35. Letter from Revd Lionel Lewis to Mrs Powell, no. 4781, dated 30 September 1938, held at the National Library of Wales.
36. NLW Facs 202, op. cit. This is dated at the bottom of the text: 26 October 1938.
37. Letter from Revd Lionel Lewis to Mrs Powell, no. 4783, dated 17 October 1938, held at the National Library of Wales.
38. It was John Bacon, who in 1937, founded a society for collectors and dealers of antique glass known as the Glass Circle – this society exists to this day. See http://www.glasscircle.org/History/Glass%20Circle%20 History.html. Accessed 9.01.15.
39. According to Lewis, this was the continuation of Stow's Chronicle published in 1615 by Edmund Howes. The dedication to Prince Charles was penned by Howes.

40. Words of John Bacon, quoted by Lionel Lewis in his letter to Mrs Powell, 4784, dated 31 October 1938, National Library of Wales.
41. Letter from Revd Lionel Lewis to Mrs Powell, no. 4785, dated 2 November 1938, held at the National Library of Wales.
42. Letter from John M. Bacon to Mrs Powell, no. 4582, dated 1 November 1938, held at the National Library of Wales.
43. Letter from Revd Lionel Lewis to Mrs Powell, no. 4784, dated 31 October 1938, held at the National Library of Wales. The text appears underlined in the original.
44. Letter from Revd Lionel Lewis to Mrs Powell, no. 4787, dated 14 November 1938, held at the National Library of Wales.
45. Nanteos letter 4595, Library subscription reminder from Boots Library, dated 10 November 1938.
46. Letter from Revd Lionel Lewis to Mrs Powell, no. 4788, dated 18 January 1939, held at the National Library of Wales.
47. NLW Facs 202 is not the original (which had a cover), but the content would have been the same.
48. NLW Facs 202, op. cit.
49. NLW Facs 202, p.3. Lionel Lewis.
50. *Leland's Itinerary in Wales*, Lucy Toulmin Smith edn, p.120.
51. NLW Facs 202, op. cit.
52. *Dugdale's Monasticon*, 1817 edn, Vol. 5. p.632, Footnote h.
53. Willis, Browne, *Mitred Abbies*, Vol. II. p.311.
54. The inventory is in the box 'Nanteos Miscellaneous Manuscripts' at the National Library of Wales.
55. *Catalogue of the Valuable Surplus Furnishings and Effects at Nanteos to be Sold by Auction on the premises* by Russell, Baldwin & Bright, Ltd. on Wednesday and Thursday, 9 and 10 October 1957.
56. Nanteos Sale Prices, *Cambrian News*, 25.10.57, p.7.
57. Williams, Stephen, *The Cistercian Abbey of Strata Florida*, Whiting and Co., 1889, p.190 and *Archaeologia Cambrensis*, 1888, Fifth Series Vol. V. p.171.
58. Letter from Revd Lionel Lewis to Mrs Powell, no. 4789, dated 27 January 1939, held at the National Library of Wales.
59. Letter from Revd Lionel Lewis to Mrs Powell, no. 4789, dated 27 January 1939, held at the National Library of Wales.
60. Letter 4789, op. cit.
61. Letter 4789, op. cit.
62. Letter 4860 to Margaret Powell from F. G. Rendall of the British Museum, held at the National Library of Wales.
63. Waite, A. E., *The Hidden Church of the Holy Graal* (Rebman, 1909), p.441.
64. Letter from Revd Lionel Lewis to Mrs Powell, no. 4791, dated 9 February 1940, held at the National Library of Wales.
65. Letter from Revd Lionel Lewis to Mrs Powell, no. 4792, dated 11 March 1940, held at the National Library of Wales.
66. Letter from Revd Lionel Lewis to Mrs Powell, no. 4781, dated 30 September 1938, held at the National Library of Wales.

67. See for example the foreword to Lewis's Glastonbury – Her Saints, Second and Enlarged Edition (A. R. Mowbray & Co. Ltd, 1927), pp. ix-xviii.

68. Lewis, Lionel S., *St. Joseph of Arimathea at Glastonbury or The Apostolic Church of Britain*, 3rd edn (A. R. Mowbray & Co. Ltd, 1924), p. 8.

69. See section below: The Glastonbury Crusade.

70. Letter to the *Western Mail* from Frederick M. S. Blight, Plaistow, Sussex, 21.3.53.

71. Letter from Lionel Smithett Lewis to Sir George Fossett Roberts, dated 21 May 1950, kept with FACS 202 at the National Library of Wales.

72. Von Harten, Marjorie and Marston, Melissa, *Man of Wolverhampton* (Coombe Springs Press, 1979), pp.203-204.

73. Marston, Charles, *The Bible Comes Alive* (Eyre & Spottiswoode, 1940) (1st impression 1937), p.175.

74. Cohen, Ralph, Moses and the ABC, *Jewish Daily Bulletin*, Thursday 31 January 1935, p.5.

75. Letter from Revd Lionel Lewis to Mrs Powell, no. 4788, dated 18 January 1939, held at the National Library of Wales.

76. Lionel Lewis in NLW Facs 202 simply says that Warrilow had 'also been in Palestine'.

77. 'Nomination Database'. Nobelprize.org. Nobel Media AB 2014. Web. 5 December 2014. http://www.nobelprize.org/nomination/archive/show. php?id=8386

78. Nanteos Letter 4956 to Margaret Powell from Barbara Waylen, dated 8 January 1943.

79. Nanteos Letters 4956-8 to Margaret Powell from Barbara Waylen, 1943.

80. Nanteos Letter 4957 to Margaret Powell from Barbara Waylen, dated 17 February 1943.

81. Waylen, Barbara, *Evidence of Divine Purpose*, Edward Hamilton, Sussex, 1950.

82. Waylen, Barbara, *Evidence of Divine Purpose*, op cit., p. 50.

83. Waylen, Barbara, *Evidence of Divine Purpose*, op cit., p. 51.

84. *Cambrian News*, 1 July 1932, p.5.

85. Waylen, Barbara, *Evidence of Divine Purpose*, op cit., plate opposite p.52.

86. Letter from Revd Lionel Lewis to Margaret Powell, Nanteos Collection 4788, dated 18 January 1939. Held at the National Library of Wales.

87. Davenport, Cyril, *British Heraldry*, Methuen 1921, pp.151-2.

88. Fox-Davies, A. C., *A Complete Guide to Heraldry* (London: Orbis, 1985), p.276.

89. See The British Israelite Connection, below.

90. See discussion in Chapter 6.

91. See http://www.philvaz.com/apologetics/HolyGrail.htm accessed 3.3.15.

92. The inventory is kept at the National Library of Wales in a box marked 'Nanteos Miscellaneous Manuscripts'.

93. Nanteos Miscellaneous manuscripts, Inventory of Library after 1861.

94. Oldmixon, John, *The history of England during the reigns of Henry VIII, Edward VI, Queen Mary, Queen Elizabeth* (London: Printed for T. Cox, and R. Hett, 1739).

95. Smollett, Tobias, *A Complete History of England from the Descent of Julius Caesar to the Treaty of Aix La Chapelle 1748. Containing the transactions of One Thousand Eight Hundred Years*, Volume the Sixth (London: James Rivington and James Fletcher, 3rd edn, 1759).

96. See later in this Chapter: The British Israelite Connection.

97. Nanteos Mansion, *Nanteos Mansion* [Guide], Aberystwyth: Cambrian News Ltd., c. 1966. Held at Ceredigion library.

98. Nanteos Letter 4924 to Margaret Powell from P. I. Turner, dated 30 December 1938, held at the National Library of Wales.

99. Nanteos Letter 4924, op. cit.

100. Obituary notice for Margaret Powell, *Welsh Gazette*, 15 March 1951.

101. Obituary for Margaret Powell, *Welsh Gazette*, 22 March 1951.

102. NLW Deed 1492.

103. See later in this Chapter: Legal Battles over Nanteos.

104. Evans, Henry Tobit, *Rebecca and Her Daughters. Being a History of the Agrarian Disturbances in Wales Known as 'The Rebecca Riots'*, Educational Publishing Company, 1910.

105. Evans, Gwladys Elen, *A Collection of the Place Names of the Parish of Llandysilio-go-go together with their meanings*, Carmarthen: printed at 'The Journal' Office, 1901, front cover.

106. *Welsh Gazette*, 26 April 1951, p.6.

107. NLW MS 20963C, A volume of material by H. Tobit Evans towards an ecclesiastical history of Cardiganshire, undated.

108. Bowen, E. G., *A History of Llanbadarn Fawr* (Gomer, 1979), pp.24-25.

109. Fraser, Maxwell, Letter to 'Mr Aubrey' 25 August 1952, National Library of Wales. Ref. No: A/2179

110. Fraser, Maxwell, *Wales – Volume Two – The Country*, Robert Hale Ltd., 1952, p.334.

111. Elder, Isabel Hill, *The Cup of the Last Supper* (Bangor, Co. Down: H. McGowan & Son).

112. Covering letter from Isabel Hill Elder, kept with booklet sent to Edgar Phillips, 1958. NLW Trefin 58.

113. Elder, Isabel Hill, *The Story of Glastonbury* (Bangor: Spectator, 1965), p.20.

114. Elder, Isabel Hill, *The Story of Glastonbury* (Bangor: Spectator, 1965), p.18.

115. Elder, Isabel Hill, *George of Lydda – Soldier Saint and Martyr* (London: Covenant, 1949), p.75.

116. Nanteos Letter 4656, Florence de Ste. Croix to Margaret Powell, dated 2 December 1942. Held at the National Library of Wales.

117. Elder, Isabel Hill, *The Story of Glastonbury* (Bangor: Spectator, 1965), p.2.

118. Nanteos Letter 4656, Florence de Ste. Croix to Margaret Powell, dated 2 December 1942. Held at the National Library of Wales.

119. Nanteos Letter 4656, Florence de Ste. Croix to Margaret Powell, dated 2 December 1942. Held at the National Library of Wales.

120. Nanteos Letter 4656, Florence de Ste. Croix to Margaret Powell, dated 2 December 1942. Held at the National Library of Wales.

121. See this chapter, under 'The Postcards'.
122. Capt. E. Raymond, *The Traditions of Glastonbury* (Artisan, 1987 edn), pp.102-104.
123. See section on Michael Poynder, Chapter 6.
124. Obituary for Frederick M S Blight, *Welsh Gazette*, 27 June 1963, p.6.
125. Frederick Blight is mentioned as a donor in the National Library of Wales Annual Reports for 1953-54 (p.53) and 1954-55 (p.58). The works he donated are listed on an index card system as follows: Echoes of the Nineties – drawings & articles from various sources – filed in cupboard to left of main Entrance into Print Room (PB2022); two copies (framed) of drawings by Aubrey Beardsley (PB1962-3); a collection of 53 drawings copied from works of A. Beardsley, M. Beerbohm & others, etc., Misc. (PB2824).
126. Letter to the *Western Mail* by Frederick M S Blight, published 22 May 1953, p.6.
127. Letter to the *Sunday Times* by Frederick M S Blight, published Sunday 12 August 1951, Issue 6695, p.8.
128. Letter to the *Sunday Times* by Frederick M S Blight, published Sunday 12 August 1951, Issue 6695, p.8.
129. *The Healing Cup in Safe Custody, Welsh Gazette*, 31 May 1951, p.6.
130. Robinson, Joseph Armitage, *Somerset Historical Essays,* Published for the British Academy, by H. Milford, Oxford University Press, 1921.
131. Blight, Frederick M S, Letter to the *Welsh Gazette*, 13 September 1951, p 4
132. Letter from Frederick M S Blight to Dr Thomas Jones, dated 24 September 1951. WW3/40
133. Letter from Frederick M S Blight to Dr Thomas Jones, dated 24 September 1951. WW3/40
134. Letter from Frederick M S Blight to Dr Thomas Jones, dated 4 October 1951. WW3/41
135. Blight, Frederick M S, Letter to the *Welsh Gazette*, 1 November 1951, p.4.
136. Letter from Revd Lionel Smithett Lewis to Margaret Powell, National Library of Wales, Ref. 4791, 9 February 1940.
137. Letter to Sir George Fossett-Roberts from Revd Lionel Lewis, kept with FACS 202, National Library of Wales.
138. Letter from Frederick M S Blight to Dr Thomas Jones, dated 4 October 1951. WW3/41
139. Lambeth Palace Library, MS 1729 ff. 294-308, Account of the Nanteos Cup, or Grail, by the Revd Lionel Smithett Lewis, Vicar of Glastonbury, with correspondence on the same subject with Archbishop Fisher, 1951. Geoffrey Francis Fisher, Baron Fisher of Lambeth (1887–1972) was appointed Archbishop of Canterbury in 1945.
140. It is interesting to note that Revd Knapman graduated from St David's College, Lampeter, in 1933.
141. Is this the cup that was used at the Last Supper? *Sunday Express*, 8 January 1961. The initials of Revd Knapman are incorrect in the article. His full name was Hugh William Hartly Knapman.
142. Blight, Frederick M S, Letter to the *Welsh Gazette* – 1 November 1951, p.4.

143. Lewis, Lionel S., *Glastonbury – Her Saints,* 2nd and enlarged edn, A. R. Mowbray & Co., 1927, pp. ixxviii.
144. Blight, Frederick M S, Letter to the *Welsh Gazette* – 1 November 1951, p.4.
145. Blight, Frederick M S, Letter to the *Welsh Gazette* – 1 November 1951, p.4.
146. Blight, Frederick M S, Letter to the *Welsh Gazette* – 1 November 1951, p.4.
147. Blight, Frederick M S, Letter to the *Welsh Gazette* – 15 May 1952, p.4.
148. Blight, Frederick M S, Letter to the *Welsh Gazette* – 15 May 1952, p.4.
149. Blight, Frederick M S, Letter to the *Western Mail* – 21 March 1953, p.6.
150. Blight, Frederick M S, Letter to Miss Megan Ellis, kept with a scrapbook entitled 'Booty', NLW 20695B.
151. Obituary for Frederick M S Blight, *Welsh Gazette* 27 June 1963, p.6.
152. The Healing Cup in Safe Custody, *Welsh Gazette*, 31 May 1951, p.6. According to Byron Rogers, it was kept at Lloyd's bank in Aberystwyth, c.f. Rogers, Byron, *The Bank Manager and the Holy Grail* (Aurum Press, 2003), p.265.
153. *Welsh Gazette*, 'Nanteos Estate Dispute', 29 December 1955.

6 Exile and Return

1. Betty also had a daughter from her first marriage to Lt.-Col. Jocelyn Arthur Garnons-Williams.
2. Libby, Willard, Radiocarbon Dates II, *Science*, Vol. 114, 1951, p.291.
3. Light Ray Test for Nanteos Healing Cup, *Cambrian News*, 9 August 1957, p.5.
4. Bowman, Sheridan, Radiocarbon dating at the British Museum – the end of an era, *Antiquity*, Vol. 76, No.291, March 2002, pp.56-61.
5. Barker, H. & Mackey, C. J., British Museum natural radiocarbon measurements I, *American Journal of Science Radiocarbon Supplement* 1: 81-6.
6. Nanteos Tenants Entertain, *Cambrian News*, 16.8.57, p.8.
7. See Chapter 5. This work mentions that there were seven monks at Strata Florida at the time of the dissolution.
8. *Catalogue of the Valuable Surplus Furnishings and Effects at Nanteos*, Russell, Baldwin and Bright, 1957.
9. *Three sermons on the Nanteos Cup preached by Fr Wharton*, Additional Notes, p.17. Held at Birmingham Archdiocesan Archives, P292/7/46.
10. *Sunday Express* 'Is this the cup that was used at the Last Supper?' Peter Bloxham, 8.1.61.
11. See Chapter 3 – 'The Placebo Effect'.
12. Stedman-Jones, Fred, 'The Grail in Wales: The Nanteos Cup', *Pendragon* Vol. XVIII No. 3, Easter 1987.
13. Cottrell, John 'My Search for the Holy Grail', *Ladies Home Journal*, April 1971, Vol. LXXXVIII, No 4.
14. Cottrell, ibid.
15. Private e-mail from Fred Stedman-Jones to Ian Pegler and John Matthews, 3 September 2015.
16. *Three sermons on the Nanteos Cup preached by Fr Wharton*, op. cit.
17. *England and Wales National Probate 1966*. James H. S. Wharton passed away on 22 February 1966.

18. £10,400 Grant for Nanteos, *Cambrian News*, 22 May 1959, p.6.
19. Nanteos gets a grant, *Cambrian News*, 31 October 1959, p.6.
20. National Library of Wales, *Annual Report*, 1961, p.68.
21. Obituary for Gildas Tibbott by E. D. J., *Ceredigion: Journal of the Cardiganshire Antiquarian Society*, Vol. 8, nos. 1-4 1976-1979, p.479.
22. 'Crowds Flock to Home of Holy Grail', *Cambrian News*, 7 August 1961, p.1.
23. *Sunday Express*, 'Holy Grail' to go on show, circa 1958/9.
24. *Radio Times*, (Welsh Edition), Sept. 21, 1961, Vol. 152, No. 1976, p.30 & p.33.
25. Davies, Cynric Mytton, The Treasure House of Wales, *Country Quest*, Vol 3., Summer 1962, pp.28-31.
26. Cottrell, op. cit.
27. Fred Stedman-Jones archive, letter from 'Bob' Danvers-Walker to Fred Stedman-Jones dated 12 February 1985.
28. Danvers-Walker, Cyril Frederick aka 'Bob', The Chalice of Nanteos, *Coming Events in Britain*, April 1963.
29. See below: The Aberystwyth 700 exhibition
30. Fred Stedman-Jones archive, letter to Fred Stedman-Jones dated 12 February 1985.
31. *Woman* 'The Cup that Cherishes a Legend', Joyce Robins, 3 May 1969, Vol. 64, No. 1664, p.43. IPC magazines.
32. *Country Life* 1967, Vol. 142, 12 Oct, pp.904-906.
33. *Woman* 'The Cup that Cherishes a Legend' op. cit.
34. Fred Stedman-Jones archive, handwritten notes by Fred S. J. 4.9.85 'I saw and handled the Cup'.
35. *Woman* 'The Cup that Cherishes a Legend', op.cit.
36. Advertised in the *Cambrian News*, 24 June 1977, p.5.
37. *National Library of Wales journal* – Cyf. 20, rh. 3 Haf 1978, Professor E. G. Bowen, 'Aberystwyth 700' pp.300-308. Available online from http://welshjournals.llgc.org.uk
38. *Cambrian News*, Friday 24 June 1977, p.14.
39. Bowen, ibid, p.302.
40. *Cambrian News*, Friday 24 June 1977, p.14.
41. *Archaeologia Cambrensis*, Vol 127 (1978). p.162. The AGM was advertised as part of Aberystwyth 700, see advert in the *Cambrian News*, 12 August, p.13 under 'Aberystwyth 700 Events'.
42. Cambrian Archaeological Association Annual Meeting, 1977. E [sound recording], 19 August 1977, Casgliad Llyfrgell Ceredigion. (WlAbNL) 006507206.
43. Douglas Hague: An Appreciation, *Cambrian News*, 28.9.90. p.7.
44. Hague, Douglas B., *Lighthouses of Wales – Their Architecture and Archaeology*, edited by Stephen Hughes, Royal Commission on Ancient and Historical Monuments of Wales, Crown Copyright, February 1994.
45. Fred Stedman-Jones archive, Letter from Douglas B. Hague to Fred Stedman Jones, dated 8.10.85.
46. Document held at RCAHMW – C45742, letter to Douglas Hague from J. Brazier of Forest Products Research Laboratory, 8.10.1970.

47. Royal Commission on Ancient and Historical Monuments in Wales, *An Inventory of the Ancient Monuments in Glamorgan, Vol III Part II, Mediaeval Non-defensive Secular Monuments*, Cardiff: Her Majesty's Stationery Office 1982, pp.xxiii-xxiv.

48. Examination of several volumes of *The Civil Service Yearbook* and its predecessor *The British Imperial Calendar and Civil Service List*, showed that Edleston House was the headquarters of the RCAHMW from 1965 to 1991.

49. The R.C.A.H.M. Wales in my Time 1949-89 by Peter Smith, in *Transactions of the Ancient Monuments Society Volume 34, 1990.* p.63.

50. Hague, Douglas B., *Aberystwyth Trail*, 1975.

51. RCAHMW Catalogue Number C45744.

52. RCAHMW Catalogue Number C41705.

53. The University College of Wales, Aberystwyth, *Prospectus 1978-80*, printed June 1977, p.4.

54. NLW ex 682-3, Autograph copy of 'In Arthur's Land: An Account of the traditions and antiquities relating to Arthur and his knights in South Wales & Monmouthshire' by Ada Mary Merry. Presented by Douglas Hague.

55. Hague, Douglas B., NLW ex 720, 16.3.85, p.1.

56. Letter from Douglas Hague to Fred Stedman-Jones, op. cit.

57. NLW ex 720.

58. Presumably these were provided by the wood-turner.

59. Hoadley, R. Bruce, *Understanding Wood – a Craftsman's Guide to Understanding Wood Technology* (Taunton Press, 2000), Chapter 3, pp.47-49. Also, Jane, F. W., *The Structure of Wood* (London: Adam and Charles Black, Second Edition Revised and Reset, 1970).

60. Jane, F. W., *The Structure of Wood* (London: Adam and Charles Black, Second Edition Revised and Reset, 1970), p.413.

61. NLW ex 720.

62. NLW ex 720.

63. P. E. Damon, D. J. Donahue *et al.*, *Radiocarbon dating of the Shroud of Turin*, Nature 337 (16 February 1989), pp.611-615

64. Letter by Douglas Hague: 'Made of Wych Elm', *Country Life*, April 1985, p.1125.

65. *New York Times*, 'A Prince Eternal', Kathryn Shattuck, 3 April 2005.

66. IMDB.com, accessed 2.8.2016.

67. IMDB.com, accessed 1.4.2018.

68. http://www.eworldwire.c om/pressreleases/14275 accessed 2.8.16.

69. De Saint Simone, Ysatis, 'My Quest for the True Holy Grail,' http://www.biblicalcatholic.com/apologetics/HolyGrail.htm accessed 4.8.16.

70. Private e-mail from Fred Stedman-Jones to John Matthews and Ian Pegler, 13.3.15.

71. Graves, Tom, *Needles of Stone* (30th Anniversary Edition), Grey House in the Woods, 2008, pp.7-11.

72. Underwood, Guy, *The Pattern of the Past*, first published by Museum Press, 1969.

73. Gawn, Billy & Twinn, Nigel, *Beyond the Far Horizon: Why Earth Energy Dowsing Works* (Penwith Press, 2012), p.346.

74. Underwood, op. cit., p.14.
75. Underwood, op. cit., p.165 & p.169.
76. Poynder, Michael, *PI in the Sky – A Revelation of the Ancient Wisdom Tradition*, Rider, 1992, from the blurb.
77. Poynder, Michael, *The Price Guide to Jewellery 3000 B.C. – 1950 A.D.*, Antique Collectors' Club, 1976, inside back jacket blurb.
78. Poynder, Michael, *The Lost Magic of Christianity – Celtic Essene Connections*, Collins Press, 1997, p.1.
79. Poynder, 1997, p.3.
80. Poynder, 1997, p.93.
81. Kersten, Holger, *Jesus Lived in India: His Unknown Life Before and After the Crucifixion* (Element Books, 1994).
82. Poynder, 1997, p.69.
83. See Poynder, 1997, pp.74-80.
84. This idea derives from the writings of Edward Williams (1747–1826) better known as Iolo Morganwg, a known forger. He implies that Joseph of Arimathea was known in Wales as 'Ilid' – but this was his own invention.
85. Poynder, Michael, *The Lost Magic of Christianity – Celtic Essene Connections* (Green Magic, 2000), p.78.
86. Poynder, 1997, p.76.
87. Poynder misspells Nanteos the same way as E. Raymond Capt.
88. Poynder, 1997, p.76.
89. Poynder, 1997, p.134, Diagram 103.
90. Poynder, 1997, see diagrams on pages 136, 138, 139 and 141.
91. Poynder, 1997, p.135.
92. Underwood, Guy, *The Pattern of the Past* (Abacus, 1969), p.178 & p.179.
93. Underwood, 1969, p.184.
94. Graves, Tom, *Needles of Stone* op. cit., p.19.
95. Huntley, H. E., *The Divine Proportion, A Study in Mathematical Beauty* (Dover Publications, 1970).
96. West elevation Strata Florida Abbey, Cardiganshire, Stephen W. Williams, Telfer. Smith, 1887, National Library of Wales, BCWC 222.
97. See http://networkofleyhunters.com/
98. *The Real Merlin and Arthur*, BBC Wales 2009, Series Director Mark Proctor, Series Producer Gillane Seaborne.
99. Bromwich, Rachel, *Trioedd Ynys Prydein – The Triads of the Island of Britain*, Third Edition (University of Wales Press, 2006), p.169.
100. Main, Laurence, *King Arthur's Camlan – A Quest for the Truth* (Meirion Publications), 2006.
101. See *The Ley Hunter* no. 103, 1987, 'At Strata Florida', Llowarch, pp.5-7. Also see *The Cambrian News*, 'Weird Wonders of Wales' by Llowarch: 'On the right lines', 30 October 1987 p.25 and 'More on 'earth mysteries', 6 November 1987, p,25.
102. Main, Laurence, *The Spirit Paths of Wales* (Cicerone Press, 2000), p.61.
103. Main, Laurence, *Camlan – the True Story?* (Meirion Publications, 1997), p.18.
104. Main, *King Arthur's Camlan*, p.29.
105. Main, *The Spirit Paths of Wales*, p.63.

106. Main, *The Spirit Paths of Wales*, p.59.
107. Edwards, Nancy, *A Corpus of Early Medieval Inscribed Stones and Stone Sculpture in Wales*, Volume II (University of Wales Press, 2007), pp.131-132 and pp.274-275 and pp.294-296.
108. Main, *The Spirit Paths of Wales*, p.61.
109. Leland, John, *The itinerary in Wales of John Leland in or about the years 1536-1539; extracted from his mss.* arranged and edited by Lucy Toulmin Smith (London: G. Bell & Sons, 1906), p.118.
110. Main, *The Spirit Paths of Wales*, p.63.
111. Main, *The Spirit Paths of Wales*, p.65. See also Main, *King Arthur's Camlan*, p.33.
112. Evans, George Eyre, *Cardiganshire: A Personal Survey of Some of its Antiquities, Chapels, Churches, Fonts, Plate and Registers* (Aberystwyth: The Welsh Gazette, 1903), pp.32-33.
113. Main, *King Arthur's Camlan*, p.33.
114. Griffiths, Graham K., *Behold Jerusalem!* (Longinus, 2003).
115. Maltwood, K. E., *A Guide to Glastonbury's Temple of the Stars – Their Giant Effigies Described from Air Views, Maps, and from 'The High History of the Holy Grail'* (James Clarke & Co. Ltd, 1964), p.1.
116. Griffiths, op. cit., pp.97-98.
117. Joel, Janet, *The Nanteos Cup (Holy Grail)* (self-published, 2016), p.6.
118. Sound-recording held at the National Library of Wales, Cambrian Archaeological Association Annual Meeting, 1977. dated 19 August 1977. 1 sound-tape reel: analogue, 1/4in. Casgliad Llyfrgell Ceredigion. (WlAbNL)006507206.
119. Information from Fred Stedman-Jones.
120. Information from eBay, in the Fred Stedman-Jones archive.
121. Private e-mail from John Matthews sent to Ian Pegler and Fred Stedman-Jones, sent 3.4.15.
122. Website of Adrian Wagner, http://www.adrianwagner.com/awbiog.html, accessed 29.8.16.
123. Gardner, Laurence, *Bloodline of the Holy Grail: The Hidden lineage of Jesus revealed* (Dorset: Shaftesbury, 1996).
124. See Chapter Four.
125. See the blurb for the cassette recording of *Sought and Found* by Adrian Wagner.
126. Baigent, Michael, Leigh, Richard & Lincoln, Henry, *The Holy Blood and the Holy Grail*, originally published by Jonathan Cape, 1982.
127. Wagner, Adrian, *The Feminine Element in Mankind*, 1994.
128. Sabor, Rudolph, *The Real Wagner* (Cardinal, 1989), p.22.
129. *Film and Television Handbook*, BFI, 1995 (Garden House Press), p.300.
130. Goddard, Sue, Search for the Holy Grail Continues, *Cambrian News*, 14.1.94.
131. Gorman, D., 'Errors flow from Nanteos Cup tale' and Morgan J., 'Talk to the local people!', *Cambrian News*, 21 January 1994.
132. Garlick, Raymond, *A Sense of Europe*, Collected Poems 1954-1968, Gwasg Gomer, 1968.
133. Prys-Jones, A.G., *A Song of Caldey*, *Poems of Wales* (Oxford: Basil Blackwell, 1923), pp.2-3.

134. Koch, John, T. (ed.), *Celtic Culture – A Historical Encyclopaedia*, Vol., 3, ABC-Clio Inc., 2006, p.957.

135. Bromwich, Rachel, *Trioedd Ynys Prydain: The Myvyrian 'Third Series' Part II*, The Transactions of the Honourable Society of Cymmrodorion, 1969, Part I, p.147.

136. Letter from Frederick M S Blight to *Welsh Gazette*, published 13 September 1951, p.4.

137. Peter Scothern's website: http://www.peterscothernministries.co.uk/page. asp?pid=498 accessed 6.2.20.

138. Fred Stedman-Jones archive, Typed/printed summary of a Peter Scothern audio tape, 'The Holy Chalice', 1997.

139. See discussion in Chapter 3.

140. Not all claimed cures are linked with the waters. Some might occur, for example, during a procession.

141. Marchand, A., *The facts of Lourdes and the Medical Bureau* (London: Burns Oates and Washbourne Ltd, 1924), p.22.

142. See Chapter 5, section on The Lionel Lewis letters.

143. Fred Stedman-Jones archive, *Sunday Express* 'Is this the cup that was used at the Last Supper?' Peter Bloxham, 8.1.61.

144. Fred Stedman Jones archive, 'I saw and handled the Cup', op. cit.

145. *Pendragon* Vol. XVIII, No.3, Easter edition, reprinted in *Pendragon* xxvii, Spring 1997 and in the *Pendragon Jubilee Souvenir volume*, 2010.

146. Fred Stedman-Jones archive, email from Fred S. J. to Rachel Whitfield, Teliesyn, 10 June 2002.

147. Information from Janet Joel.

148. See Chapter 4.

149. *Chasing the Wind II - Return of the Crystal Skulls* and *Vampire Lust* by Keith Fauscett, 2009.

150. Davies, Tom, *Fire in the Bay*, William Collins & Co., 1989.

151. Clynes, Michael, *The Grail Murders*, Penzler, 1993.

152. Davies, D. H., *Flight from Glastonbury*, Lulu, 2015, p.295.

153. *Cambrian News*, 23 January 2014.

154. Holy Grail quest set to bring tourist boom to 'magical' Nanteos House in Wales, *The Guardian*, Vanessa Thorpe, 26.1.14.

155. *The Guardian*, 26.1.14. *op cit.*

156. *Cambrian News*, Search for the 1930s Nanteos Cup re-enactment script, 3.7.14, p.28. See Chapter 5 for discussion on Hugh Lunt and the pageant play.

157. Statement from West Mercia police, reproduced in *The Cambrian News*, Police on Crusade to find stolen Nanteos 'Holy Grail', 24.7.14, p.4.

158. In Search of the Holy Grail, *Town and Country*, Spring 2015.

159. Information from Fred Stedman Jones.

160. Fred Stedman-Jones archive, letter from Diane Powell, 1993.

161. http://stats.grok.se/en/201408/Nanteos_Cup accessed 20.1.17.

162. Blog: *On Myths and Misinformation at Nanteos*, by 'The Curious Scribbler', dated 7 December 2015. http://www.letterfromaberystwyth. co.uk/on-myths-and-misinformation-at-nanteos/ accessed 20.1.17.

163. See discussion in Chapter 3.
164. From notes made by Ian Pegler, who was present at the talk.
165. Press Release: Discover the 'Holy Grail' at The National Library of Wales, National Library of Wales, 16.6.16, https://www.llgc.org.uk/en/information-for/press-and-media/press-releases/2016-press-releases/discover-the-holy-grail-at-the-national-library-of-wales accessed 27.1.17.
166. Taken from *Llyfr Ffoto G. E. Evans, Album 4 [graphic] 240 A*. Held at the National Library of Wales.
167. BBC Website article: 'Holy Grail' cup on show at national library in Aberystwyth, http://www.bbc.co.uk/news/uk-wales-mid-wales-36562685 18.6.16, accessed on 27.1.17.
168. *Cambrian News* report: New home for cup that was thought to be Grail, 23.6.16, p.4.
169. BBC report, Tackle 'terrifying' environment issues, Prince Charles says, http://www.bbc.co.uk/news/uk-wales-mid-wales-40560949 accessed 3.4.18.

Bibliography

For those wishing to visit the Nanteos Cup, it is currently to be found in a special display curated by the National Library of Wales / Llyfrgell Genedlaethol Cymru, Aberystwyth, Ceredigion SY23 3BU Opening Hours: Monday - Friday 09:00 - 18:00 Saturday 09:30 - 17:00 Sundays: closed,

Primary Sources
The following book list contains texts and other books consulted during our research. For details of journals and newspapers see the Notes section.

Bede, *The Ecclesiastical History of the English Nation* (London: J. M. Dent, 1903)

Brut y Tywysogion, ed. and trans. Thomas Jones (Cardiff: University of Wales Press, 2000)

Chrétien de Troyes, *The Complete Story of the Grail: Chrétien de Troyes' Perceval and Its Continuations,* trans. Nigel Bryant (D. S. Brewer, 2018)

Didot Perceval (The Romance of Perceval in Prose), trans D. Skeels (University of Washington Press, 1960)

Guto'r Glyn, trans. Ian Pegler, in *Valle Crucis and the Grail* (Burnham-on-Sea: Llanerch Press, 2010)

Leland's Itinerary in Wales, Lucy Toulmin Smith (New York: Franklin Classics, 2018)

The Mabinogion, trans. Sioned Davies (Oxford: Oxford University Press, 2000)

Malory, Sir Thomas, *Le Morte D'Arthur,* ed. John Matthews (London: Cassell, 2000)

Perlesvaus (The High Book of the Grail), trans N. Bryant (Woodbridge: D. S. Brewer, 1978)

Robert de Boron, *Perceval*, trans. N. Bryant in *Merlin and the Grail* (D. S. Brewer, 2008)

'The Estoire de Saint Grail' *in The Lancelot-Grail – The Old French Arthurian Vulgate and Post-Vulgate in Translation*, ed. Lacy, Norris J. et al; trans. Carol Chase (D.S. Brewer, 2010)

The Voyage of Saint Brendan: Journey to the Promised Land, trans. J. J. O'Meara (Gerards Cross: Colin Smythe, 1991)
Wolfram von Eschenbach *Parzival*, trans. A. T. Hatto (Penguin Books, 1980)

Further Reading
Amery, Ethelwyn Mary, *Sought and Found – A Story of the Holy Graal* (Aberystwyth: William Jones, 1905)
Apperley, Newton Wynne, *A Hunting Diary* (Pirton: Nisbet & Co. Ltd, 1926)
Ashdown, Paul, *The Lord Was at Glastonbury* (Glastonbury: Squeeze Press, 2010)
Ashe, Geoffrey, *Avalonian Quest* (London: Fontana, 1984)
Augustine, Saint, Bishop of Hippo, *The City of God* (*De Civitate Dei*) translated by the Revd Marcus Dods MA (Edinburgh: T & T Clark, 1884)
Baigent, Michael, Leigh, Richard & Lincoln, Henry, *The Holy Blood and the Holy Grail* (Jonathan Cape, 1982)
Benham, Patrick, *The Avalonians* (Glastonbury: Gothic Image, 2nd edn, 2006)
Bernard, J. H., *The Pilgrimage of S. Silvia of Aquitania to the Holy Places*, c. AD 385, transl. with introduction and notes (London: Palestine Pilgrims' Text Society, 1891)
Bourdillon, Hilary, *Women as Healers – A History of Women and Medicine* (Cambridge: Cambridge University Press, 1988)
Bowen, E. G., *A History of Llanbadarn Fawr* (Llandysul: Gomer, 1979)
Brock, M. G., Curthoys, M. C. (editors), *The History of the University of Oxford, Vol. VII Nineteenth-Century Oxford, Part 2* (Oxford: Clarendon Press, 2000)
Bromwich, Rachel, *Trioedd Ynys Prydein – The Triads of the Island of Britain*, Third Edition (University of Wales Press, 2006)
Brooks, Michael, *13 Things That Don't Make Sense* (London: Profile Books, 2000)
Burton, Jane & Stöber, Karen, *Monastic Wales – New Approaches* (Cardiff: University of Wales Press, 2013)
Capt, E. Raymond, *The Traditions of Glastonbury* (California: Artisan, 1987)
Clynes, Michael, *The Grail Murders* (Penzler, 1993)
Cripps, Wilfred Joseph, *Old English Plate, Decorative, and Domestic, Its Makers and Marks* (London: Spring Books, 1967) (original edition, 1878)
Davenport, Cyril, *British Heraldry* (London: Methuen 1921)
Davies, D. H., *Flight from Glastonbury* (Lulu, 2015)
Davies, James Douglas, *The Antiquities of the Abbey or Cathedral Church of Durham: Also, a Particular Description of the County Palatine of Durham, Compiled from the Best ... and Original Manuscripts* (London: Forgotten Books, 2018)
Davies, Tom, *Fire in the Bay* (William Collins & Co., 1989)
Dunning, R. W. (ed.), *The Victorian History of the Counties of England, Glastonbury and Street* (Woodbridge: Boydell & Brewer, 2006)
Edel, Leon (ed.), *Henry James Letters*, Vol IV 1895-1916 (London: Belknap, 1984)
Edwards, Nancy, *A Corpus of Early Medieval Inscribed Stones and Stone Sculpture in Wales*, Volume II (University of Wales Press, 2007)
Elder, Isabel Hill, *The Cup of the Last Supper* (Bangor, Co. Down: H. McGowan & Son)

Bibliography

Elder, Isabel Hill, *The Story of Glastonbury* (Bangor: Spectator, 1965)

Elder, Isabel Hill, *George of Lydda – Soldier Saint and Martyr* (London: Covenant, 1949)

Evans, Henry Tobit, *Rebecca and Her Daughters. Being a History of the Agrarian Disturbances in Wales Known as 'The Rebecca Riots'* (Cardiff, Educational Publishing Company, 1910)

Fox-Davies, A. C., *A Complete Guide to Heraldry* (London: Orbis, 1985)

Gardner, Laurence, *Bloodline of the Holy Grail: The Hidden lineage of Jesus Revealed* (Dorset: Shaftesbury, 1996)

Garlick, Raymond, *A Sense of Europe*, Collected Poems 1954-1968 (Gwasg Gomer, 1968)

Gosse, Edmund, *Portraits and Sketches* (London: William Heinemann, 1912)

Graves, Tom, *Needles of Stone – Revisited* (Glastonbury: Gothic Image, 1986)

Gregor-Dellin, Martin and Mack, Dietrich, Cosima Wagner's *Diaries*, trans. Geoffrey Skelton, Volume II 1878-1883 (London: Collins, 1980)

Griffiths, Graham K., *Behold Jerusalem!* (Longinus, 2003)

Hague, Douglas B., *Lighthouses of Wales – Their Architecture and Archaeology*, ed. Stephen Hughes (Royal Commission on Ancient and Historical Monuments of Wales, 1994)

Hague, Douglas B., *Aberystwyth Trail* (1975)

Hall, W. R., *Aberystwyth: What to See and How to See It – A Guide to Walks, Excursions and Places of Interest* (Aberystwyth: J. Gibson, 1880)

Harris, Ruth, *Lourdes: Body and Spirit in the Secular Age* (London: Penguin, 2008)

Harte, Negley, *The University of London 1836-1986: An Illustrated History* (London: Athlone Press Ltd, 1986)

Henderson, George, *Early Medieval* (London: Penguin Books, 1977)

Hoadley, R. Bruce, *Understanding Wood – A Craftsman's Guide to Understanding Wood Technology* (Taunton Press, 2000)

Hope, Sir William Henry John, et al. (ed.), *Rites of Durham, being a description or brief declaration of all the ancient monuments, rites, & customs belonging or being within the monastical church of Durham before the suppression* (London: Facsimile Publisher, 2015)

Hopkinson-Ball, Tim, *The Rediscovery of Glastonbury* (Stroud: Sutton Publishing, 2007)

Horsfall-Turner, E. R., *Walks and Wanderings in County Cardigan* (Bingley: Thomas Harrison & sons, 1902)

Howells, W. D., *Seven English Cities* (New York: Harper & Brothers, 1909)

Huntley, H. E., *The Divine Proportion: A Study in Mathematical Beauty* (Dover Publications, 1970)

Jane, F. W., *The Structure of Wood* (London: Adam and Charles Black, 2nd edn, revised and reset, 1970)

Jeffs, H., *'J.B.' – J. Brierley, His Life and Work* (London: James Clarke & Co., 1916)

Jeffreys, Diarmud, *Aspirin – The Remarkable Story of a Wonder Drug* (London: Bloomsbury, 2005)

Joel, Janet, *The Nanteos Cup (Holy Grail)* (self-published, 2016)

Jowett, B., *The Dialogues of Plato Translated into English* (Oxford: Clarendon Press, 1892)

Kersten, Holger, *Jesus Lived in India: His Unknown Life Before and After the Crucifixion* (Element Books, 1994)

Koch, John, T. (ed.), *Celtic Culture – A Historical Encyclopaedia*, Vol., 3 (ABC-Clio Inc., 2006)

Lane, Cecily, & Shannon Jr, Edgar F. (eds), *The Letters of Alfred Lord Tennyson*, Volume 1, 1821-1850 (Oxford: Clarendon Press, 1982)

Lang, Cecil Y. (ed.), *The Swinburne Letters,* Vol. 1 (New Haven: Yale University Press, 1959)

Leland, John, *The Itinerary in Wales of John Leland in or About the Years 1536-1539; Extracted from His MSS,* arranged and edited by Lucy Toulmin Smith (London: G. Bell &Sons, 1906)

Lewes, Mary L., *Stranger Than Fiction: Being Tales from the Byways of Ghosts and Folklore* (London: W. Rider, 1911)

Lewes, Mary L., *The Queer Side of Things* (London: Selwyn & Blount, 1923)

Lewis, Lionel S., *St. Joseph of Arimathea at Glastonbury or The Apostolic Church of Britain* 3rd edn (A. R. Mowbray & Co., 1924)

Lucan: *Pharsalia* ed. and trans. Jane Wilson Joyce (New York: Cornell University Press, 1993)

Machen, Arthur, *The Great Return* (London: Faith Press, 1915)

Machen, Arthur, *The Secret Glory* (London: Martin Secker, 1922)

Machen, Arthur, *Selected Letters,* ed. Dobson, Roger, Brangham, Godfrey and Gilbert RA (London: Aquarian Press, 1998)

Machen, Arthur, *The Shining Pyramid* (London: Martin Secker, 1925)

Maltwood, K. E., *A Guide to Glastonbury's Temple of the Stars – Their Giant Effigies Described from Air Views, Maps, and from 'The High History of the Holy Grail'* (James Clarke & Co. Ltd)

Marchand, A., *The Facts of Lourdes and the Medical Bureau* (London: Burns Oates and Washbourne Ltd, 1924)

Marston, Charles, *The Bible Comes Alive* (London: Eyre & Spottiswoode, 1940 (1st impression 1937)

Mackay, Christopher S., *Malleus Maleficarum* (Cambridge: Cambridge University Press, 2006)

Main, Laurence, *King Arthur's Camlan – A Quest for the Truth* (Meirion Publications, 2006)

Main, Laurence, *The Spirit Paths of Wales* (Cicerone Press, 2000)

Main, Laurence, *Camlan – The True Story?* (Meirion Publications, 1997)

Matthews, Caitlín and John, *The Lost Book of the Grail* (Rochester: Inner Traditions, 2019)

Matthews Caitlín, *King Arthur's Raid on the Otherworld* (Glastonbury: Gothic Image Press, 2000)

Matthews, John, *Temples of the Grail* (Woodbury: Llewellyn Publishers 2019)

Matthews, John, *Taliesin: The Last Celtic Shaman* (Rochester: Inner Traditions, 2002)

Meyrick, Sir Samuel Rush, *The History and Antiquities of the County of Cardigan* (London: T. Bensley for Longman, 1808)

Miller, Hamish & Broadhurst, Paul, *The Sun and the Serpent* (Launceston, Pendragon Press, 1990)

Oldmixon, John, *The History of England During the Reigns of Henry VIII, Edward VI, Queen Mary, Queen Elizabeth* (London, printed for T. Cox and R. Hett, 1739)

Pegler, Ian, *Cwpan Saint Greal (The Cup of the Holy Grail): A One Act Pageant Play Based on the Traditional West Wales Tale of the Nanteos Cup* (privately printed by Ian Pegler, Ceredigion, 2017)

Pick, Bernard, *The Apocryphal Acts of Paul, Peter, John, Andrew and Thomas* (Chicago: The Open Court Publishing Co., 1909)

Poynder, Michael, *PI in the Sky – A Revelation of the Ancient Wisdom Tradition* (Rider, 1992)

Poynder, Michael, *The Price Guide to Jewellery 3000 B.C. - 1950 A.D.* (Antique Collectors' Club, 1976)

Poynder, Michael, *The Lost Magic of Christianity – Celtic Essene Connections* (Collins Press, 1997)

Prys-Jones, A. G., A Song of Caldey, *Poems of Wales* (Oxford: Basil Blackwell, 1923)

Rahtz, P., Watts, L., *Glastonbury – Mythology and Archaeology* (Stroud: Tempus, 2003)

Rainsford, K. D., *Aspirin and Related Drugs* (Boca Raton: CRC Press, 2002)

Rhys, John, *Studies in the Arthurian Legend* (Oxford: Clarendon Press, 1891)

Robinson, David M. *Strata Florida Abbey, Talley Abbey* (Cardiff, Cadw Welsh Historic Monuments, 2007)

Robinson, Joseph Armitage, *Somerset Historical Essays* (published for the British Academy, by H. Milford, Oxford, Oxford University Press, 1921)

Rubin, *Corpus Christi – The Eucharist in Late Medieval Culture* (Cambridge: Cambridge University Press, 1991)

Sabor, Rudolph, *The Real Wagner* (Cardinal, 1989)

Saunders Lewis, *Meistri'r canrifoedd: ysgrifau ar hanes llenyddiaeth Gymraeg*, Gwasg Prifysgol (Cymru, 1982)

Shoesmith, Ron & Richardson, Ruth (eds), *A Definitive History of Dore Abbey* (Little Logaston: Logaston Press, 1997)

Smollett, Tobias, *A Complete History of England from the Descent of Julius Caesar to the Treaty of Aix La Chapelle 1748. Containing the transactions of One Thousand Eight Hundred Years*, Volume the Sixth (published by James Rivington and James Fletcher, 3rd edn, London 1759)

Somner, William, *Dictionarium Saxonico-Latino-Anglicum, voces, phrasesque praecipuas Anglo-Saxonicas . . . cum Latina et Anglica vocum interpretatione complectens . . . Aecesserunt Aelfrici Abbatis Grammatica Latino-Saxonica cum glossario suo ejusdem generis,'* 2 parts (Oxford, 1659; 2nd edn, with additions by Thomas Benson, 1701

Spenser, Edmund, The Complete Works, ed. T. Hughes (1715)

Steegmuller, Francis, *Maupassant* (London: Collins, 1950)

Sweetinburgh, Sheila, *The Role of the Hospital in Medieval England: Gift-Giving and the Spiritual Economy* (Dublin, Ireland: Four Courts Press, 200)

Swinburn, Algernon Charles, *Tristram of Lyonesse* (London: Chatto & Windus, 1882)

Trzebiatowska, Marta & Bruce, Steve, *Why Are Women More Religious Than Men?* (Oxford: Oxford University Press, 2012)

Twinn, Nigel, *Hamish Miller – A Life Divined* (Hayle: Penwith Press, 2010)

Underwood, Guy, *The Pattern of the Past* (Abacus, 1972)

Ussher, James, *The Annals of the World, deduced from the Origin of Time, and continued to the beginning of the Emperour [stet] Vespasians Reign* (London, 1658)

Von Harten, Marjorie and Marston, Melissa, *Man of Wolverhampton* (Coombe Springs Press, 1979)

Von Heusinger, *Sabine and* Annette Kehnel (eds) *Generations in the Cloister – Youth and Age in Medieval Religious Life*, Vita Regularis Abhandlungen 36 (Berlin, 2008)

Wagner, Adrian, *The Feminine Element in Mankind* (1994)

Wagner, Richard, *Mein Leben* (München: F. Bruckmann A-G, 1911)

Wagner, Richard, *My Life*, Constable & Co. Ltd (London, 1911) (1994 reprint)

Waite, A. E., *The Hidden Church of the Holy Grail* (London: Rebman Ltd, 1909)

Ward, C. H. Dudley, *History of the Welsh Guards* (London: John Murray, 1920)

Waylen, Barbara, *Evidence of Divine Purpose* (Sussex: Edward Hamilton, 1950)

Wilkinson, John, *Egeria's Travels* (London: SPCK, 1971)

Williams, David Henry, *Atlas of Cistercian Lands in Wales* (Cardiff: University of Wales Press, 1990)

Williams, Stephen W., *The Cistercian abbey of Strata Florida: its history, and an account of the recent excavations made on its site* (London: Whiting & Co., 1889)

Wolff, Robert Lee, *Strange Stories and Other Explorations in Victorian Fiction* (Boston: Gambit Incorporated, 1971)

About the Authors

JOHN MATTHEWS is an independent scholar living in Oxford. He published his first book in 1980 and has since gone on to publish over a hundred titles on myth, folklore, and ancient traditions. He has worked in the film industry as an historical advisor and won a BAFTA for his work on the movie *King Arthur* (2004). He has made a lifetime study of every aspect of the Arthurian legends, from its origins to modern retellings, and wrote a bestselling work on piracy. *Pirates* (Carlton/Athenaeum) was a number one *New York Times* bestseller for 22 weeks in 2005 and was translated into 18 languages. Among his forthcoming titles are *Artorius: The Roman King Arthur* (written with Linda Malcor, Amberley 2022) and *The Great Book of King Arthur* (Harper 2022)

IAN PEGLER has been familiar with Welsh mythology and the Welsh take on Merlin and King Arthur from an early age. He knew about the Black Book of Carmarthen and the tales of the Mabinogion from primary school. In the summer of 1977 aged eleven he learned about the story of the Nanteos Cup which culminated in his work on this book. In 2003 Ian won the Bell Essay award from the British Society of Dowsers and completed his first book, *Valle Crucis and the Grail* published by Llanerch in 2010. In 2017 he produced *Cwpan Seint Greal*, which was inspired by his discovery that a long-forgotten pageant-play had been written about the Nanteos Cup in the 1930s.

FRED STEDMAN-JONES, after leaving the RAF in 1952, studied English and Drama at Caerleon and Rose Bruford Drama Colleges and went on to teach drama in Slough and East London. In 1966 he studied for a BA in Drama & English at Hull University. Fred graduated in 1969 and took up a post at Liverpool University's new department of drama, where he taught for twenty years. Through his interest in the genealogy of the Stedmans, Fred became interested in the Nanteos Cup and spent countless hours in archives, art galleries, ancient sites, abbeys, churches and libraries, in Wales and further afield. Fred died in 2016.

Index

Also available from Amberley Publishing

'A remarkable book ... an inspiration from
the heart of the Shire'
ROBERT PLANT

THE
MAGICAL
HISTORY OF
BRITAIN

MARTIN WALL

Also available from Amberley Publishing

FOREWORD BY RICHARD CARPENTER
PREFACE BY MARK RYAN

ROBIN
HOOD

JOHN MATTHEWS

Available from all good bookshops or to order direct
Please call **01453–847–800**
www.amberley-books.com